1969

This book may be kept

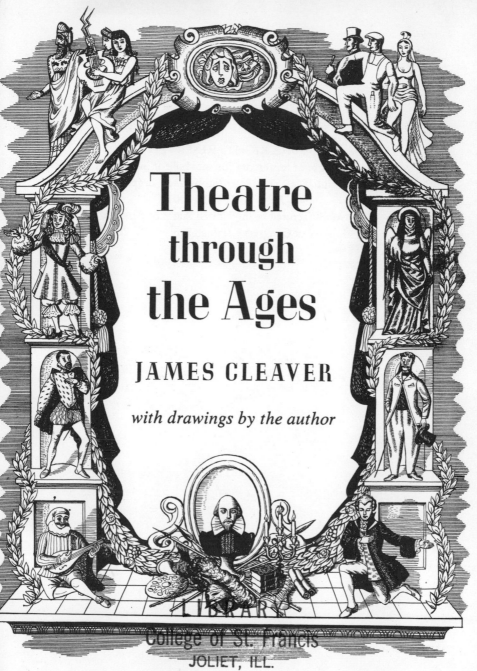

Theatre
through
the Ages

JAMES CLEAVER

with drawings by the author

Hart Publishing Company, Inc.   •   *New York City*

Theatre
through
the Ages

Contents

THE RESTORATION THEATRE

THE EIGHTEENTH CENTURY

List of Illustrations

THE RISE OF THE AMERICAN THEATRE

THE RUSSIAN THEATRE

THE ENGLISH THEATRE OF THE
TWENTIETH CENTURY

THE AMERICAN THEATRE OF THE
TWENTIETH CENTURY

The Greek Theatre

THE EARLIEST THEATRE

The theatre as we know it today had its origins in the early days of
Greece. Dionysus (or Bacchus as the Romans called him) was the god
of wine and fertility; every year the Greeks held a number of festivals
in his honor. On these occasions, the worship of Dionysus took the
form of a combination of song and dance, accompanied by music and
much flowing of wine. These festivities, at first improvised in a spirit
of lively religious fervor, became formalized in the seventh century
B.C. by a poet named Arion.

THE DITHYRAMBS

Dionysus was supposed to have been enclosed in the thigh of Zeus,
the father of all the gods, and then reborn. So the name *dithyramb*,
meaning twice-born, was given to the poem composed in his honor.
The dithyrambs were performed by a chorus of fifty men dressed as
satyrs. Their costume was a shaggy goatskin embellished with a
horse's tail worn around the middle. Each actor wore a mask with a
snub nose, a beard, and long, animal-like ears. Each also wore the

phallus, a purely symbolic representation of the male organs in the religion of the Greeks. The chorus did not impersonate the character of the satyr; rather, their costumes were regarded as the outward trappings of their religion.

BOAT CAR This drawing of Dionysus and his satyrs is sometimes called the Thespis Car. Thespis, according to legend, brought the first tragedy to Attica on wagons in the sixth century, B.C.

THESPIS

The idea of impersonation is popularly supposed to have been the innovation of Thespis, a leader of the satyr chorus about 550 B.C. Instead of wearing the satyr's costume, he donned the traditional costume of Hermes, but retained the satyr mask. The next step was for him to wear the mask of Hermes—and so he became for the first time a definite character, and as such was separated from the chorus, who appointed another leader. Dialogue between the actor (as Thespis had become) and the chorus was then introduced. The actor gradually developed his scope and impersonated other gods, and also the heroes of ancient Greek legend.

The subjects of all the early plays were, primarily, the life and adventures of Dionysus and, secondly, the ancient epics of Homer. On many of the Greek vases that have survived, the painted decorations give us much information concerning the Greek theatre. Thespis is usually depicted seated in a cart, and for this reason all touring actors have subsequently been known as *thespians*.

AESCHYLUS

None of the plays of Thespis has survived. The first great writer for the theatre whose work we know today was Aeschylus, who lived from 525 to 456 B.C. and is considered the father of Greek tragic drama. Aeschylus wrote over seventy plays, of which only seven have come down to us. They were all tragedies, comedy being a much later development. Fortunately, those plays that have survived were written at various periods of Aeschylus' life, and are very representative of his whole work. The *Agamemnon, The Choephorae (The Libation Bearers)*, and the *Eumenides (Furies)* are a trilogy (called the *Oresteia*) on the house of Agamemnon and the tragedies that befall its members; *The Persians, Seven Against Thebes, The Suppliant Women*, and *Prometheus Bound* are his other extant works.

Aeschylus was nourished on Homer, and his work reflects the grand sweep as well as the legends visible in Homer's epics. Aeschylus began competing in the dramatic contests in 499 B.C., but he did not win first prize until 484. Thereafter, he was Athens' most popular playwright.

One of his greatest achievements in the drama was his expression of lofty religious ideals—at a time when many of the Greek gods had lost much of their luster. *Prometheus Bound*, which is the first and only remaining part of a trilogy, deals with the relationship between Prometheus and Zeus, the godhead, whom Aeschylus presents as purified and righteous. He interprets the theological idea further in the *Oresteia*, in which the goodness and benevolence of Zeus are contrasted with the avenging justice of the Furies.

Aeschylus surpassed his contemporaries and his successors in his great tragic power (as in *Agamemnon*, with its dire prophecies by the Chorus, Cassandra's rantings, Agamemnon's scream of death, and Clytemnestra's remorseless gloating over Agamemnon's murder), dramatic effects, and originality of ideas.

From the simple arrangement of chorus and one actor reciting long lyrical passages of an epic poem, Aeschylus gradually developed a more creative and living drama. In *The Persians,* one of his earliest plays, a drama on the defeat of the Persians at Salamis (to which he was an eyewitness), he introduced a second actor, and consequently much more dialogue. As his work developed, more characters were added, and stage effects were inaugurated. Simple properties and settings were introduced. An altar or a tomb, for instance, gave point to the action of a particular part of the play, while trumpets were blown to emphasize other points. Ghostly apparitions and Furies made their dramatic appearance. Aeschylus is also credited with the use of paintings as a symbol for a particular scene, rather than as a pictorial background to the actors.

SOPHOCLES

The rapid development of the theatre in the fifth century B.C. was, of course, not entirely due to the innovations of Aeschylus. Plays were selected for production in open competition. The City or State authorities, who governed all theatrical activities, would invite poets to submit plays for a coming festival, and to have a play accepted became a great honor.

The first great rival of Aeschylus was Sophocles, who first appeared as a protagonist in the competition in 471 B.C. Sophocles is considered the very pinnacle of Greek poetic drama. He brought Greek tragedy to its perfection.

Sophocle's outlook differed considerably from Aeschylus'. He was of a younger generation than Aeschylus, and he did much to humanize both the language and the characters of the tragedy. He also actually helped in the development of Aeschylus' work, as the older man adopted some of Sophocles' innovations. It was Sophocles who introduced the third actor, and in 458 B.C. Aeschylus followed suit in the *Oresteia.*

Sophocles wrote well over a hundred plays, but, as with Aeschylus, only seven survive: *Oedipus the King, Oedipus Coloneus, Antigone, Electra, The Trachinian Women, Ajax,* and *Philoctetes.* His first

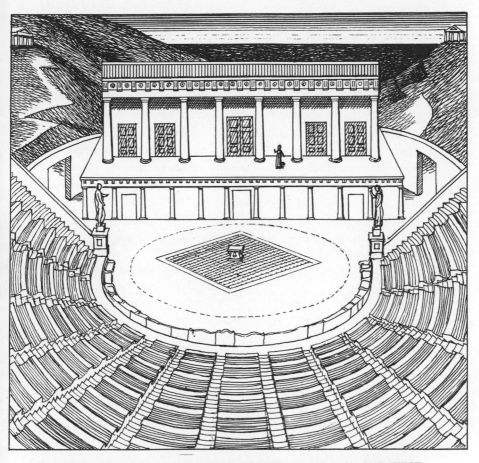

RECONSTRUCTION OF THE GRAECO-ROMAN THEATRE OF THE FIRST CENTURY, A.D. The dotted circle represents the position of the ancient Greek orchestra. Note the altar in the middle of the paved orchestra.

success was in 468 B.C., at the age of twenty-seven, when his work was chosen in preference to that of Aeschylus; and for nearly three decades after, he was repeatedly first, and never below second.

Oedipus the King is often considered the greatest of all Greek tragedies. The powerful dramatic impact of Oedipus' gradually coming to realize that he has, in ignorance, killed his father and married his mother, is unsurpassed in dramatic literature. This impact becomes overwhelming when Oedipus refuses to plead his ignorance and accepts full moral responsibility for his acts and blinds himself. In addition to its flawless structure and high moral purpose, *Oedipus the King* has further proved its universality by lending its name to an important aspect of modern psychological interpretation—the *Oedipus complex.*

In *Antigone,* Sophocles deals with the conflict between the laws of God and the laws of man. Creon, King of Thebes, has ordered that burial rites not be administered to his nephew, Polyneices, who was killed during a treasonable assault on Thebes. Antigone, Polyneices' sister (and daughter of Oedipus), feels that she must follow the law of God, which holds that burial rites must be accorded the dead. She stands by her belief, even when it leads to her death. The dialogue between Creon and Antigone is a powerful discussion of moral versus legal right. Sophocles obviously feels that the laws of God must stand above the laws of man.

EURIPIDES

Euripides followed Sophocles as the third great tragic poet. He did not achieve the early success of his predecessors, and had a hard struggle before his plays were accepted. Three years after his first victory in the competitions, he was again defeated by Sophocles. He won first prize in the competitions only four or five times altogether.

Euripides was skeptical of established authority, and is considered to have been a more profound thinker than either Aeschylus or Sophocles, giving greater psychological insight into his characters and their motives. He scoffed at the gods, usually showing them as immoral or ridiculous, and imputing few of the lofty motives to them that

Aeschylus and Sophocles did. He was often called a "woman-hater" and attacked for his portrayals of the emotions of women in love. However, some of the greatest feminine characters in drama appear in his plays: Medea, Iphigenia, Phaedra, Alcestis, Evadne. Because of his modern ideas, many of which had never before been presented on a stage, Euripides was satirized by many conservative critics, among them Aristophanes in *The Frogs* and *Women at the Thesmophorian Festival*.

Seventeen tragedies and one satyr-play (afterpiece) survive of the approximately ninety-two plays composed by Euripides, among them: *The Trojan Women*, which depicted the horrors of war and its aftermath; *Hippolytus*, which introduced the first *human* (though illicit) love story ever acted in a theatre; *Medea; Iphigenia in Tauris;* and *The Bacchae. The Bacchae*, perhaps because it was written later in his life, when he lived as an exile in Macedonia, seems to return toward old religious beliefs which Euripides had rejected earlier.

THE GROWTH OF COMEDY

The next stage was the growth of comedy. Tragedy transported the enrapt audience into the past; it made them sad, and it made them weep. Comedy brought them down to earth; they wiped their eyes, began to smile, and finally laughed uproariously. Comedy was officially admitted to the City Dionysia at Athens in 487 B.C. Early comedy abused and satirized prominent people, and its growth was probably considered a democratic measure.

The performances at the competitions lasted three days, and three tragedies were given each day. The performances began at sunrise and continued without a break until early evening, when a short interval for refreshment was given. After this, a comedy was performed, at the conclusion of which the citizens returned to their homes in a joyful mood.

ARISTOPHANES

Aristophanes was the great writer of comedies. His extant work was produced from 425 to 388 B.C. His plays were particularly noted for their outspoken topical allusions to unpopular people and causes, for which he suffered imprisonment several times in the course of his career.

GREEK CONTEMPORARY DRESS   The long chiton and the short cloak were the basis for stage costume developed in the fifth century, B.C.

The Clouds is an attack on the educational theories of the Sophists, and contains a caricature of Socrates. *The Birds* concerns a Utopia set up in the clouds by two Athenians, and contains the "Bird Chorus," which is so remarkably lyrical that it seems to transport one to birdland. *The Frogs* satirizes Euripides and Aeschylus discussing their tragedies in Hades. *Lysistrata* is a plea for peace, in which the women of Athens withhold their sexual favors to force their husbands to make peace. Despite its many quite bawdy passages, it is an earnest plea. *Plautus* is a moral allegory, and *The Wasps* satirizes the popular courts and the Athenian jury system.

THE COMPETITIONS

Although these four writers are the great figures of Greek drama, their achievements were probably due in no small measure to the spirit of competition which was the basis of all Dionysiac festivals. The State selected the poets who were to take part in the competitions. For the tragedies, three poets were usually selected; for the comedies, in later times, the number was five.

There were ten judges, who were selected from the citizens, partly by election and partly by appointment. The judges sat in seats of honor in the front rows of the theatre, and made their choice at the conclusion of the performances, placing their votes in an urn. Only five selections were taken from the urn, and the majority of these decided the result of the competition.

To win victory in the competition was considered a great honor, and the poet's name was inscribed in the public archives and carved on a tablet in the theatre. The prize was originally a goat for the winning tragic poet, and a basket of figs and a jar of wine for the writer of the winning comedy. Later, however, money prizes were given.

The lively spirit of the competitions kept the poets very active and stimulated them to their best efforts throughout their lives. Aeschylus died at the age of sixty-nine, and was producing plays right up to a few years before his death. Both Sophocles and Euripides also produced plays late in life.

Poets who were unsuccessful in the competitions were allowed to revise or rewrite their plays and submit them again at subsequent festivals. Euripides gained several victories with plays which had been rewritten after unsuccessful performances.

THE FESTIVALS

The drama in Greece, then, arose from the religious festivals, of which there were four during the year. Only two of these, however, were associated with dramatic performances: the *Lenaea* and the *City Dionysia*. Comedies were given at both festivals, but tragedies were presented only at the chief festival, the City Dionysia, which was held in the early spring.

The festival began with a procession through the city by priests, officials, poets, actors, the *choregi* (the wealthy citizens who were called upon to finance the productions as a State tax), the members of the various choruses, and the musicians, followed by the populace of the city and the many strangers who had come to join in the celebrations. With the participants attired in brilliantly colored garments richly ornamented with gold, the procession marched to the temple of Dionysus, carried out the statue of the god, and set it up in state in the theatre. Announcements were then made of the plays to be performed on the following day.

The performances were usually preceded by the choral competitions, in which choruses of men and boys sang as representatives of the various communities in the State. After this, the poet came forward and announced his plays which were to be performed that day. The plays were then given.

The audiences of those days would sit on stone benches through a whole day, from sunrise to sunset, with only one interval, in rapt attention to the spectacle before them and the alternating voices of actor and chorus. That this was possible was, in the first place, a triumph of art, and in the second a measure of the extraordinary enthusiasm of all members of the State. Perhaps religious fervor had something to do with it, but the plays of the great poets of the fifth century B.C. would seem to have little in common with the wine-induced ecstasy of the early Dionysiac festivals.

The performances continued on the following days, and the judges then made their choice of the winning and second-best poets. The winning poet was brought to the stage and crowned with a chaplet of ivy, a solemn sacrifice was made, and the proceedings wound up with a grand banquet given by the poet to his actors, chorus, and friends.

THE PERFORMANCES

The theatre belonged to the State, and a public official, the *archon*, had the responsibility of bringing the various people together to produce a play. The poets were selected previously by the State. The actors, who were also paid by the State, were attached to the poets by lot. No poet was allowed to choose his own actors—a condition which was a constant source of worry to the poets.

The State then nominated to each poet a *choregus*, who was called upon to finance the production, paying the chorus, the supers, and the musicians, providing the costumes and properties, and meeting all the expenses involved in the performances. Here, again, the poet had his worries, for a niggardly choregus would not spend more than he thought necessary, and the judges' verdict might depend on the actual mounting of the play.

The system became more practical when the choregus was honored along with the winning poet for, generally, the choregus coveted the honor and consequently went to considerable expense to secure the best chorus and costumes available. Nicias and Antisthenes were two choregi who spent money lavishly and, with their poets, won many victories in the competitions.

Although there were only three actors in each play, a considerable number of what we should call *supers* were used as soldiers, attendants, and other characters, who appeared on the stage but were not required to speak.

The chorus for the tragedies was composed of fifteen men, who were all highly trained in declamation, music, and dancing. In the comedies the chorus was rather larger, and the number was generally

GREEK TRAGIC COSTUMES Elaborately patterned stage costumes are illustrated by these figures from Attic vases of the sixth and fifth centuries, B.C. The tiara worn by Andromeda indicates that she is an oriental princess. The hero from the Pronomos vase holds the mask of an oriental king.

twenty-four. The choregi had to pay the chorus a wage, provide their keep, and attend to their training. In the days of the great poets, they themselves trained the chorus; but after Euripides, they no longer took an active part in production, and a special chorus-trainer was appointed, thus causing a further drain on the resources of the choregi. During the time of the Peloponnesian Wars, when money was rather scarce, the authorities allowed the expenses of each play to be shared by two or more choregi. Eventually, at the end of the fourth century B.C., the State took over complete responsibility, and bore the entire cost.

Originally, the performances were given free to the entire population. The consequence was that many people would arrive at the theatre the day before the performances to take the best seats. There were also many complaints about foreigners taking all the seats. The State therefore decided to charge a small fee, and issued tickets for the seats.

All citizens, however poor, were entitled to see the plays. In cases of dire need the State officials provided the cost of admission. As the performances were part of a sacred festival, even prisoners were released from gaol in order that they might attend. During the several days of the festival, all citizens were expected to be on their best behavior, any offenses committed during the period being punished severely and the offenders publicly castigated at the close of the festival.

As there were few books and only a small proportion of the people could read, the plays, with their largely historical content, had a useful educational value. The poet, therefore, exercised considerable influence on the people in the role of teacher, and the theatre was vastly more important to the intellectual life of the time than it is today.

During the sixth and fifth centuries, successful plays were given only one performance (with the exception of the plays of Aeschylus, which were continually revived after his death). The fourth century produced no great tragic writers, so the revival of the old plays became a regular custom. This being the period when the art of acting reached its highest level, the old plays, being well known (so that interpretation became more important), sometimes suffered under the drastic adaptations carried out by some actors.

THE THEATRES

The early theatres were temporary affairs, consisting of a wooden platform used as a stage with a tent or booth at the rear for the use of the actors. The audience sat on rough wooden benches. By the time of Thespis, the theatre had become more permanent. The platform and booth had developed into permanent stage buildings and the wooden benches into a stone amphitheatre.

The theatre at Athens was the original of all the ancient theatres. Building began about 500 B.C., and work continued for nearly two hundred years. A natural position on a hillside was chosen for the site, the rows of stone seats following the contours of the ground, rising up the hill and roughly forming the shape of a horseshoe. In the center was the circular *orchestra*, or dancing place, in which the chorus performed. Behind was the stage, a platform which, though wide, was only a few feet in depth. Behind the stage was the facade of the stage buildings, embellished with columns and other architectural features; in the center was a large door, flanked on either side by one or two smaller doors, all of which were used by the actors when making their entrances and exits.

The theatre at Athens faced south, and a convention arose out of the natural position of the stage. To the right of the stage was the distant sea, and to the left the country inland. When a character in a play was supposed to come from a distant land across the sea, the actor would make his entrance from the right-hand door; conversely, it seemed quite natural for a character coming from the nearby countryside to make his entrance from the left-hand door.

The chorus also used the side doors to come down into the orchestra. In later times, when the chorus occasionally took part in the action on the stage (as in the plays of Aristophanes), a temporary wooden staircase was erected in the center of the stage. As the stage was nearly twelve feet higher than the orchestra, the use of this staircase must have been a rather awkward procedure. Generally, the chorus remained below in the circular orchestra, and the dialogue between chorus and actors took place with the actors speaking from the stage and the chorus from below. While the actors were speaking, the chorus stood with their backs to the audience, facing the stage. When it came their turn to speak, they turned and faced the audience —a simple, formal arrangement which gave emphasis to various parts of the play.

The stage buildings at the back of the stage were as high as the last row of seats in the amphitheatre. This arrangement suited the excellent acoustical properties of the theatre. The audiences were entirely at the mercy of the weather, there being no protection from sun or rain; but as the performances were held in the early spring, the sun would be rather welcome, and the rain the only trouble.

SCENERY AND PROPERTIES

Mention has been made of Aeschylus' using painted scenery as a background to the presentation of his plays. There is little knowledge of its specific use, but information is available of certain scenic devices which were used, not in the modern pictorial fashion, but rather in a symbolic sense. On each side of the stage, a three-sided screen was erected on which three different pictures were painted. The screens were made to revolve so that any of the three pictures could face the audience. It is not known whether a backcloth was used in the early days, but its use certainly developed in Roman times. The simple arrangement of easily changed pictures gave the audience sufficient understanding of a change of scene. The revolving of one screen alone meant that the scene represented was in the immediate neighborhood of the preceding scene, while the movement of both screens represented a complete change of locality. Most of the plays of Sophocles and Euripides have their scenes laid before a temple or a palace, and the stage buildings, with their columns, thus formed a very suitable background.

If a backcloth was used it was in two sections, the lower part painted to represent buildings or natural surroundings and the upper part to represent the sky. This was because in many of the plays an actor personifying a god often made his appearance at the top of the buildings. The complicated tangle of plots and counterplots in Euripides was usually straightened out toward the end of the play by a god's making his appearance out of the sky. Sometimes a crane was used to convey him to the ground or stage level, and also to carry characters such as Trygaeus, in Aristophanes' *The Peace,* who, in order to meet the gods, flew up to Olympus on the back of a giant beetle. The use of this contrivance originated the phrase *deus ex machina,* which has come to mean a device introduced in order to bring the action of a play to a convenient, if artificial, conclusion.

Another device frequently used by the Greeks was a trolley, which was pushed onto the stage through the large central door, and on which a tableau of characters would be arranged. Scenes of violence were taboo in the Greek theatre, and all murders were committed offstage. As all scenes were exteriors, any important action that took place indoors was also conveyed to the audience by the expedient of pushing out the trolley with the characters in a set pose. There was no attempt at realism, but a simple use of stage convention which, once established, could be employed with great dramatic effect.

Trapdoors were used in bringing ghosts, Furies, and other subterranean beings onto the stage. Certain properties were continually used as part of the setting, altars, tombs, and statues of gods being constantly referred to in the Greek plays. In much later times, horses and chariots were brought onto the stage. The theatre at Epidaurus, which is considered the most beautiful of the ancient theatres, had a stage which, although only eight feet deep, was seventy-eight feet wide, thus making it quite easy to gallop a horse or bring a chariot across. The rush of movement so caused would create a dramatic contrast to the rather static performance of the actors. Nevertheless, this practice was never widely used, and remained something of a novelty.

THE ACTORS

There were only three actors in a Greek play, but there were, of course, many characters, both male and female, and each actor was called upon to play a number of parts. The great advantage of this system was that even the minor parts were excellently played. There were never more than three characters involved in dialogue together. If a fourth character did appear on the stage, he had no lines to speak, so the part could be played by a super or a minor actor. The actors wore masks and costumes, which made it simple to change from one character to another.

The continual change of character did, of course, stress the importance of the actor's voice. It had, primarily, to be powerful, as the theatre held nearly thirty thousand spectators. It also had to be flexible, to change with the character—from youth to old age, from man to woman. Some actors could imitate all kinds of weird noises—the rush of the wind, the roar of the seas—and a whole repertoire of animal cries. Actors with bad taste would indulge any abilities they had in this direction, as it was always a sure method of attracting applause. Discerning writers deplored this rather cheap method of winning over an audience. Aristotle, when writing of the tragic actor Theodorus, commends the thoroughly natural quality of his voice, saying that unlike the other actors, he seemed to speak with his own voice. Tragic plays were delivered in a loud, sonorous style, and all movements were dignified and restrained. A more conversational style was used in comedy, and the movements were much more active.

Acting reached its heights of achievement during the fourth century, particularly as the old tragedies could be revived and their interpretation assumed new importance. After Euripides, there was a decline in the use of the chorus by the tragic writers, and more dialogue was given to the actors.

The actors' professional status was honorable, almost comparable with that of the priests. As they wished to maintain their privileges, the actors formed a guild around the middle of the fourth century. The Artists of Dionysus, as they were called, brought in as members of the guild poets, actors, chorus and trainers, and musicians. Among the privileges they were granted was permission to travel through foreign, and even hostile, states to give performances. Two famous actors traveled from Athens to Macedonia during the height of the war against Philip of Macedon to give performances, and they actually assisted in negotiating the peace. Another privilege they obtained from the State, though not without some trouble, was exemption from the compulsory period of military service.

MASKS

Thespis is supposed to have invented the tragic mask, although Aeschylus and others developed its use. The characters in Greek tragedies are general types rather than individuals, so a certain number of set masks were evolved. They indicated by simple outline and shape the general attributes of the particular character. Facial expression, which is so important to the actor's craft today, was quite out of the question in the enormous Greek theatres.

Once the masks were evolved, they changed only in detail throughout the centuries. The masks varied in size according to the importance of the character, and the coiffure was built up from the forehead accordingly. That is to say, a king's mask would have the hair built up considerably, the actor thus gaining inches in height, while the mask of a minor character would have no such built-up effect.

The masks were originally made of stiffened linen, but it was later found that cork or wood had better acoustical properties. Some masks had a small megaphone arrangement concealed inside the open mouth which amplified the voice of the actor to some degree. The masks entirely covered the head, and were painted to emphasize the expression and to delineate the character further. Even the eyes were painted in, with only a small hole through which the actor could see.

The tragic masks of the Roman period, first century, B.C., were characterized by elaborate coiffures, with wide openings for the mouth and eyes.

TYPICAL GREEK AND ROMAN MASKS   The tragic masks of the Roman period, first century, B. C., are characterized by elaborate coiffures and wide eye and mouth openings. The other masks represent stock characters of the Greek New Comedy of the fourth century, B. C.

TRAGIC HERO

TRAGIC HEROINE

PARASITE

OLD MAN, NEW COMEDY

MESSENGER

COURTESAN

COSTUMES

The costumes of Greek tragedy were neither strictly historical nor contemporary. Although the action of the tragedies took place in Homeric times, there was no attempt at historical accuracy. At the same time, the Greeks considered that common, everyday dress was not sufficiently dignified to be worn by their gods and heroes; so a special costume was evolved.

A long-sleeved robe decorated with bright colors was the basis of the costume. With this would be worn either the *himation,* a long mantle usually worn over the right shoulder that covered most of the body, or the *chlamys,* a short cloak which was flung across the left shoulder. Buskins with high soles of six inches or more gave the actor greater height and dignity, while the mask gave the clue to the character. With the extra height gained by the use of buskins and the size of the mask, the body of the actor tended to look puny, so it was necessary to pad the costumes to equalize matters.

The trailing gowns worn by women characters were longer than those of the men, and were usually of a particular color. A queen's costume, for instance, was purple. In the days when theatre programs were unheard of, it was important that the audience be able to recognize a character at once; therefore, if certain characters were always dressed in a costume of a particular color, recognition was made easy. Color was also used to signify the condition of a character. If in misfortune or exile, the character wore a mantle of black or gray over the tunic.

In Greece, hats were worn only on journeys, so the audience could readily appreciate the change of scene implied when a hatted character appeared.

All the male characters in tragedies wore the same kind of tunic, girdled high under the breast and falling in long, graceful folds. The tunics differed only in decoration, which was designed in patterns of varied colors. These patterns were based on floral designs or simply drawn animal or bird shapes.

To differentiate among gods and heroes, certain easily recognizable properties were carried. Thus, Apollo had his bow, Hermes his magic wand, Hercules his club and lionskin, and Perseus his cap of darkness. Warriors usually appeared in full armor, with a short scarlet cloak wrapped around the arm. Old men carried a bent staff, and messengers of good tidings wore crowns of olive or laurel. Kings wore a crown and carried a scepter; they also wore an extra short tunic over the usual long one.

The costume of comedy was rather different, the tunics being much shorter and with much padding fore and aft. The tradition of the old boisterous Dionysiac festivals was continued by the wearing of the phallus. In the plays of Aristophanes, the chorus, in some cases, did not represent human beings, so special costumes were used. At times other writers used this device, and the chorus were represented as birds, fishes, insects, frogs, goats, and even clouds. In Aristophanes' *The Birds,* the chorus wore a delightfully conventionalized bird costume, complete with wings and crests.

The buskin was never worn in comedy; a soft-soled shoe known as the *soccus* was used, and it has always since been associated with comic acting.

THE NEW COMEDY

Toward the end of the fourth century B.C., when Athens had lost its political importance but held the lead in art, science, and philosophy, the last important development took place in Greek drama. The subject of comedy shifted from the satirical political themes of Aristophanes to scenes of everyday domestic life. Athens, no longer a democracy, was under the domination of Macedonia, and the freedom of speech enjoyed by Aristophanes was no longer possible. Political reasons, then, conditioned the creation of the New Comedy, as it has been called.

The greatest writer of New Comedy was Menander (343–292 B.C.), who wrote over a hundred plays, of which more than 1,100 fragments have survived. He presented his first play in Athens around 321 B.C., and he set the standard in comedy for Terence and all comedy until Molière. Menander's comedies had certain typical

figures or stock types, and the costumes approximated more closely
to everyday life, although the convention of using certain colors to
give the clue to the character still held good. Many of these stock
characters still appeared repeatedly on the early Elizabethan stage.

A character which appeared in most of the plays was the roguish
slave, who had a very distinctive mask and red hair, and wore a short
white tunic. Old men also wore white, and were always clean-shaven,
with closely cropped hair. Beards were worn only to denote mature
manhood or middle age. Young men wore purple, parasites black or
gray, and old women yellow or light blue. Courtesans were easily

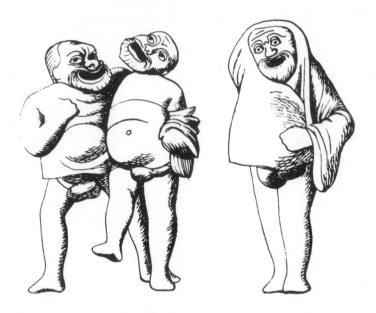

GREEK COMIC CHARACTERS OF THE FOURTH CENTURY, B.C.
They wear the costume of Menander's New Comedy: the short
jerkin, the large phallus, and the grotesquely grinning masks.

recognized by having their hair bound up with golden ornaments and brightly colored bands.

The actors of New Comedy, by discarding the phallus and wearing costumes similar to the everyday garb of the Greeks, developed a more realistic style of acting. They appeared in amusing situations and developed more individualism in their performances.

It was inevitable that the general theme of the plays was that of human failings and vanities. The dissolute rake of wealthy parents with his amorous adventures—largely engineered by his slave—the courtesan, the stern parent, the seduced daughter, were all typical figures. The tragedies of the past were still being revived at this period, but the old comedies were dead and buried and New Comedy reigned in their stead.

THE CHORUS

The chorus reached its peak of importance under Euripides, when it consisted of fifteen men. These moved in a military formation of three files, each of five men, and were usually characterized as old men, women, or maidens, being generally supposed to represent "the public." They wore masks, and their dress was usually contemporary, except, as mentioned previously, when they were not representing human beings. In the *Eumenides* of Aeschylus, they were dressed in black costumes, wore masks with distorted features, and had artificial snakes entangled in their hair.

Normally, the chorus was grouped in a rectangular formation in the circular orchestra, and had various forms of delivery. They either sang, spoke, or delivered their lines in the form of recitative, accompanied by a flute. The chorus was also required to perform various dances, those of the tragic plays being slow and dignified, while in the comedies the movements were more lively, and often lascivious and coarse.

All singing in those days was in unison, harmony having yet to be discovered, and the music was written to suit the words. Since it was chiefly the lyrical parts of the play that were allocated to the chorus, all dancing and music were subordinated to the poetry. The members of the chorus had to be highly skilled men, and the leader had a position almost as important as that of the actor. It was necessary for the chorus to be well trained, not only individually, but as a group, and their attainments must have been a considerable contribution to the stature of Greek drama.

GREEK COMIC CHORUS   The actors are dancing in a Komos, the earliest form of Greek comedy. Animal costumes were conventional stage dress in the Komos.

THE AUDIENCES

Audiences at the theatre at Athens numbered nearly thirty thousand, and included strangers and foreigners who were attracted to the festivals. Ambassadors and representatives of allied states came to pay the annual tributes, sums of money which were displayed on the stage. The front rows of the theatre were reserved for these important people, and for the various priests, State officials, and judges. The priest of Dionysus had a throne of honor in the center of the front row, and other thrones were set up for the rest of the officials. Successful generals also sat among the elite. The remainder of the seats in the theatre were backless stone benches, built very close together. Rich men brought rugs and cushions, and no doubt proved very unpopular with the more democratic citizens.

The Athenians were a very lively audience, and it was necessary to have a team of staff-bearers to keep order. They patroled the narrow gangways which divided the audience into twelve blocks.

Although it was customary in Greece at that time to relegate women to seclusion, they were allowed to see the performances. They all sat together in one place, probably at the back of the theatre. Boys were also admitted, and they too had their special place in the auditorium. Slaves were sometimes taken when they were lucky enough to have a benevolent master.

Among the audience of the Greek theatre were types which will always be found throughout the ages. There was the man of taste and discernment who hissed when everyone else was applauding and applauded when everyone else was silent. There was the boy who continually whistled the popular tunes, and the young man of the city who took pleasure in hissing a play off the stage.

Aristotle divides the audiences into two parts: the refined and cultured citizens and the rough and ignorant artisans. It is interesting in the study of Greek drama to see how the poets have met the two almost contradictory demands. Superb poetry goes with simple and sometimes very amusing stage devices, and the sublime is very happily wedded to the ridiculous.

The Roman Theatre

GREEK ORIGINS

The young and aggressive Roman republic borrowed its drama, like most of its art, from the Greeks. About the middle of the third century B.C., Livius Andronicus presented a comedy and a tragedy in Rome which had been adapted from the Greek and translated into Latin. The success of these performances ensured that future plays would be modeled on those of the Greeks.

Livius Andronicus had been taken captive as a child and brought to Rome as a slave. His command of both Latin and Greek enabled him to become a tutor and, eventually, a freedman. He translated the tragedies of Sophocles and Euripides, as well as some Greek comedies. Naevius, a contemporary of Livius Andronicus, also translated many of the old plays. Consequently, the Roman playwrights had the advantage of ready-made material—an advantage which they certainly took. Plautus and Terence borrowed wholesale from the New Comedy of Menander, and most of our knowledge of his work is based on the study of their plays. Seneca wrote tragedy which was to prove the model for all subsequent periods in the theatre, notably the

Elizabethan period in England and the French theatre of the seventeenth century.

Roman dramatic performances were not altogether religious festivals, but often merely public holidays or special performances in honor of victorious generals. The number of official holidays at which dramatic performances took place steadily increased through the years until in A.D. 354 there were over a hundred days set aside for that purpose. On some occasions after the victorious return of an expedition the spoils of war were carried across the stage by hundreds of mules—a spectacle which may have delighted the multitude, but was, to the intelligent writer of the time (Cicero, for instance), a boring substitute for drama.

THE THEATRES

The theatres changed considerably under Roman influence, and eventually all the ancient theatres were adapted to the new conditions. The use of the chorus further declined, and the orchestra subsequently became smaller. The new theatres built by the Romans differed fundamentally from those of the Greeks in that they were usually built on level ground instead of on a hillside. The reason for this, it has been suggested, was the love of architectural embellishment which the Romans were able to lavish on the outside walls of these theatres.

The stage was provided with a sloping roof, which probably acted as a sounding board and improved the acoustics. The stage was also enlarged, and the facade of the stage buildings elaborated with many statues and architectural features. Eventually, the Romans abolished the choral part of the performances, and all spectacle took place on the stage.

A curtain was introduced to mark the beginning and end of the play. Instead of being raised to open the play, the curtain was lowered, a slit trench being excavated in the floor of the stage to house it during the performance. Details of the arrangements for operating the curtain are not available, but probably pulleys were attached to the roof of the stage and the ropes went through to the rear of the stage buildings. As dramatic performances in Rome went on throughout the year, huge canvas awnings were erected to give shelter to the audience.

DECLINE OF TRAGEDY AND COMEDY

Under the Romans, tragedy and comedy declined in favor of farces, burlesques, and pantomime, which were nearer the vaudeville shows of our own time. In place of the tragedies, solo performances were given by tragedians or famous personalities. Nero himself delighted in giving tragic recitations, and he appeared on the stage as Apollo, Hercules, Orestes, and the blinded Oedipus, accompanying himself on the cither.

THE ACTORS

The Greeks had laid great stress on the unity of production: actors, chorus, and musicians worked together in perfect harmony as a team. The Romans made more of individual performances by the leading actors.

Until the first century B.C., the Roman actors played without masks and specialized in one particular kind of role. This meant that the original three actors of the Greek tragedies, who played many parts, switching from one character to another by changing masks, gave way to a troupe of specialists in the various roles of women, old men, youths, and parasites.

Without masks, the Roman actors were able to develop facial expression, which led to further specialization. The Romans were born improvisers, and with their lively and expressive gestures took naturally to the stage. Acting reached its height of perfection in Rome when the writing of plays was in its decline, during the first century B.C.

The greatest actor the Romans produced was Roscius, who specialized in comedy. When drama had begun to decline in favor of spectacle, he reintroduced many of the ancient Greek customs, including the use of masks, and succeeded in re-establishing the individuality of the actor. His name has subsequently always been associated with the height of perfection in acting.

In spite of Roscius, however, the acting profession lost its status under the Romans. Actors even lost their elementary rights as citizens, and were considered little better than slaves. This was partly due to managers' forming permanent troupes consisting of slaves, whom they could treat as they wished. Floggings and beatings were the reward of such actors should they not be well received and thus bring discredit on the manager. In the Roman theatre most of the acting profession were probably of foreign extraction and mostly slaves, while a few of the leading actors may have been freedmen who very occasionally received civic honors. Women appeared in dramatic performances, chiefly as dancers and instrumentalists—a thing unheard of in the days of the Greeks.

DEGENERATION OF THE THEATRE

The Romans differed greatly from the Greeks in their love of bloodshed and scenes of violence. Actors were made to resort to kicks and blows in their performances. Ear-boxing, acrobatic feats, and juggling with knives became common accomplishments. Sometimes scores of warriors, mounted and in full armor, presented mimic battles. These gave way to the actuality of gladiatorial fights and animal baitings.

Life was cheap in the days of the Empire, and slaves, captives, and robbers were thrown to their deaths to wild beasts made ferocious by judicious starving. Sometimes the unfortunate victims were subject to dramatic performances which culminated in their execution. At the time of Trajan, a musician dressed as Orpheus was torn to pieces by wild animals. On the day Caligula was murdered, during the performance of a mime, a robber was brought onto the stage and actually nailed to a cross, the audience apparently enjoying his slow and painful death. In later times the robbers and slaves were replaced as victims by the early Christian martyrs. The worst effect of Roman life on the theatre was not the decay of acting and drama, but such degenerate spectacles.

THE THEATRE DURING THE DECLINE OF THE EMPIRE

With the decline of the Roman Empire came the breaking up of all dramatic traditions inherited from the Greeks. The theatres, however, continued to flourish. They had become a very popular feature in the life of the Romans, and their numbers grew from forty-eight under Augustus to over a hundred under Constantine. They were very large, and each was capable of holding tens of thousands of the polyglot peoples living within the Roman Empire.

Apart from being the source of entertainment, theatres were the only meeting place for slaves and people without rights, who were debarred from Forum and Senate. In addition to being the rallying point for possible disturbers of the peace, the theatre was also a convenient instrument for winning over the populace. For these reasons, the authorities tightened their control over the theatres and passed many laws imposing restrictions on the actors. They were treated little better than slaves, and both Julius Caesar and Augustus enforced laws which in effect deprived actors of their civic rights.

THE MIMES

The large popular audiences did not care much for literary drama, and the numerous tongues spoken in the Empire dismissed the possibility of any subtlety in the performances. From these conditions, a new form of entertainment arose, the mime. It was found expedient to have intervals in the long tragic dramas during which certain actors would come forward and perform a short interlude in which singing, dancing, and acrobatics were mingled with dialogue. The subject of these so-called *farces* was to be found in the low life of the times. Certain stock types developed—a fat, talkative fool; a malicious character; a stupid, rustic fool; a foolish old man; and, as women also played in the mimes, equivalent female roles. The dialogue was usually improvised, and naturally had a close relationship to contemporary life.

The mimes became so popular that they expanded and became the principal part of the program. They achieved success for the same reason that variety is popular today: because of the intensely human qualities contained in their vulgarity.

The actors in the mimes wore short tunics with a yellow or parti-colored cloak, and they generally discarded the traditional mask. There is a tradition that the actresses played in the nude, and although this probably was not general, it is certainly conceivable that it might have happened when we consider the way the Romans lived during the late years of the Empire. Furthermore, it is hardly necessary to point out the nudes on our own variety stage.

The tragic actors were influenced by the mimes, and had to adopt the new technique. The long lyrical passages in the tragic plays were now sung by one player, accompanied by musicians, while the actor spoke only the dialogue. Later the dialogue was completely dropped by the actors, who then concentrated on miming the action while a large choir sang or chanted the story. The *histriones,* as the tragic actors were called, were in continual rivalry with the mimes until the last years of the Empire, when they merged in order to survive the growing difficulties.

EARLY CHRISTIAN OPPOSITION TO THE THEATRE

By far the greatest opposition to theatres and actors in general came from the early Christian leaders, and as Christianity spread it began to have some influence on the civil legislation of the Empire. In the fourth century A.D., the so-called *Canons of Hippolytus,* presumed to be the work of the leader of the Christian Church at that time, prohibited the theatre to the clergy. Also, the players had to quit their profession if they wanted to become Christians, or even if they wanted to marry a Christian. The Church forbade theatrical performances on Sundays and on religious festival days. St. John Chrysostom in the East and St. Jerome in the West continued to issue edicts on the evils of the theatres.

In spite of this growing opposition, the theatres continued, and during the last years of the Empire there was actually a lessening of official restrictions. This may have been partly due to the Emperor Justinian, whose wife Theodora had been an actress before becoming his mistress and, subsequently, his wife and Empress.

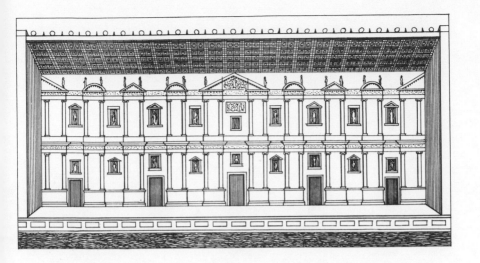

ROMAN STAGE This drawing of the Theatre of Aspendus in Asia Minor, shows the highly ornamented scene wall (scaena frons), the enclosed sides and the pulpitum, the rectangular playing area in front of the scaena frons.

END OF THE THEATRE IN ROME

By A.D. 400, the theatres were doomed, not because of early Christian opposition, but from an entirely new danger. Within a few years Rome was sacked by the invading Goths, and in order to find a scapegoat for their defeat, the authorities blamed the degeneration of the Roman defenders on the loose morals of the theatre. But when Rome was again sacked in A.D. 467, a theatre was still there. Theodoric, the Ostrogoth who invaded Italy in 488, found it expedient to continue the theatres, and they had further years of grace until 568, when the Lombards—the hard, tough Germans from the north—descended on Italy. After this, although the Lombards did not conquer the city itself, there is no more mention of theatres in Rome.

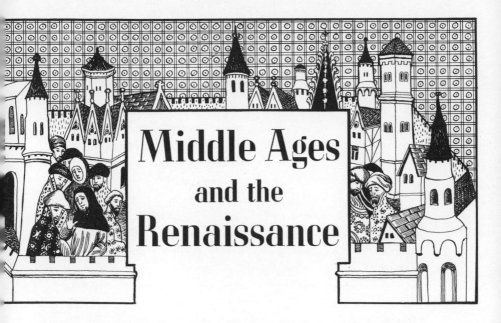

Middle Ages and the Renaissance

TOURING COMPANIES

Theatrical performances did not come to an end after the decline of Rome. Although the actors had to leave the theatres, they formed small companies which took to the roads and wandered through the country from hamlet to village and city, giving private performances at weddings, baptisms, and other festivities. Even though the theatres were closed, the Church showed itself to be still alive to the purported evils of the stage, and the officiating clergy were ordered to leave before the actors began their performances.

MINSTRELS

For centuries the actors wandered the roads, rubbing shoulders with acrobats, rope dancers, and beast tamers. The best of them became minstrels and gleemen, the well-paid servants of nobles and kings. The rest merged with the lower class of entertainers and were little better than wandering vagabonds. The earliest English poem is about a famous minstrel named Widsith, an epic singer who wandered across Europe to Egypt, Persia, and even as far as India.

The minstrels and gleemen were well established in England by the time Christianity came, in the sixth century. Their performances were in the nature of songs sung in praise of heroes and great deeds, and during the Middle Ages, when Europe was continually at war, they had no difficulty finding the necessary material. Wandering minstrels were usually made very welcome wherever they stayed. They had practically a free right of entry into all the great houses and castles of the nobles of the land; for, in addition to entertainment, they also brought news of foreign parts, which they no doubt carefully colored to suit the particular audiences. Sometimes they would settle down permanently in the service of a king or noble.

The Church looked with disfavor on the activities of the minstrels, and the bishops were continually issuing orders prohibiting the clergy from welcoming or watching the performers. A priest of Ripon minster was charged, in 1312, with breaking the canons in this respect. In spite of the edicts of the bishops, however, the clergy looked forward to occasional visits from wandering minstrels, certain bishops even receiving them favorably, and they were usually assured of a warm welcome in the monasteries. The clergy, of course, were only human, and the minstrels certainly satisfied the very human need for news and entertainment.

By the eleventh century, the minstrels were popular among all classes, and they gave their performances in tavern, castle, guild hall, and marketplace. They appeared in great strength at festivities such as weddings. There were 426 of them at the marriage of Margaret of England and John of Brabant in 1290.

Some of the more famous minstrels made large sums of money. Rahere, who was chief minstrel to Henry I, made a fortune. Deciding to quit the profession, he founded the great priory of St. Bartholomew, of which he became the first prior.

In France, at Beauvais, Lyons, and Cambrai, were some famous minstrel schools, where minstrels from all over Europe would gather during Lent, when no performances were given. There they would learn new songs and fresh news and material.

MEDIEVAL MINSTRELS In this drawing, the minstrels wear the typical parti-colored costumes of the period. The ancient instruments of the Middle Ages which they carry are, from the left: trumpet, vielle, cymbals, hand organ and harp.

The first requirement for a successful minstrel was a pleasing voice and personality; the second was a suitable accompaniment. The usual accompanying instruments were the harp and a fiddle-like instrument known as the *vielle*. Trumpets were also used, not so much as an accompaniment as for sounding fanfares to punctuate the dramatic moments of the performance. Other instruments of the time were a kind of hand organ, cithers of various shapes and sizes, bagpipes, drums, and cymbals.

When several minstrels performed together, they sang alternately in the form of dialogue based on question and answer. There are many illustrations in old illuminated manuscripts of minstrels and musicians and other entertainers of the Middle Ages wearing the usual costume of the period, but in much bolder colors and decoration. We can well imagine them presenting a pleasing and colorful entertainment to the simple, illiterate people of the time. Certain stage properties, such as the old favorite, the ass's head, were common, and animal mimicry reached a fine art.

At the beginning of the fifteenth century, there were small groups of minstrels in the service of the municipal corporations of the larger towns, such as London, Bristol, York, Canterbury, Shrewsbury, Chester, and Norwich. They wore the town livery and played at local festivities and celebrations. The *waits,* as they were called, had other duties to perform, including the very odious one of piping the watch at certain fixed hours of the night.

The fifteenth century saw the invention of printing, and when books became available in large numbers and the upper classes learned to read, the popularity of the minstrels waned. They flourished between the eleventh and thirteenth centuries, and had quite disappeared by the sixteenth century. The lower class of entertainer still continued in the marketplace, together with the jugglers and acrobats, while some of the best were no doubt absorbed into the companies of stage players that were established in the early sixteenth century.

MEDIEVAL FOOL In typical motley dress, the jester wears a close-fitting hood. The peaks, representing asses ears, is thought to derive from the ancient Roman mime, Mimus Calvus.

RELIGIOUS PLAYS

In spite of the importance and popularity of the minstrels during the Middle Ages, the development of the theatre owes more in this period to the activities of the people themselves. The Middle Ages was, indeed, the great period of amateur theatricals. Apart from the folk drama arising from very ancient celebrations connected with farming and the land, such as the May Day festivals, the Mummers, and the Sword Dance, the chief contribution to the history of the theatre came through the medium of the Church.

This drama began in a very simple way, developed and established its own conventions, and brought to the common people that pageantry and entertainment so necessary to relieve the monotony of the daily round and the common task. From 970 onward there are records that show the introduction of drama into Church services. It probably came about through the desire of the clergy to make the incidents in the life of Christ appear more real to the congregations.

A beginning was made with the Easter morning service, when a short, simple scene was played before the altar. A seat representing the Sepulcher was placed where all could see, with two priests dressed as angels on either side. Three women would enter and wander up to the angels, one of whom then asked, "Whom do you seek in the Sepulcher, O Christian women?" They would reply, "Jesus of Nazareth, who was crucified, O heavenly ones." The angel would say, pointing, "He is not here. He has risen even as He foretold. Go announce that He has arisen from the Sepulcher." After this all would join with choir and congregation in *Te Deum Laudamus,* and the church bells would chime out in an effective climax.

When treated formally this little scene must have had a tremendous effect on the congregation. The dialogue was chanted in Latin and the angels' wings looked very unconvincing, but such was the pattern of the scene and the earnestness of the players that the performance was really effective.

The success of this small beginning was followed by other short scenes, such as the meeting of Mary Magdalene and Christ in the garden, Peter and John running to the Sepulcher, and the incredulity of Thomas. Later, at Christmas, other scenes were introduced, showing the shepherds, the star, and the three kings at the Manger. From being chanted in Latin the dialogue came to be spoken in English, and gradually the religious play evolved, quite separately from the service. The actors were the people of the church, the priests, nuns, and choirboys. Their costumes consisted of the usual ecclesiastical dress: the surplices, copes, and chasubles of the time.

MEDIEVAL DEVIL MASKS   As seen in these drawings, these false faces were grotesque and fearsome. They were often animal-like, with snouts of beasts and a variety of large horns.

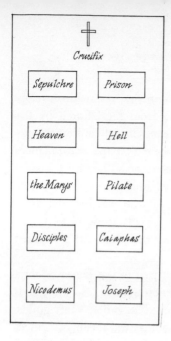

Crucifix

Sepulchre	Prison
Heaven	Hell
the Marys	Pilate
Disciples	Caiaphas
Nicodemus	Joseph

MIRACLE PLAY PLAN This diagram shows the mansions of the "Resurrection," a twelfth century miracle play. The placement of the settings was determined by the interior structure of the church and became fixed by tradition.

The whole interior of the church was used, and short scenes were played in various parts of the building. The setting in each case symbolized a particular place or scene, and for certain scenes a permanent structure was built in the church. Thus, instead of being represented by a seat, the Sepulcher became a wooden or iron construction, complete with hinged lid. The beautiful interiors of the early churches provided plenty of opportunity for dramatic effect, and the lighted candles carried by the actors heightened the emphasis on the individual scenes.

An example of a twelfth-century Resurrection play shows the various scenes arranged as in the diagram, with the crucifix naturally represented at the altar. The play would begin with the actors performing one scene, possibly near the entrance of the church, and then, having played it, moving on to the next scene, and so on right around the church. The content of these religious plays varied considerably, and incidents from the Old Testament were introduced. The increasing number of scenes, together with the larger congregations the plays attracted, made it necessary for the plays to be produced outside, on the church steps.

GUILD PRODUCTIONS

From the thirteenth to the fourteenth centuries, the main development was the taking over of the drama from the Church by the people themselves. This was because the Church authorities resented the enormous popularity and appeal that the performances themselves (as distinct from the Church services) had for the common people. The Church understood the latent power of the drama well enough, and it saw that the people who watched the plays showed no signs of spiritual uplift, but simply came to be entertained. So the Church stopped producing the plays and prohibited the clergy from taking part in them.

The plays, however, were an accepted part of the Easter celebrations, and the people demanded their entertainment, so the guilds took over the responsibility of production. The various craft guilds, which also had other responsibilities such as the repair of bridges and roads and the building of chapels and charitable institutions, took turns producing the plays and providing the actors, the costumes, and the various scenes and effects. From the steps of the church the spectacle moved to marketplace and guild hall.

The guilds took their responsibility for production very seriously, and they spent considerable sums on scenery, costumes, and effects, and even paid the actors for their part in the performance. Thus, a man at Coventry was paid 3s. 4d. for playing God; another was paid 4d. for cock-crowing; while at Hull, a certain Jenkin Smith received Is. Id. for taking the part of Noah.

MIRACLE PLAYS

The plays grew in length as more scenes from the Old Testament were added, and the performances lasted several days. The dialogue became more in keeping with daily life, and therefore more easily managed by the simple amateur actors.

The plays followed the tradition of the earlier church performances by having separately erected settings for each scene. The various settings were built of wood and canvas on elevated stages for all to see. If one can imagine a modern fairground arranged in a rectangle with all the sideshows distributed around the sides, which perhaps one or two in the central open space, it will give some idea of the staging of the miracle plays as played on the Continent.

A painting by the artist Jehan Fouquet shows an incident from one of the French miracle plays. Behind the central group of actors can be seen the several stages for the various scenes in the play. One of the most prominent figures in the painting is the prompter, who stands among the actors with the book of the play in one hand and a stick in the other. The prompter was very important because there was only one complete copy of the play (in manuscript). The actors were given their own lines to learn, but they had no idea of the rest of the play, so it was necessary for the prompter to indicate, by pointing his stick, the actor whose turn it was to speak.

The open space in the middle of the marketplace was used for various scenes, being very useful because it could represent any place for which there was no particular setting. It could also be used in conjunction with one of the set stages. In the Fouquet miniature, the king has left his throne on one of the stages, descended the steps to the ground, and joined the group of actors in the center. As much more movement was possible by the use of this central space, a further development had been made in the history of the theatre. The foundations of many of the Elizabethan stage conventions were laid in the Middle Ages, and it becomes easier to understand how audiences could imagine the place at which the scene was laid without the visual aid of scenery when we realize that it was done in the miracle plays.

In England the miracle plays did not develop in the same way that they did on the Continent. Instead of having set stages around the marketplace, the scenes were built on wagons. A contemporary description reads:

> . . . a highe place made like a howse with ij rowmes, being open on ye tope: the lower rowme they apparrelled and dressed them selves; and in the higher rowme they played: and they stood vpon 6 wheeles.

Of their progress we are told:

> They first beganne at ye Abbaye gates; & when the firste pagiente was played at ye Abbaye gates, then it was wheeled from thence to the pentice at ye highe crosse before ye mayor; and before that was donne, the seconde came, and ye firste wente in-to the watergate streete, and from thence vnto ye Bridge-streete, and soe all, one after an other, tell all ye pagiantes weare played.

Something of this arrangement still survives in London in the Lord Mayor's Show, although the "pageants" are only tableaux, and there is no acting or dialogue.

THE HELL MOUTH

One of the most popular scenes in the miracle plays was the Hell Mouth, with its assortment of demons rushing about making horrible noises, carrying fireworks and flaming spars on which powdered resinous pitch was thrown, causing clouds of smoke and flame. The Hell Mouth was usually provided with some device for opening, in order to render the effect of fire and smoke belching forth.

The demons appeared in most of the scenes, and as they had no lines to speak there must have been great competition for these parts. One rather suspects that the apprentices, being younger and more agile, took most of these devil parts, and when they came into contact with the older citizens (perhaps their masters) their devilry was no doubt most realistic.

HUMOR IN THE MIRACLE PLAYS

Although the plays were based on incidents from the Bible, a good deal of comic byplay crept in. Apart from the devils, such characters as the shepherds would probably have a short interlude before the appearance of the angel in which some invented "business" could be introduced, possibly some low humor which would evoke an immediate response from the audience. The playing of saints and other

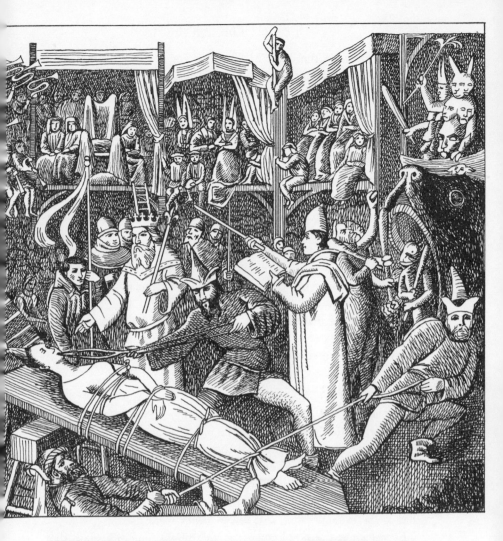

PERFORMANCE OF "THE MARTYRDOM OF ST. APOLLONIA" The mansions in the background progress from Heaven at the left through intermediate mansions to Hell, with the traditional Hell Mouth, at the right. Note the dominant position of the prompter.

sacred figures, on the other hand, called for no such relation with life, and the acting resolved itself into a series of formal and stilted movements.

THE ACTORS IN MIRACLE PLAYS

In England all the acting of both male and female characters was undertaken by men or boys, a convention that was to last right up to Restoration days. On the Continent, however, women took part in the miracle plays from time to time, and at Metz in 1468 a young amateur actress appeared as St. Catherine and had a large number of lines to speak.

The players had to be ready by 4:30 A.M. As the whole cycle of plays lasted for two or three days, they must have found it a very fatiguing business, especially as they had to repeat their performance at every stop on the route. On the Continent, where the plays took place in the market square, they were more fortunate in being able to join the rest of the audience in watching the other scenes when their own performance was over.

THE MORALITY PLAY

Together with the miracle plays, the morality play developed in the later years of the Middle Ages. The morality play had one central figure representing man, and all the abstract qualities of vice and virtue were characterized as real persons. Being more ethical than religious in theme, the morality play was a further step away from the Church's influence in the drama. The staging was similar to that of the miracle plays, but fewer scenes were used.

Everyman is the best-known example of the morality plays that have survived. In Cornwall certain amphitheatres were set up in the country where morality plays were performed. There are records of a play called *The Castle of Perseverance* being performed during the reign of Henry VI in which it is mentioned that Mercy was dressed in white, Ruthlessness all in red, Truth in a sad green, and Peace all in black.

RETURN OF THE PROFESSIONAL ACTOR

During the fifteenth century, the professional actor began to make his appearance again. It is quite possible that the professional wandering entertainer occasionally played in the miracles. The cycles took so long to perform that interludes of pure entertainment would have been welcome to both players and audience, and no doubt professional advice in acting was frequently sought and given.

THE RENAISSANCE

The fifteenth century saw a great change in social life in Europe, which was reflected in the treatment of the miracle plays. Pageantry became more and more important, and the spoken drama consequently declined. The performances took place more often in the banqueting hall than in the marketplace. With the invention of printing, the renaissance of learning, and the many colleges and educational centers that were being founded, the ruling class became more dominant. The miracle plays gradually declined in popularity, and drama rediscovered its old form. Scholars began writing plays, using for subject matter much of what they had read in the classic Roman writers.

Gian Giorgio Trissino was probably the first Italian writer of tragedy *in Italian*. His best-known plays were *Sofonisba,* written in 1515 and first performed in 1562, and *Italia Liberata*. Other dramatists of the time were Rucellai, Cinthio (*L'Orbecche*), Dolce, and Tasso, the great writer of pastoral plays, of which his *Aminta* had tremendous influence outside Italy for many years, and was widely translated. Ludovico Ariosto, whose great epic poem *Orlando Furioso* is more famous than any of his dramas, was probably the most important of the Renaissance playwrights; several of his dramas survive, and are highly regarded in Italy even today. Niccolo Machiavelli (*Mandragola*) and Pietro Aretino were among the best of the comedy writers.

RENAISSANCE STAGE DESIGN

Italy was the center of the Renaissance, and there, at the famous

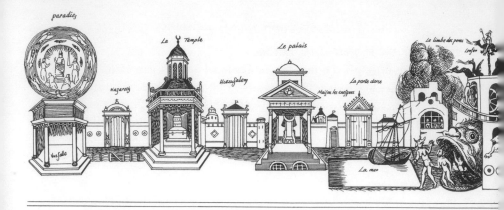

SIXTEENTH CENTURY MYSTERY PLAY In Valenciennes, spectators were faced by a straight stage with the traditional mansions from Paradise on the left to Hell at the right. The acting area is the open space directly in front of the mansions. Note the elaborate Hell Mouth on the right.

academies of Vicenza, Mantua, Milan, Naples, Florence, and Venice, new theatres were built, chiefly for the private performances of plays written by their scholars. Great artists such as Raphael designed the theatres and scenery, setting standards which have not been surpassed in the theatres of the whole world.

A manuscript by Vitruvius, a Roman architect of the first century B.C., came to light which gave information about architecture in general and the architecture of the Greek theatre in particular, and the architects of the Renaissance modeled their work on the ancient classic principles expounded in this manuscript. Perspective was one of the fascinating discoveries of the Renaissance. Artists and architects (in those days there was very little difference between the two) vied with each other in producing stage settings in which painted perspective was employed to the full. Serlio produced a work of his own on theatre architecture early in the sixteenth century, based very closely on Vitruvius' work. From Serlio we have illustrations showing the principles of stage setting for tragedy, comedy, and pastoral drama, into which trinity all plays of that time could be placed.

The scene for tragedy was a street of grand palaces with a dignified archway in the background and many statues and architectural adornments associated with grandeur. Comedy had an everyday street scene, with an inn, shops, and many balconied windows at greatly varying levels. It was essentially a lively and human setting, much closer to reality than was the tragic scene. The pastoral scene emphasized the lyrical qualities. It was a landscape with trees in the foreground and a rocky path wandering between laborers' cottages, such as could be seen anywhere in Italy.

Serlio's and other published works on the theatre eventually found their way to England and formed the basis of stage design in the seventeenth century, when Inigo Jones was designing the scenery for the Court masques.

THE INTERLUDES

By the sixteenth century the miracle plays had fallen into disuse, except in a few isolated instances, but companies of professional players were being formed which gave performances of the Interludes, as they were called, in halls and inns. The Interludes were short comic pieces based on everyday life. They more closely resembled our variety sketches than plays, but they certainly proved acceptable to the people of the times.

THE SCHOLAR-PLAYWRIGHTS

As printing became more universal, scholars in England were busy studying the ancient works and writing plays based on classical principles. The first plays by the scholar-playwrights were performed at the universities, and as they were written without any practical knowledge of the theatre, they seem stilted and pedantic to us. It was left to Shakespeare to infuse that profound knowledge of life, together with practical stagecraft, into the poetry of English drama by producing plays which have remained, and will remain, models for all time.

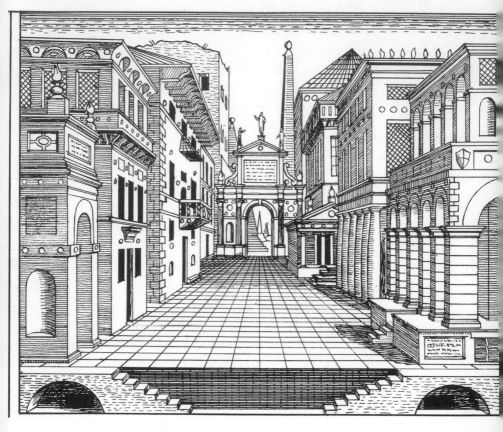

TRAGIC SCENE This drawing of the famous stock setting by Serlio, shows the Tragic Scene, distinguished by its palaces.

COMIC SCENE Serlio characterized his comic scene by the use of ordinary houses. Both settings comprised a masterly blend of perspective paintings and built up houses made of lath and canvas.

The Elizabethans

INN-YARD PLAYS

From about the middle of the sixteenth century, the traveling companies of players, which were now well established, began to give their performances on stages set up in the courtyards of certain inns in London. In those days, these inns were large and important establishments, being used as stations by the great network of carriers plying their trade over the entire country. When travel was necessary, or when goods were dispatched into the country, the inn was inevitably the starting place. Horses were hired, goods were transferred from carrier to carrier, and there was much bustle and excitement. In the early days, the actors had to take turns with the carriers in the use of the courtyard; but later, when the performances attracted large audiences, the proprietors of certain inns gave up the business with the carriers and concentrated on the drama.

The inns were generally of a standard design, the building being in four sections around a rectangular courtyard, with entrances at the back and front for the wagons and horses. The courtyard was open to the sky, and around it, on the walls of the inn, two or three galleries were constructed at different levels; they were roofed over but open at the sides.

The stage would be set up at one end of the courtyard, near the stairs which gave access to the galleries. At the back of the stage there would probably be a curtain, behind which space would be provided for the actors to use as a dressing room. The gallery immediately above the stage would sometimes be used in the action of the play, and was generally reserved for the actors.

These courtyards could comfortably hold some three or four hundred of the common people, who would pay a penny or two-pence to stand and watch the performance. The nobility and people of quality, who were also attracted to these inn-yard plays, would take seats in the galleries. Often, in certain parts of the courtyard, a simple platform or ramp would be constructed to give a better view of the stage, and possibly a seat would be provided on payment of a further sum.

The innkeepers reaped quite a harvest in providing refreshment to the audience, and as they also retained the admission fees to the galleries, the actors had to rely on what the courtyard provided them. In some towns the innkeeper was quite an important person. Davenant's father, for instance, was an alderman at Oxford, and eventually became Mayor of the city. In London, however, they were not so important or highly respected, or they might have helped to mitigate the growing hostility of the City Fathers toward the players.

PURITAN AND CIVIC HOSTILITY TOWARD THE THEATRE

All through the history of the theatre actors have had to contend with prejudice and hostility from either the civic authorities or the Puritans. The charges of the Puritans against the stage and the players were the old charges of the early Christians—ungodliness, idolatry, lewdness, profanity, and evil practices: in brief, that the players were pretending to be what they were not in real life. There was also the eternal complaint about Sunday performances.

The charges of the City Corporation were more practical. They complained that the public performance of a play was an opportunity for idle apprentices, who met with the sole purpose of creating disorders, and that it was an "unthrifty waste of money of the poor." They also made much of the accidents that occasionally happened on the stage or among the audience: "sundry slaughters and maimings of the Queen's subjects have happened by ruins of scaffolds, frames, and stages, and by engines, weapons, and powder used in plays."

About 1570 the Lord Mayor and the Corporation were also Puritans, so the players suffered under a double attack. The Lord Mayor would have stopped all performances of plays had not the players foreseen this danger years before. Therefore, when forming their companies, they had placed themselves under noble patronage and called their companies after the names of their patrons. Thus we have the Earl of Leicester's Men, the Queen's Men, the Admiral's Men, and so on. Attempts by the City to regulate the players were therefore often interfered with by higher authority, usually through the Privy Council.

TOURING COMPANIES

There was one circumstance, however, in which the City Fathers had their way in stopping the performances, and that was in times of great plague. During a hot summer, the open sewers and conduits that ran in the streets would do their deadly work, and as the plague was most infectious, all public gatherings would be prohibited. In these times the players would take to the road and tour the country.

From 1573 to 1587 there were twenty-three visiting companies giving performances in Stratford, so that Shakespeare must have seen plenty of acting in his youth. The companies also gave private performances at Court, in noble households, at the universities, and at the Inner Temple. They had a universal appeal to all classes of the community, and it is interesting to note how Shakespeare includes in his plays characters and episodes especially written for the scholar, the courtier, the poet, and the common people. However, a statute of 1572 directed that all strolling players who had not been licensed by a lord be treated as vagabonds.

THE FIRST PUBLIC THEATRES

In 1576 the players had been having a bad time, what with the plague and the City Fathers, so the leading player of the Earl of Leicester's Men launched out with spirit and shrewdness. James Burbage, a carpenter turned player, decided to build a public theatre for plays just outside the City limits, at Shoreditch. This region was rural in those days, and there had been a pleasure ground (Moorfields) nearby which had been set aside for sports and picnics. It was close enough to the City to attract an audience, and had the great advantage of being outside the jurisdiction of the Corporation.

There is little information about the "Theatre," as it was called, but we can imagine that it did not differ greatly from later theatres concerning which we are better informed. It was a wooden structure, and probably circular in plan. The Earl of Leicester's Men found their new home very successful, and crowds flocked to their performances. The same year another theatre was built quite near, and called the Curtain, and this also came under the management of the astute Burbage.

When Shakespeare first came to London in his early twenties, he went to live at Shoreditch, and was soon at work at one or the other of the two theatres. In 1596 another theatre, the Blackfriars, was opened in the City. Although it was within the City limits, it was outside the jurisdiction of the Corporation, being Crown property. It was part of the old abbey of the Black Friars which had become Crown property after the Reformation. Other theatres built outside the City limits on the south bank of the Thames were the Rose, built in 1587, and the Swan, built in 1595.

ELIZABETHAN PLAYHOUSE   Traditional features were the tapered stage (partially roofed over), the curtained "tiring house" (behind), and the balconies, used by both spectators and actors.

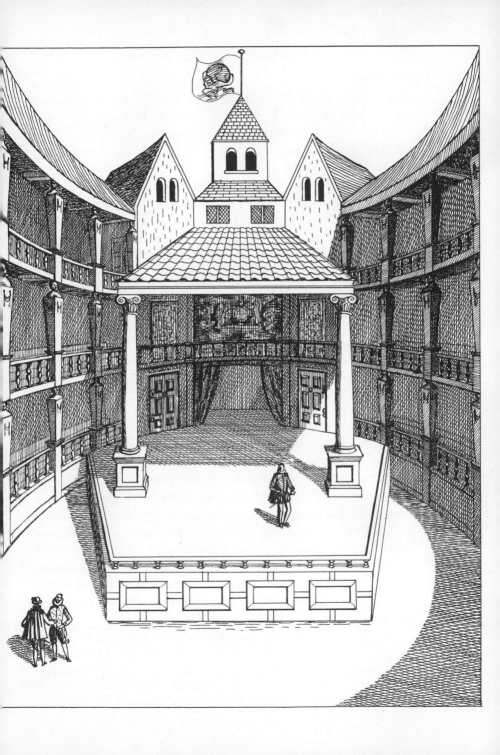

THE SWAN

There exists a rough sketch of the Swan, made by a visiting Dutchman, Johan de Witt. It shows that the designers of the early theatres compromised between the rectangular inn yard, with its galleries, and the circular arena used for bull-baiting, a popular amusement of the time.

The stage was square and projected well into the arena, or pit. Around this roofless arena were covered galleries, very much as in the old inn yards. The rear part of the stage was roofed over either with tiles or with thatch, and at least one gallery was provided at the rear of the stage for use in staging the plays. There was a central opening in the rear wall with a curtained alcove, or inner stage, and a large door on either side. Above the roof of the stage there was a small hut or turret, which may have housed some primitive machinery for the stage. From the turret a trumpeter blew warning blasts announcing the commencement of the performance. A flag also flew from it, and could be seen from across the river, indicating that a performance would be given that afternoon.

THE GLOBE

On the death of James Burbage his two sons, Richard and Cuthbert, carried on at the Theatre; but owing to some difficulty about the renewal of the lease by the ground landlord, they decided to move elsewhere. In 1598 they formed a syndicate with some of the Lord Chamberlain's Men who were playing at the Curtain. The players were Shakespeare, John Heming, Augustine Phillips, Thomas Pope, and William Kemp. At the end of the year, with carpenters and laborers, they began pulling down the Theatre for the timber and fittings, which were to be used (for financial reasons) in building the new theatre. This was called the Globe, and was built in accordance with the latest stage developments on the south bank of the river, at Bankside.

By this time Shakespeare had written about twelve of his plays, including *Romeo and Juliet, A Midsummer Night's Dream, The Merchant of Venice*, and *Henry IV*, and he was already acknowledged as the greatest living dramatist. But the Globe was yet to witness the full flower of his genius in the great tragedies he wrote later.

The company contained the leading actors of the day, and the Globe outshone all other theatres in the standard of its plays and the quality of its productions. The company was organized on a profit-sharing basis. The original syndicate of the two Burbages and the five leading actors was known as the "House-keepers," and received a certain proportion of the takings. The rest of the company received shares of the receipts according to their status in the company. When these actors became more important by virtue of their increasing skill, they were promoted to be house-keepers, and received a further share in the receipts.

When James I came to the throne, he was so pleased with the Globe company that he allowed them to call themselves the King's Men. Their success was further assured when they acquired the Blackfriars Theatre in the City for use as winter quarters, for this theatre was entirely roofed in, and with a few braziers of burning coal distributed about the house was reasonably comfortable for cold winter afternoons. Indeed, the company played as often at the Blackfriars as at the Globe, for the Blackfriars was a semiprivate theatre and attracted a better class of audiences. This was naturally more profitable to the company, as charges could be raised, with a resulting increase in the takings.

THE FORTUNE

The nearby Rose Theatre suffered greatly from the competition of the Globe, so the managers, Henslowe and Alleyn, decided to build a new theatre in the City between Golden Lane and Whitecross Street, which they called the Fortune. Although it was a square building instead of circular like the Globe, its stage was identical, the dimensions being recorded as forty-three feet wide by twenty-eight feet deep. To give some idea of the real size of this stage, it is worth mentioning that the average theatre in London today has a proscenium opening of about thirty feet.

QUEEN ELIZABETH AT 59
Here is a portrait of the Queen in elaborate court dress. The "cannon" sleeve, long stomacher and the farthingale (hooped petticoat) were characteristic of the costume.

SHAKESPEARE AND THE SCHOLAR-PLAYWRIGHTS

Shakespeare brought real life to Elizabethan audiences, not only in his presentation on the stage of such characters as Sir John Falstaff and Mistress Quickly and the atmosphere of the tavern and the city street, but even in his verse, which had the familiar ring of the town and countryside. It is only necessary to read the works of dramatists immediately prior to Shakespeare to realize the contrast he afforded. They were primarily scholars and literary men, and their verse seems dry, pedantic, and lifeless. They resented the fact that Shakespeare, a common actor, could also write successful plays.

John Lyly, who was born ten years before Shakespeare, wrote several plays inspired by the classics, developing a prose style made up of puns and the fashionable jugglery of words. George Peele, Thomas Lodge, Thomas Nashe, and Thomas Kyd (whose *Spanish Tragedy* was one of the most popular plays of the time) all wrote plays modeled on the works of the Roman dramatist Seneca. Robert Greene has become famous chiefly for his attack on Shakespeare; in the publication of one of his plays he advised his university friends to give up writing plays because the actors had "one, an upstart crow, of their own to supply their needs." Even Marlowe, although he wrote some fine poetry, wrote plays that were difficult to act and bring to life.

Shakespeare, with his feet firmly planted on the stage and his acute powers of observation, re-created in dramatic form life in England as he saw it. It was politic, of course, to make the action of the plays take place in some foreign country and to give the important personages, the nobles and princes, foreign names so that there could be no chance of recrimination by some lord who thought he saw himself caricatured on the stage. But he could not resist placing the famous tavern of South London, the Elephant, even in the mythical country of Illyria *(Twelfth Night)*; and near Athens *(A Midsummer Night's Dream)* he introduced a group of rustics who were given uncommon but typically English names, and who behaved exactly as Shakespeare may have seen them behave in the fields and hamlets of Warwickshire.

CHRISTOPHER MARLOWE

Among Shakespeare's immediate predecessors, however, was one true poetic genius—Christopher Marlowe. Marlowe wrote only four plays (he was killed in a tavern fight when he was only thirty years old): *Tamburlaine, The Tragical History of Doctor Faustus, The Jew of Malta,* and *Edward II.* No one before him had written such glorious blank verse, and probably no one after him but Shakespeare. He is regarded as the greatest Elizabethan dramatist next to Shakespeare.

BEN JONSON

Among Shakespeare's contemporary dramatists, his immediate friends were Ben Jonson, Beaumont, and Fletcher. Jonson was continually in trouble, for he was hot-headed and quarrelsome. He was in prison three times for various reasons. He was, however, a fine scholar and wrote some good comedies. Shakespeare's company gave Jonson his first success, putting on *Every Man in His Humour* in 1598. Jonson followed this with *Sejanus* in 1603, *Eastward Ho* in 1604 (a collaboration with his old friends and rivals, Marston and Chapman), *Volpone* in 1606, *Epicoene* in 1609, *The Alchemist* in 1610, and *Bartholomew Fair* in 1614.

Jonson was rather overbearing, and at times, no doubt, patronized Shakespeare for his lack of classical learning, although he was always envious of Shakespeare's success. He was honest enough to admit Shakespeare's greatness, however, and when the latter died in 1616, Jonson wrote a sincere memorial in verse.

BEAUMONT AND FLETCHER

Francis Beaumont and John Fletcher, who worked and lived together, were prolific writers and produced over fifty plays between them. They wrote romantic comedies, pastorals, tragedies, and the new kind of play, tragicomedy, which had some tragic incidents but a happy ending. Among their works were *The Maid's Tragedy, The Knight of Malta* (a tragicomedy), *Rule a Wife and Have a Wife,* and *The Knight of the Burning Pestle.*

OTHER CONTEMPORARIES OF SHAKESPEARE

Shakespeare's other contemporaries were Thomas Dekker, John Webster, John Ford, Philip Massinger, John Marston, and George Chapman. Dekker wrote some good comedies (*Shoemaker's Holiday, The Honest Whore*), and understanding the new realism that Shakespeare was achieving, he introduced many scenes from the low life of the times into his plays. Webster and Ford wrote tragedies, Webster's most popular plays being *The Duchess of Malfi* and *The White Devil;* Ford's, *'Tis Pity She's a Whore.*

SIR WALTER RALEIGH In this drawing, based on the portrait of the Armada year, 1588, the famed courtier is shown wearing the close-fitting doublet and carrying the cloak which were adapted to Elizabethan stage dress.

ACTING

Hamlet's directions to the players in Act III, scene ii, are very illuminating, as they give us Shakespeare's own ideas about acting, which can be summed up as "be natural but not too natural."

Speak the speech, I pray you, as I pronounced it to you, trippingly on the tongue: but if you mouth it, as many of your players do, I had as lief the town-crier spoke my lines. Nor do not saw the air too much with your hand, thus, but use all gently; for in the very torrent, tempest, and, as I may say, the whirlwind of passion, you must acquire and beget a temperance that may give it smoothness. O, it offends me to the soul to hear a robustious periwig-pated fellow tear a passion to tatters, to very rags, to split the ears of the groundlings, who for the most part are capable of nothing but inexplicable dumbshows and noise. . . . Be not too tame neither, but let your own discretion be your tutor: suit the action to the word, the word to the action; with this special observance, that you o'erstep not the modesty of nature: for any thing so overdone is from the purpose of playing, whose end, both at the first and now, was and is, to hold, as 'twere, the mirror up to nature; to show virtue her own feature, scorn her own image, and the very age and body of the time his form and pressure. Now this overdone, or come tardy off, though it make the unskilful laugh, cannot but make the judicious grieve; the censure of the which one must in your allowance o'erweigh a whole theatre of others. O, there be players that I have seen play, and heard others praise, and that highly, not to speak it profanely, that, neither having the accent of Christians nor the gait of Christian, pagan, nor man, have so strutted and bellowed that I have thought some of nature's journeymen had made men and not made them well, they imitated humanity so abominably.

. . . And let those that play your clowns speak no more than is set down for them [probably a dig at Will Kemp, whose habit of introducing his own gags on the stage must have caused Shakespeare a deal of annoyance]; *for there be of them that will themselves laugh, to set on some quantity of barren spectators to laugh too; though, in the mean time, some necessary question of the play be then to be considered: that's villanous, and shows a most pitiful ambition in the fool that uses it.* . . .

The players at the Globe were capable of delivering Shakespeare's lines with great speed and zest, and with the constant stream of characters coming and going, they could complete their performance of the play within two hours.

Shakespeare himself played various parts in his plays, including the Ghost in *Hamlet* and Theseus in *A Midsummer Night's Dream*, parts that had little personal character, but needed a dignified and poetic interpretation. His chief activity apart from the writing of his

COUNTRYWOMAN'S COSTUME
The drawing shows the ruff and the farthingale, typical of Elizabethan dress.

plays was in the direction of their production. Some of his chief actors were Richard Burbage, Edward Alleyn, John Heming (who was later to publish his plays), and Will Kemp as leading comic actor. Other clowns of the time were Robert Wilson, John Singer, and Thomas Pope.

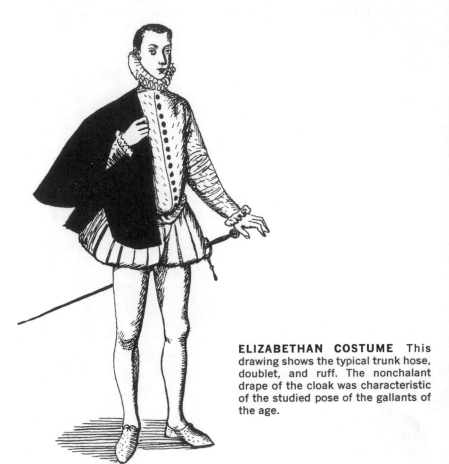

ELIZABETHAN COSTUME This drawing shows the typical trunk hose, doublet, and ruff. The nonchalant drape of the cloak was characteristic of the studied pose of the gallants of the age.

RICHARD BURBAGE

Richard Burbage played all Shakespeare's great tragic parts and, as Shakespeare wrote his plays to suit the actors of his company, he must have had Burbage in mind when writing *Hamlet, Othello, King Lear,* and *Macbeth.*

Little has been recorded about Burbage, except that his movements were graceful and he was perfectly natural on the stage, while his musical voice gave beauty to quite commonplace verse. Besides playing in Shakespeare's plays, he also appeared in many of Ben Jonson's, in Kyd's *Spanish Tragedy,* and in Webster's popular tragedy *The Duchess of Malfi.*

Burbage was also a painter, and he has left several portraits of his fellow actors which are now in the Dulwich Gallery.

EDWARD ALLEYN

The other great tragic actor of the time was Edward Alleyn. He was noted for his acting in Marlowe's plays, especially in *Tamburlaine,* and he also played in many of Shakespeare's early plays. When Shakespeare was at the Globe, Alleyn was in partnership with his father-in-law, Henslowe, first at the Rose and later at the Fortune. He also shared with Henslowe certain interests in bear-baiting and, being a shrewd man of business, he made a fortune; bought Dulwich Manor for £10,000, and founded Dulwich College.

Alleyn was a typical example of the Elizabethan: a scholar, poet, courtier, and adventurer—a man with a wide variety of interests and one always ready to break new ground. He was a very tall man, of splendid physique, and was best in majestic parts.

RICHARD TARLTON

About 1580 the chief comic actor was Richard Tarlton, whose popularity was probably mainly due to his improvisations. The audience would suggest a theme or verse, to which he would extemporize some doggerel or cap it with another. He was also noted for his jigs, which were humorous dances accompanied by comic patter. The jig usually took place at the end of the play, and was not really

RICHARD TARLTON The greatest of Elizabethan clowns is shown performing the jig for which he was so famous. The drawing derives from the title page of a contemporary manuscript.

connected with it. Tarlton has been associated by many scholars with *Hamlet*'s Yorick. He died in 1588.

WILL KEMP

Will Kemp took Tarlton's place as the leading comic actor. Kemp, who modeled his style largely on Tarlton's, played with Shakespeare's company and went with them to the Globe. He appeared in many of Shakespeare's early plays, playing Peter in *Romeo and Juliet,* Dogberry, one of the Dromios, and Launcelot Gobbo.

He did not remain long at the Globe, however, possibly because of differences of opinion with Shakespeare, and left to join the Earl of Worcester's Men. He also traveled extensively on the Continent, where he was very popular. He is chiefly noted for his "nine days' wonder"—his wager, which he won, that he would dance all the way from London to Norwich.

WILL KEMP Reproduced from the title page of his "Nine Days' Wonder," written in 1600, this drawing shows the actor dancing a morris. The book gave an account of Kemp's memorable dance from London to Norwich in 1599, which he performed on a wager and won.

THE BOY ACTORS

Shakespeare had a certain limitation in the writing of his plays, in that all the female parts had to be played by boys or men. Women had never achieved any importance in the theatre of the past. The theatre was essentially a masculine domain, and while women did appear in the Roman theatres, it was chiefly as singers or dancers. The female parts in the old plays had always been acted by men.

Women were very much in the background in the everyday life of Elizabethan times, and not until Restoration days was it considered possible for them to act.

Here was a practical stage problem which Shakespeare solved very well. A boy could easily put on a woman's costume and, with the necessary makeup and decoration, pass as a woman. Being a mere boy, however, he would hardly have sufficient experience of life to do justice to the interpretation of the role. Shakespeare therefore arranged for the most difficult acting to be done by the male characters.

Typical of this procedure is the opening scene of *Twelfth Night* in which the Duke Orsino discusses his mistress at length, so that when she finally appears her character has already been established in the minds of the audience. Another useful device was that of making his heroines assume male attire. When one considers the dress of the time it will be seen that a youth with a slight figure could easily give a very convincing interpretation of a woman in man's costume. In the men's costume, the padded doublet and full breeches or trunk hose would quite conceal a feminine figure and, conversely, the women's costume, with its enormous skirts and padded sleeves, would easily conceal a boy's figure.

The boy players were thoroughly expert at female impersonation, and some of them continued with their feminine roles even after their voices broke. The part of Lady Macbeth was probably played by one of these "senior" boys, who would naturally be much more experienced, and capable of playing a more difficult part.

Unfortunately, there is little record of the boy actors, although some must have continued playing female parts until they were middle-aged. Nat Field was the best known, but he graduated from one of the companies of boy players and did not play women's parts with Shakespeare's company. When the Globe company took over the Blackfriars Theatre in 1608, they retained the leading boy actors, Ostler, Underwood, and Eggleston, but little is known about them.

No doubt the boys were a constant problem to the companies: they were growing up all the time, their voices would crack, and they would then have to be replaced. Suitable boys must have been scarce, and that is probably why there are rarely more than two or three female characters in Shakespeare's plays.

COMPANIES OF BOY ACTORS

Apart from the boys who served an apprenticeship with the regular companies, there were two troupes composed entirely of boy actors.

JAMES I AS A BOY This portrait was painted in 1574, showing James I wearing engorged pantaloons called Venetians, a style imported from Venice.

They were the choirboys of St. Paul's, who played near the Cathedral, and the choirboys of the Chapel Royal, who played at the Blackfriars Theatre before the Globe company acquired it. That they were extremely popular in London is proved by the serious rivalry they created with Shakespeare's company at one time, as is shown by Hamlet's discussion with Rosencrantz, which concludes:

> *Hamlet.* Do the boys carry it away?
> *Rosencrantz.* Ay, that they do, my lord; Hercules and
> his load too.

"Hercules and his load" is a reference to the Globe, which had a sign outside its entrance of Hercules holding up the world.

Ben Jonson wrote plays for the Chapel Royal boys, while Marston and Dekker wrote for the boys of St. Paul's. There was great rivalry between Jonson on the one hand and Marston and Dekker on the other, and they attacked each other in successive plays. The popularity of these companies did not last, however, and the public soon deserted them for the regular companies.

STAGING

The stages in those days were well supplied with trapdoors, used not only in the action of certain plays, such as the gravediggers' scene in *Hamlet,* but also for passing small pieces of scenery or furniture onto the stage. This would be done in full view of the audience, but at the time there would be some action on another part of the stage which would distract their attention.

Shakespeare's plays were not split up into separate scenes as they are usually played today, but were played with a continuous flow of characters coming on and going off the stage. Often certain characters in a scene would still be speaking when players in the following scene were already in view and approaching another part of the vast stage. The changing atmosphere of successive scenes—from comedy to tragedy, from the bustle of the public square to the more intimate interior—was created almost entirely by dialogue. When a definite break was required it was effected by a dance or procession, or by the use of rhyming couplets, a stage convention that existed well into the eighteenth century.

The study of *Hamlet* gives much information about the acting and staging of plays in these times. It is possible by reading the play to reconstruct the way in which it was staged.

For example, in Act I, scene iv, Hamlet confronts the ghost of his father. This takes place, as Hamlet says earlier, on "the platform," otherwise the gallery above the stage. The Ghost appears and does not speak, but, beckoning Hamlet to follow, makes an exit. Hamlet does so, in spite of protestations from his friends, Horatio and Marcellus. After Hamlet goes they have six lines of dialogue, which gives the Ghost and Hamlet just sufficient time to descend the stairs onto the main stage, where they make their entrance and the Ghost begins to speak. After the Ghost has made his long speech he makes an exit, presumably through a trapdoor (the old convention was that ghosts were subterranean beings). Horatio and Marcellus then make their entrance and after some conversation with Hamlet are made to swear secrecy about the night's happenings. The Ghost echoes the order to swear; the stage directions read, "Ghost cries under the stage."

When the play is read with all the facilities of the Elizabethan stage in mind, some idea of the continual flow of movement is gained. On a modern stage it does not seem so convincing, and some change of setting, such as a drop curtain, is usually necessary between the two scenes.

COSTUMES

The costumes worn by the players were most important, as they formed almost the only feature of decoration on the stage. The actors who played nobles and princely characters wore the simple but very richly decorated dress of the period. The fools and clowns wore the costume of the common people. There were also certain special costumes not associated with everyday dress.

Eastern characters, such as Othello, usually wore a turban of some kind, long, baggy trousers gathered in at the ankle, and a short coat ornamented with the Elizabethan idea of Arabic decoration.

Some form of Greek or Roman costume was also used, probably a tight seamless tunic after the style of a cuirass with a short pleated skirt. Buskins and a helmet plentifully decorated with feathers completed the costume which, as can be seen in old engravings, was in use until the nineteenth century.

Robes and gowns were also used for friars and other characters of a special kind. From Henslowe's diary we find that a costume for Cardinal Wolsey cost the company £38 12s. 2d. for "coats, velvets, satins, and lace," a princely sum in those days. The costumes for the female characters were also expensive, £9 being spent on a taffeta gown, while a skirt of silver camlet cost £2 15s.

The women's dress of the period, as worn by the boy players, was very rich in decoration, although simple in shape. The curious stilted shape of the figure was obtained by a leather corset which had two semicircular sidepieces around the waist at right angles to the bodice. The petticoats and the skirt were drawn in over the sidepieces, which had the effect of bunching out the skirt at the waist so that it fell in long, straight folds to the ground. It can be seen that the boys could easily manage these rather stiff and all-concealing costumes.

The fashionable color for hair was red (after the false hair of the Queen), and red wigs were naturally very popular among the ladies of the Court, another point which gave conviction to the boys' use of them.

There was a great deal of stage jewelry to give the finishing touches to the richness of the costumes. There is a considerable use of pageantry in Shakespeare's plays, and the richness of the costumes played an important part in the many processions and formal dances which punctuated the performances at the Globe and the other theatres. The costumes of the numerous heralds, with their surcoats emblazoned with heraldic devices, would, with their bold decorative qualities, help to achieve a dramatic and pleasing spectacle.

Costumes were the big expense to the Elizabethan actors, and they generally spent a considerable proportion of the takings in providing additions to their wardrobes.

MUSIC IN THE THEATRE

Music also played an important part in the productions. Shakespeare's innumerable songs and the stage directions in *The Tempest,* for example, called for a small orchestra. In de Witt's sketch of the Swan the word *Orchestra* is written under the first gallery at the left side of the stage, which would be a very suitable place for it.

At the end of the various acts a formal dance was given in which all the players took part. Music and a flourish of trumpets also accompanied the many processions which are mentioned in the stage directions of Shakespeare's plays. If a character was killed on the stage a procession was formed to bear off the body. No doubt, there was also considerable stage business not mentioned in the plays.

ARTIFICIAL STAGE LIGHTING

Artificial lighting was first used in England in Shakespeare's time. Although the Globe was open to the sky and performances were given only on summer afternoons, the stage balcony would be in shadow, and in some scenes candlelight could be used for effect. In *Romeo and Juliet* the balcony became Juliet's bedchamber, and probably had some lighted candles to denote that the action was taking place at night. In the first scene in *Hamlet,* which we presume took place on the balcony, there is Horatio's reference to "the morn, in russet mantle clad, walks o'er the dew of yon high eastern hill," which might indicate the use of a concealed lighting effect, which the Italians were using before this time. The Blackfriars Theatre was roofed in, so artificial lighting was necessary. Chandeliers holding numerous candles were probably the chief source, as they must have been at the performances held at Court.

COURT PATRONAGE OF THE THEATRE

The development of Shakespeare's art and the Elizabethan theatre was bound up with the growth of Court influence in the drama. Henry VIII was very fond of pageants, masques, and dramatic diversions, and when Elizabeth came to the throne she also developed a taste for plays. Shakespeare's company continually played at Court, and the patronage the players enjoyed from various nobles saved them many times from extinction at the hands of the City Fathers.

Some of Shakespeare's plays are said to have been written to the order of the Queen, and there is an old tradition that *The Merry Wives of Windsor* was the outcome of her wish to see Falstaff in love. There is no doubt that it is not of the same quality as the other plays in which the immortal Sir John appears, and we can guess what Shakespeare thought of it.

COURT MASQUES

As the performances at Court increased, it became apparent that the needs of the Court were rather different from the demands of the public audiences. The public wanted plenty of dramatic action, passionate acting, and low-comedy relief, while the Court audiences wanted a more poetic spectacle in which the ladies and gentlemen of the Court could take part.

There is a hint of this in one of Shakespeare's last plays, *The Tempest,* in which Prospero conjures up a masque to celebrate the betrothal of Miranda and Ferdinand. It was been suggested that Shakespeare was influenced by the masques that were especially written and produced for the Court. Some years before 1611 (when it is presumed that *The Tempest* was written), Ceres and Juno appeared in a masque by Samuel Daniel. Nymphs called *naiads* and reapers performing a country dance appeared in other masques which Shakespeare, with his connections at Court, may have seen. Some writers even suggest that Prospero's explanation of the abrupt ending to the masque in *The Tempest*—the dissolving of "the cloud-capp'd towers, the gorgeous palaces"—is a direct reference to the scenic devices of Inigo Jones. While the speech has a deeper, philosophical meaning, it is certainly possible that in writing it Shakespeare was influenced by the scenic splendor of the Court masques.

Ben Jonson began writing exclusively for the Court performers, and produced a large number of masques, which were a combination of spectacle, dances, and formal recitation. No great acting was required in the performances, which were, in effect, a dramatization of the courtly qualities of beautiful and dignified appearance, refined speech, and graceful movement.

INIGO JONES

Inigo Jones, artist and architect, produced the masques and designed the scenic backgrounds and the costumes. Jones had studied art in Italy, and he returned with a store of information about the Italian theatres, which by then had developed the art of staging to a great extent, evolving stage devices for moving the elaborate scenery, colored lighting, and many other elements of the theatre which we associate with much later times.

A large number of sketches, plans, and diagrams by Inigo Jones survive and give us information about the staging of the masques. Considerable sums were spent, £3000 being recorded as the cost of a masque produced for the Queen.

Ingenuity as well as lavishness was displayed in some of the devices for moving scenery, which was usually done in full view of the audience. The movement of the scenery was, indeed, an integral part of the masque. Gods and goddesses were made to appear and vanish at will by clouds which moved across the scene.

This emphasis on setting was a source of irritation to Jonson, and finally resulted in a quarrel with Jones. Jones, however, was in the stronger position and continued to direct the masques, while other writers provided the scripts.

THE LEGACY FROM THE ELIZABETHANS

Within the space of fifty years, drama had developed from the pedantic, lifeless verse of the scholar-playwrights to the great force of a Shakespearean tragedy, full of deep penetration of character, in a language that reached heights of perfection that have never been approached since. Acting must also have reached its greatest heights, with Burbage its paragon—for what other actor has had a *Hamlet,* an *Othello,* a *Lear,* written for him? And the masques, with the sumptuous settings and costumes, and with Inigo Jones to direct, achieved new levels of artistic endeavor which, although never reached again, bequeathed to the public theatres a tradition of spectacle that played a large part in the theatres of later centuries.

The
Commedia
dell 'Arte

A TRAVELING THEATRE

With the coming of the Renaissance in Italy and the magnificent
theatres that were built to house the spectacular productions of
classic plays and opera, the popular *commedia dell'arte,* or companies of comedians, developed quite separately. These comedians
refined their art and performances to such a high standard of execution that their work had a strong influence on the theatre in Europe
for nearly two hundred years.

The entertainment they provided was enjoyed by all classes of
the community, and they traveled across Europe with great success, even though they rarely spoke other than their own tongue.
Their success was partly due to the contrast they provided to the
regular theatres—which were presenting classic dramas of the past
—by drawing the themes and characters of their plays from real
life and the people of their own times. They drew largely from
observation, playing on the weaknesses and vanities of human
beings. In Italy they often used the dialect of the district in which
they were playing.

ORIGINS OF THE COMMEDIA DELL'ARTE

The Italian comedians had their origins in the dim past of the Roman Atellan theatre, and possibly earlier still. The farces which had become so popular when the Romans became tired of the Greek tragedies were also improvised from a simple plot or scenario. The pantomime, which developed from the actor's having his lines chanted by a chorus while he acted his part in mime, was to be exploited to great advantage by the Italian comedians.

Other links with the ancient classical theatres were the masks worn by the comedians and the character of the Captain, who is almost an exact counterpart of a character in a comedy by Plautus. Also, in the early days of the Italian comedians, the phallus was worn by Pantalone, and there were numerous other analogies to indicate that the *commedia dell'arte* owed much in its development to the theatre of the past.

THE ACTORS

All the dialogue of the plays was improvised by the players themselves, so the acting became highly developed and specialized. Each actor developed the presentation of a particular character, which had its own unique personality, and he usually played that character until the end of his career. Each character had its own canons of behavior on the stage, and the actors had an extensive repertoire of speeches, cracks, and gags which could be used in any given situation. The speeches were so fashioned that they could be lengthened or compressed according to need. In order to give a performance it was only necessary to put up the *scenario* (the bare outline of the plot) in the wings before the performance to serve as a guide to the actors in their comings and goings on the stage. The actors cooperated so closely and understood their roles so well that the performance went with a swing from the very beginning. This could have been done only by highly practiced professional players who were masters of their craft.

The players often intermarried, as women also had their part in the companies, and the traditions of their craft were handed down

SIXTEENTH CENTURY ITALIAN PLATFORM STAGE Note the open stage, often supported by wooden trestles, and the characteristic back curtain.

from father to son and from mother to daughter. Thus the company was often a family in the real sense of the word.

The most famous actors of the *commedia dell'arte* were Flaminio Scala, Andreini, Biancolelli, and Riccoboni, all cultured men and distinguished as poets and writers. These actors were probably the original writers of much of the dialogue used by the comedians, which was handed down through generations of players. The most famous company was probably the Gelosi, of which Scala and Andreini were members, as was Andreini's wife, the lovely Isabella, a cultured, witty, and beautiful woman who gave her name to the heroines of the plays.

THE COMMEDIA DELL'ARTE IN FRANCE

The influence of the *commedia dell'arte* was felt chiefly in France. There, after a period of insecurity during which they were sometimes invited to perform by the King or the nobles of the Court, followed by their expulsion from Paris by Parliament, they became firmly established in the seventeenth century.

At first they performed in their own language, but later they were able to perform in French, and their performances underwent a change in spirit. The characters became more elegant and witty, and the costumes and presentation were adapted to suit the change of style. The French playwright Molière was greatly influenced by the comedians, and at one time his company shared a theatre with them.

In 1680 the existing theatres in Paris were unified by the King, and the Theatre Français was established and given the monopoly for spoken drama. The Italians were allowed to continue their performances at their own theatre, the Hôtel de Bourgogne, but they were limited to pantomime and music which, however, had always played a great part in their presentations.

At the end of the seventeenth century, they were again driven out of Paris, having become unpopular with the authorities. They came back in 1716, after which they had many years of popularity. They began to perform plays by French writers, and with the influx of French actors into their companies they finally merged into the native drama. By 1780 there were no longer any Italian comedians at the Theatre des Italiens, although in their own country certain companies of comedians were playing in the old traditional style until the nineteenth century. Some additional characters, such as Gros-Guillaume, Gaultier Garguille, and Turlupin, were created by the French actors who played in comedies in the Italian style. The *commedia dell'arte* helped to shape the theatre in France, and was finally absorbed by it.

INFLUENCE IN ENGLAND

From France, their influence passed to England with Charles II who, having spent part of his exile in France, must have seen them often in Paris, and gave them permission to play a season in London during which they proved very popular. Pepys, in the *Diary*, mentions having seen "Polichinelly" several times. (*Polichinelle* was the French version of *Punchinello*.) No doubt Charles enjoyed their performances and found the women players witty, amusing, and beautiful, for after the Restoration he was partly responsible for the acceptance of the actress as a new convention on the English stage.

A company had been in England as far back as 1527. Shakespeare must have known of them, as he describes Pantaloon in *As You Like It*, while the comic letter scene in *Twelfth Night* might easily have been a scene played by the comedians. Indeed, is there not something of the Captain, Harlequin, Brighella, Columbine, and the Doctor in Sir Toby, Sir Andrew, Fabian, Maria, and Malvolio?

CREATION OF CHARACTERS

The characters of the *commedia dell'arte* were of two main types: the comic characters, who performed the most important parts in the plays; and the "straight" characters, who provided the love interest, giving a rather poetic or romantic interpretation of their roles. The characters, being actually created by individual actors, varied with different companies, and adopted various names. Other actors created new characters, which were also handed down through the generations. Altogether, there are innumerable characters created by the comedians at various times on their extensive travels. There are, however, certain very well-known characters, whose description will serve to give a picture of the form of the *commedia dell'arte*.

THE COMIC CHARACTERS

Arlecchino (Harlequin). The most famous character of the *commedia dell'arte* originally had quite a different personality from the Harlequin who eventually found his way into the English pantomime. He was originally rather a numskull, a valet or servant, a

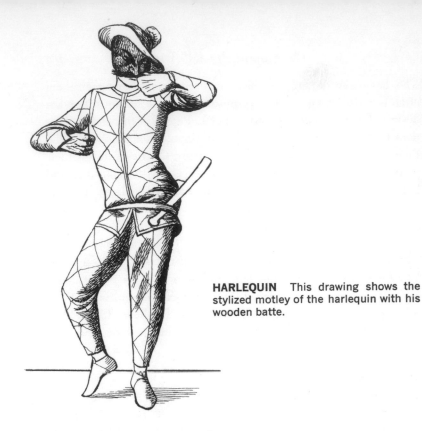

HARLEQUIN This drawing shows the stylized motley of the harlequin with his wooden batte.

simple native of Bergamo; but although guileless, he was full of pranks and always extremely agile. He would be played by an actor who was also a clever dancer and acrobat, and in many old prints he is seen on stilts, walking on his hands, and generally spending a considerable time in the air.

In the seventeenth century, a famous Harlequin named Dominique, or Biancolelli, gave a new interpretation of the character. Harlequin was no longer the rather stupid creature, but became clever and shrewd; while his character was interpreted almost entirely in mime, he had occasional flashes of brilliant wit.

His distinctive costume was originally a simple tunic and breeches with numerous patches, which were supposed to signify his status as a servant. In the seventeenth century the patches became symmetrical diamond shapes of red, blue, and green, separated by yellow or gold braid. He wore a black mask, which had a bristly moustache and sometimes a beard, and at his belt hung his magic sword-bat. He usually wore a skullcap or a large-brimmed hat decorated with a hare's foot, which symbolized his own fleetness.

In spite of the changes in the character, there has always been something indefinably gay about Harlequin that has captured the imagination of writers, musicians, and artists throughout the centuries. Even today, whenever an actor in the traditional Harlequin costume appears on the stage, we anticipate that something wonderfully exciting and amusing will follow.

Brighella was also a native of Bergamo, and also a servant; but, unlike Harlequin, he was always wily and clever, and continually busy at some sly mischief. He was a singer, musician, and dancer, always ready to tackle any undertaking, whether it was serenading his master's mistress or baiting some old man. As soon as his craft

BRIGHELLA Stock character of the Commedia dell'Arte with money pouch, dagger and guitar.

and rascality had earned him some money he was content to laze and loaf until necessity forced him to engage in some further trickery.

He looked ferocious, and indulged in frequent knife-play—provided he was dealing with someone older or weaker than himself. His mask was olive-colored and had a hooked nose and a moustache and beard. His costume was a short tunic and trousers with green braid trimmings along the seams, a short cloak, and a soft hat with a green border. At his belt he always carried the symbols of his character—the money pouch and dagger.

Scapino (Scapin), a servant and companion of Brighella, was also always ready to put out his hand for money, but where Brighella would draw his dagger Scapino would make a rapid exit. In common with the other comic characters, he was continually involved

SCAPINO Stock character of the Commedia dell'Arte in loose-fitting costume with wooden sword.

in amorous intrigues, both on his own account and on his master's. The character was not of the first importance, being actually a variation on Brighella. His costume seems to have varied considerably, but it followed the general tradition of valet costumes in having a small cape with a short tunic and loose trousers. It was usually decorated with green and white stripes to indicate that it was some kind of livery.

Mezzetino (Mezzetin) was another familiar of Brighella, with similar but milder characteristics. At the end of the seventeenth century, his costume was redesigned in France by Constantin, who played the character without a mask. The costume was similar to Scapino's, but with red and white stripes instead of green and white. Mezzetino was a great favorite in the early eighteenth century in France, and appears in many of Watteau's paintings of the comedians.

MEZZETINO Stock character of the Commedia dell'Arte often depicted as a musician. Striped tunic and trousers were common.

Pantalone (Pantaloon), the dupe, a respectable citizen of Venice, was always old and had usually retired from business. Money was his ruling passion, and his avarice constantly brought him trouble. He sometimes had a young wife or a daughter who was continually engaged in some love affair behind his back—and sometimes even before his eyes. Occasionally he would fall in love himself, but always with some young maiden who was an incorrigible flirt and used him for game and the money she extracted from him in return for her favors.

His traditional costume was a short red jacket and the tight-fitting trousers to which he has given his name, with a long trailing cloak or gown of black, similar to that worn at one time by the Venetians as a sign of mourning because of the successes of the Turkish pirates. A small brimless cap and slippers (Shakespeare mentions "the lean and slippered Pantaloon with spectacles on nose") and the all-important money pouch at his belt completed his costume. In some early engravings, the phallus is discernible, a relic of the days of the ancient theatre. His mask was brown, with a long hooked nose, gray moustaches, and a short white beard with two absurdly long points.

PANTALOON   A comic character of the Commedia dell'Arte in traditional costume of red tights and long, black coat.

THE DOCTOR A comic character of the Commedia dell'Arte in the traditional black costume, the badge of his profession.

The Doctor was another dupe. He was a product of the university at Bologna and the embodiment of all the foolish, pedantic professors in the world. His knowledge was profound in letters, medicine, philosophy, astronomy, and the law, but his knowledge of life was gained from his books, from which he could never quote correctly. He had learned everything, but of life he understood nothing. He was, of course, continually meddling in other people's affairs and laying down the law, and he naturally provided Harlequin and his fellows with great sport. Like his old friend, Pantalone, he was occasionally assailed by the gentler passion, with the result that he was caught in countless ridiculous situations.

His costume was the black dress of the man of science and letters of the time. He originally wore a long black cloak and a small hat, but in the seventeenth century the cloak became shorter, being worn draped over a black tunic, and the hat became enormously large with a great wide brim. He wore a large ruff around his neck, and under his arm or in his hand he always carried a book or a treatise. His mask was curious in that it covered only his nose and forehead, and was either black or flesh-colored. He also wore a moustache and a short pointed beard.

THE CAPTAIN A comic character of the Commedia dell'Arte in the traditional costume of military dress.

The Captain, the braggart, looked forbidding and ferocious. Armed with a long rapier, he strutted about twirling his moustaches. He had been away to the wars and performed deeds of prodigious valor, but, strangely enough, all his victims were alive and well. His long-winded, bombastic talk was, no doubt, fully punctuated with strange oaths acquired in foreign lands. Of course, he was really an abject coward, and Harlequin and his fellows had only to make the clinking noise of men-at-arms offstage for the Captain to collapse with fright on the stage and pretend to be dead.

A very famous Captain was Francesco Andreini, who played with the Gelosi troupe in Paris. He had been a soldier himself, and was for a time a prisoner of the Turks; no doubt, therefore, he drew on his own experiences in his interpretation of the character.

The Captain was originally, like his fellows, a native of Italy; but in the seventeenth century, when Spain was dominating the rest of Europe, he became a Spaniard. His costume followed the military dress of the times, and changed with each successive period. In the early seventeenth century he wore tight-fitting clothes decorated with stripes, a plumed felt hat, and, usually, the high boots of the time. His mask was flesh-colored, with a large hooked nose and great bristling moustaches. One of his most important properties was his great sword, which was never unsheathed, but was worn with the point thrust aggressively upward.

Scaramouche was originally a variation on the Captain, but of much lighter caliber. He was more adroit and less bombastic, and was something of a musician and dancer. He appeared in a completely black costume, and (as played by Fiorillo in the seventeenth century) he wore no mask. In common with the valets, he was continually involved in picking pockets and dodging blows. Like the Captain, he bragged of his imaginary feats of prowess to impress the ladies and to scare peaceful citizens.

SCARAMOUCHE   A comic character of the Commedia dell'Arte. This intriguer generally apeared in short black cloak and cap.

Pulcinella or *Policinella* (*Punchinello*), from whom our own English Punch has evolved, is considered by many scholars to be a direct descendant of a Roman comic character known as *Maccus;* some ancient statuettes have similar characteristics, including the great hooked nose and round belly. The hunched back is a more recent development.

Pulcinella usually appeared as an old bachelor, was sensual and cruel, but possessed a sense of humor and showed constant flashes of wit. His costume, based on the traditional dress of the peasants of Italy, was white; but like those of the other characters, it changed in France in the seventeenth century—to red breeches and a green-trimmed jacket. He wore a ruff and a tall conical hat, or sometimes a skullcap. His mask was chiefly all nose, although it was sometimes adorned with a moustache and beard.

PULCINELLA   A Neopolitan creation of the sixteenth century. The exaggerated hump-back, sagging belly and hooked nose, as well as the ruff and high hat, were developments of the seventeenth century.

Pedrolino (Gilles, Pierrot) was another valet, but this time a trustworthy one. He was a rather simple character, and when encouraged by Harlequin to engage in trickery he was invariably the only one to be caught and punished. He was originally closely related to Pulcinella and Brighella, but in France he developed into a more attractive and elegant personality. His costume was the simple white tunic, loose trousers with a large ruff, and a soft felt cap. In the eighteenth century he developed large buttons on his tunic and long sleeves that concealed his hands. He also acquired a strange quality of sadness. He was played without a mask, the actor's face usually being powdered white.

PEDROLINO In his loose-fitting white costume, derived from the dress of the sixteenth century zany, this character wears the large buttons added in the eighteenth century.

THE "STRAIGHT" CHARACTERS

The lovers (men) were known by various names, such as Fabio, Ottavio, Silvio, Leandro, Lelio, and Flavio. Their only character- istic was being in love and serving as foils for the comic characters. They were always good-looking and elegant, and were dressed as young gallants of the time. The actor had to interpret the part in a poetic and cultured manner, and he appeared just a trifle ridicu- lous. The Lovers (or *Inamoratos*) were usually played by men of birth and position. Sometimes the noble before whom the actors performed would play the part, and it was often played by the director of the company. The Inamoratos played without a mask, as did the *Inamoratas,* or women Lovers.

THE LOVER   His talent lay in his hand- some face. His costume reflects the fashionable dress of the day.

INAMORATA This seventeenth century character traditionally wore the dress of the day

The *Inamoratas* were also known by various names, such as Flaminia, Lavinia, Aurelia, and Isabella. Women first appeared on the stage as actresses during the sixteenth century, and were welcomed with joy in France; but in Italy they were not allowed to play in the Papal States until the eighteenth century. Their numerous names came from individual actresses, who had their own particular characteristics. Isabella, the celebrated wife of Andreini and the leading actress in the company (the *prima donna*), renowned for her beauty, her cultured wit, and her poetic writings, made of the character an idealized type of a woman in love. Her costume was the elegant dress of the period.

THE FANTESCA The costume of the sixteenth century maidservant originally indicated her status, but the costume gradually began to resemble the dress of the mistress.

The Soubrette (or servant), confidante to the Inamorata, had many names, such as Liletta, Smeraldina, Olivetta, Francheschina, or more popularly, Columbine. She was a buxom wench, and was usually in love with one of the valets. She was on close terms with Harlequin, and would willingly enter into the intrigues hatched by him and his companions. She had a ready wit and sometimes some outrageous lines to speak. She was often required to disguise herself in the costume of a cavalier, a doctor, or even as Harlequin. Originally her costume was that of the common people of the sixteenth century, particularly distinguished by a large white apron, but later, in France, her dress became indistinguishable from that of her mistress.

The *ballerinas* and *canterinas*, the dancers and singers, could sing and play several instruments, and sometimes performed acrobatic feats or danced on a tightrope. They performed in the intervals of the action of the play, and sometimes sang the story of the play as an epilogue.

BALLERINA (After an etching from Jacques Callot's "I Balli di Sfessania," 1602.) Her talents were confined to musical interludes and epilogues.

THE PLAYS

The description of the various characters indicates the usual theme of the plays, which was the very ancient one of marital infidelity. Young wives of old men and virtuous daughters of rich merchants engaged in involved and complicated love intrigues. The valets and the servant-maids engineered the innumerable ridiculous situations, while providing secondary love affairs, and there was continual plot and counterplot.

STYLE OF PERFORMANCES

The complete success of the improvisations was due to the style in which these things were done. In addition to being masters of their particular characters and having numerous appropriate speeches at their fingertips, the actors could easily mime their story, thus making it clear to the audience without giving away any information to the other characters. They also had an extensive repertoire of amusing tricks, some acrobatic and some very old and simple but effective bits of stage business. They would make themselves into fountains, or imitate statues, remaining motionless and unseen by other characters until the denouement of the plot required them to resume their own characters. Syringes for the squirting of water, and other properties which today are associated with the circus or variety stage, were greatly in use.

One can imagine that although the players were never at a loss for words, it would sometimes be effective for them to use some of this byplay as a relief to the spoken parts of their show. The comedians also had stock cues which simplified the entrances and exits of the various characters, thus ensuring smoothness of playing and giving the performance a sense of dramatic form.

SCENERY

As they could not expect to find a theatre in every town they visited, the comedians usually carried a portable stage with curtains in addition to their innumerable properties. In many old prints these portable stages can be seen set up in the marketplace. They

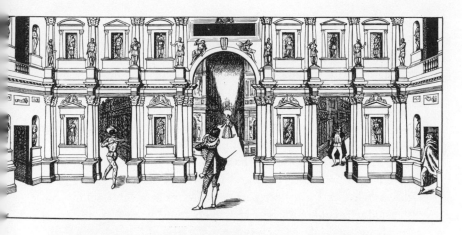

THE TEATRO OLIMPICO AT VICENZA Built between 1580 and
1584, this edifice was the most famous classical theatre of the
Renaissance. The stage wall was modeled after the Roman
Theatre in Orange, France. Note the scene of diminishing perspective through the archway.

were usually just simple square platforms with a decorated curtain
as background. The characters entered from short ladders at the
side. Some of the early troupes were hardly more than mounte-
banks, and when in a marketplace or at a fair combined the sale of
medicines, ointments, or ballad sheets with their acting.

By the nature of their art they could adapt themselves easily to
whatever setting and scenic possibilities were available. The Italians
were well ahead in stage technique throughout the sixteenth and
seventeenth centuries, and we can be sure that the comedians, professionals as they were, had the ability to make full use of scenery
and stage machinery wherever it was to be found. They were experienced in the use of colored lighting, fireworks, and fountains,
which provided dramatic and spectacular effects during their per-

formances. The settings were usually of an architectural nature, and would represent a street or marketplace in perspective.

In France, in the seventeenth century, the comedians used a great variety of settings, interiors, and outside sets, either architectural or in the form of a pastoral landscape. At the Hôtel de Bourgogne theatre they had a permanent architectural setting, in the center of which was a large arch, behind which were placed interchangeable backcloths representing various scenes.

When they performed at Palladio's famous classical theatre at Vicenza, in Italy, they had an elaborate permanent setting, with three archways giving perspective views of streets of solidly constructed wooden houses. The characters could be seen in any street, yet, being invisible to each other, several could appear simultaneously and continue with their involved plotting quite naturally. There were two further doorways at the side of the arches, so the actors had plenty of variety in their comings and goings.

HERITAGE FROM THE COMMEDIA DELL'ARTE

The companies were continually meeting opposition from either the Church or the civic authorities, so they had to be continually on the move. They often united and re-formed into new companies, and it is difficult to keep track of them in their constant travels and waves of popularity and expulsion. They traveled through most countries in Europe—Austria, Germany, France, Spain, England—and wherever they performed they left behind ideas which were adopted into the theatres of those countries, perhaps the most profound influence being felt in France.

The Restoration

LINKS WITH THE PAST

Between 1642 and 1660 the theatres in England were closed and all stage performances were prohibited by Parliament. It would be wrong, however, to assume that when the theatres were finally reopened there was a complete break with the traditions of the past. Apart from spasmodic attempts to reopen the theatres (the play usually being broken up by Parliamentary soldiers) and occasional private performances, most of the players took to the road and performed at the big fairs held all over the country. The new regime was not very welcome in certain parts of the country, so it is probable that performances went on unchecked in these places. In 1660, then, there were still a large number of players alive and active who had begun their careers during the reign of Charles I. It was a great man of the theatre of those days, Sir William Davenant, who played the chief part in providing the link with the past.

SIR WILLIAM DAVENANT

Sir William Davenant, poet and practiced writer for the theatre, was a man of great tact and diplomacy, with a genius for making friends. Although he fought for the King in the Civil War, he had friends among the Parliamentarians who were to prove very useful to him.

Born in Oxford in 1606, the son of an innkeeper, Davenant was considered by many to be a natural son of Shakespeare, who had often stayed at the inn. His mother was known as a great beauty and a very witty woman, and at all events Davenant had Shakespeare for a godfather. Inheriting his mother's wit, he achieved fame as a poet and dramatist, was knighted by Charles I, and became Poet Laureate. In his early years he lived in noble households and at Court, gaining experience of the high life of the time.

Most of Davenant's serious plays deal with the amorous and political intrigues of the society of palaces, banqueting halls, and council chambers of far-off lands, but he undoubtedly drew on his own early experiences. Davenant's plays were found morally acceptable, and even Charles I, in going over the text of *The Wits,* allowed certain parts that had been struck out by an overzealous censor.

Inigo Jones, who was producing the Court masques, turned to Davenant for material after quarreling with Ben Jonson, and Davenant rapidly climbed in Court favor. In 1634, *The Temple of Love,* a masque which was performed at Whitehall for the Queen and her ladies, gained him a reputation. Three years later Jonson died, and Davenant succeeded him (as the patent awarded by Charles I explains) as poet in the service of the Court. Although this position was not clearly defined, it can be assumed that he was recognized as holding the office of Poet Laureate. His influence with the King became greater, and he was granted a patent to build a theatre in which to present "plays, musical entertainments, scenes, and other like presentments."

Davenant proposed to introduce the spectacle and scenery of the

SIR WILLIAM DAVENANT The major theatrical figure of the seventeenth century, he kept the theatre alive during the Commonwealth with private performances of his dramatic operas. With the Restoration in 1660, he founded the famous Duke's Theatre.

Court masques into the public theatres, which were still carrying on the Shakespearean tradition of simplicity of setting. However, with political clouds on the horizon and possibly some disagreement about the site of the new theatre, it was not erected until over twenty years later.

At the beginning of 1640 Davenant wrote his last masque, in which all the art of Inigo Jones and his assistant, John Webb, brought to a climax the pride and beauty of Court pageantry.

Later in the year Davenant was made manager of a company of players at the Phoenix Theatre (also known as the Cockpit) in Drury Lane, replacing the previous manager, William Beeston, who had presented an unlicensed play containing some topical allusions that gave offense to the King. Beeston had been arrested and the theatre closed. The King, knowing of Davenant's wish to have his own theatre, appointed him to "govern, order, and dispose" the players in their plays and productions. The Phoenix was a small theatre, and there was obviously not sufficient room for Davenant to carry out his schemes of painted scenery and elaborate stage machinery.

He remained in charge until 1641, when he was forced to flee to the country to avoid being arrested by the Parliamentary soldiers, as he held some position in the royal army at this time. He was apprehended at Faversham and brought to London, where he was detained for two months. After his release he eventually reached

France. He returned, however, in 1642, when he joined the King's forces and remained with them until the defeat at Marston Moor, after which he again escaped to France.

Ill luck still dogged him, for while he was sailing to America his ship was captured by a Parliamentary frigate and he was brought to London and confined in the Tower. Tradition has it that Milton finally secured his pardon and ultimate release from imprisonment. In 1652, Davenant found himself a free man, but with no position and practically penniless. No doubt he used his ability and knowledge of the stage in some of the private performances that were surreptitiously given during the period of Puritan rule, and he must certainly have kept in touch with his old friends of the theatre.

At this time there was, among the scholars and writers particularly, a quiet but constant protest at the closing of the theatres, and in 1656 Davenant, using all his tact and political genius, actually approached the Commonwealth Secretary of State, suggesting the moral value of stage presentations for political purposes. Although this fell through, in the same year Davenant gave a private performance in a hall at the back of his own house. The play itself was a plea for the opening of the theatres, introducing Aristophanes and Diogenes in the course of the argument, and we can be sure that Aristophanes won hands down.

The success of this venture encouraged Davenant to more ambitious efforts, and there followed *The Siege of Rhodes,* an opera, so called, with the scenery designed by John Webb. The stage was only eighteen feet wide and nine feet high, and the several scenes were changed by easily movable flats. By simplification Webb successfully applied the ideas and innovations of the masque stage to a more intimate setting. The settings were composed of three sets of wings and a backcloth, which could be easily changed without machinery.

The step from a private theatre in Davenant's own house to a public theatre was the next important move, and in 1658 Davenant finally got permission from the authorities to reopen his old theatre, the Phoenix. He obtained the favor of the authorities by including some propaganda in his opening production, which he again called an opera, *The Cruelty of the Spaniards at Peru,* playing on Cromwell's hatred for Catholic Spain. The opera was merely a series of declamatory speeches, with songs and musical interludes, against a pictorial background of painted scenery. Although only a slight piece, it was the thin end of the wedge, and Davenant, becoming bolder, followed it up with *The Siege of Rhodes.*

Owing to the opposition this created, coming on top of his implication in a surreptitious attempt to bring the new King back from exile, Davenant found himself in prison again. He still had some influence in high places, however, and in August, 1659, he was again released. Performances were resumed at the Phoenix early in 1660 without much hindrance.

Davenant had sensed the changing political atmosphere, and he left for France soon after to join the royal entourage, returning in triumph the same year as a figure of importance and in a position to carry out his long-cherished ambition of presenting his plays publicly in the way for which he had worked and struggled so many years.

THOMAS KILLIGREW

With Davenant in the royal party was Thomas Killigrew, who was attached to the Court of Charles I and had joined the new King in exile. He had written plays and had them performed in the past, and he had also traveled in France and Italy and seen some of the great technical achievements developed there. While in exile he continued to write poetical works of a rather fanciful nature, which were very acceptable to the Court audiences.

THE KING'S PLAYERS AND THE DUKE OF YORK'S PLAYERS

After the Restoration, Killigrew and Davenant were granted a patent by the King giving them the monopoly of dramatic entertainment, which indirectly affected the development of the theatre in England for nearly two hundred years. They each formed com-

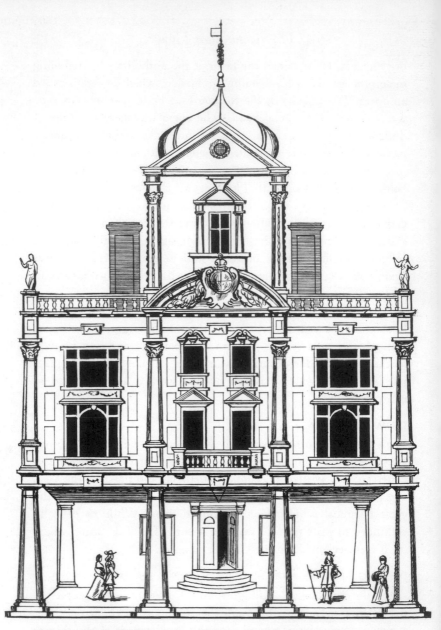

THE DUKE'S THEATRE This edifice in Dorset Garden was a baroque masterpiece designed by Christopher Wren, England's greatest architect. The theatre opened in 1671 under the management of Thomas Betterton and Charles Davenant.

INTERIOR OF THE DUKE'S THEATRE   The apron stage, the double proscenium doors, and the stage boxes were characteristic of Restoration theatres. Note the musicians' box above the proscenium arch.

panies, Killigrew's being known as the King's Players and performing at the new Theatre Royal in Drury Lane, and Davenant's as
the Duke of York's Players, performing first at a theatre in Salisbury
Court, and later in a converted tennis court at Lincoln's Inn Fields.

For the next few years, however, things did not go smoothly, and
the two companies broke up, united, and broke away again. New
theatres were built, but there were long periods when they were
closed during the years of plague and the Great Fire. The vicissi-
tudes of management were great and various, but both companies
kept on, and when Davenant died, in 1668, the management was
carried on by his wife, a shrewd businesswoman, and later by his
son, Charles Davenant, in conjunction with some of the leading
actors. Killigrew's company also carried on when he died, with his
son Charles as manager.

A great development took place in the staging of plays during
the Restoration period, and this affected the arrangement of the
theatres and the design of the new buildings. At first, only Davenant's company made wide use of painted scenery and mechanical
devices; Killigrew's company kept to the traditional simple stage of
Shakespeare. There was some outward rivalry between the two companies on this question.

Davenant decided that his current theatre was not large enough
to house the scenery he wanted, so he determined to build a new
theatre at Dorset Garden. He died, however, before it was opened.
The theatre was designed by Sir Christopher Wren, and was very
elaborate and ornate.

The other company had not been doing too well at the Theatre
Royal, and a disastrous fire made matters worse, so the two companies would occasionally join forces and act at the Duke's Theatre,
as the building at Dorset Garden was called. Later, they united
finally, and played at the new Theatre Royal.

RESTORATION PLAYS

The first productions of the two companies were chiefly the old
mainstays—Shakespeare, Beaumont and Fletcher, Ben Jonson, and

their contemporaries—but even during the Commonwealth, plays had been written and even printed. Adaptations were also made from the French dramatists, including Molière and Corneille. Davenant was too busy at management to do much writing himself, and his works were chiefly adaptations and translations, but he had works by the new dramatists to fall back on, such men as Dryden, Sir Robert Howard and his brothers, and Lord Orrery. Comedy was the vogue, although tragedy and poetical works set in distant lands were also popular. Sir George Etherege's *The Comical Revenge; or Love in a Tub* (1664), was the precursor of the Restoration comedy of manners. He wrote only two other plays, *She wou'd if she cou'd* (1668) and, his best play, *The Man of Mode; or, Sir Fopling Flutter* (1676).

The audience also shaped the conditions of a successful play— it had to be witty and contain plenty of amusing situations—and the later writers successfully conformed to these requirements. Among the more important of these dramatists were Congreve, Wycherley, Farquhar, and Sir John Vanbrugh. The plays of this time contained a wealth of topical allusions, and no doubt the performances of the players were partly based on observation of the mannerisms and excesses of the Court audiences. Today the Restoration comedies remain witty and amusing, but have a quality of coarseness which in those days was no more than commonplace.

THE AUDIENCES

The audiences of the new theatres were chiefly composed of people of the Court and gallants of the town. The common folk still regarded the theatre as an appurtenance of the Court, and the old Puritan influence was still very strong among them, few of the stolid middle class ever going to the play. The ladies and gentlemen of the Court and gallants of the town. The common folk still re- the women players, who were now accepted on the stage. Pepys was a very keen playgoer, and from his *Diary* we find that at the end of the play he would go behind the scenes to chat with the players—and perhaps steal a kiss from Nell Gwyn.

The young gallants went regularly to the theatres, not only to see but to be seen. The auditorium was illuminated as brightly as the stage itself, and witty conversation and gossip flowed continually in the audience throughout the performance of the play. People would come and go at all times, and sometimes there would be an argument in the pit leading to a duel. It is recorded that during a performance of *Macbeth* a young gallant met his end at the point of a sword. Such were the conditions under which the players performed, and yet they went from strength to strength.

THE THEATRES

The development of the theatre of this time paved the way to the modern picture stage, wedding the simple stage of Shakespeare to the wealth of spectacle of the Court masques. Theatre building in this period differed in many respects, but conformed to certain general principles. The stage projected into the center of the auditorium as in Shakespeare's day, but it also went to an equal depth back past the proscenium arch. The proscenium, heavy and ornate, had two stage doors on either side which were used by the actors; above these were stage boxes, usually occupied by the audience, but sometimes used in the play for balcony scenes.

The stage boxes on one side were reserved for the orchestra, or, as in the Duke's Theatre, a special box was provided for them at the top of the proscenium arch. Efforts were made to place the orchestra in the pit below the stage, but they met with disapproval from the audience, who liked to have nothing between themselves and the players.

SCENERY

The scenery was composed of flat wings on either side of the stage, which were fixed in slots on the stage, and with backcloths or shutters, all readily movable. There was a curtain behind the proscenium which, when lowered, cut off the scenery from the apron, as that part of the stage in front of the proscenium was called. The curtain rose after the customary prologue and revealed the setting, but it did not descend until the end of the play, and all scene changes were made in full view of the audience. This was the time when the songs or musical interludes would be given.

LIGHTING

Lighting was by lamps and candles, and as far back as 1598 the Italians were using a glass oil lamp which could be filled with colored liquid and reflected colored light. At the Court masques of Charles I, colored lighting had been used extensively, strips of colored silk being placed in front of the groups of candles and lamps situated behind the scenes.

The general lighting came from great circular fittings which held many candles and were hung above the apron. These also illuminated the auditorium, and there were probably additional candles around the boxes and galleries.

About the time of the building of the new theatre at Dorset Garden, an early form of footlights came into existence. These consisted of six oil lamps at the edge of the stage, in the center, which could be controlled to suit the action of the play. A night scene, for instance, would require some diminution of the lighting, and although the great chandeliers would be kept going, the footlights would be lowered as a concession to reality. The player would also carry a candle, to help the convention.

THE CANDLE SNUFFERS

Another stage convention founded in Restoration days was the "invisible" candle snuffer. The tallow candles in those days needed constant attention in order to make them burn brightly. There were usually two attendants who looked after the candles, one on the stage and the other in the auditorium. No matter what was happening on the stage, should a candle begin to splutter the attendant would walk onto the stage, quite unconscious of the actors, and attend to his business, having concluded which he would make a dignified exit. His appearance on the stage on these occasions was accepted in the same way that the scene shifters were accepted, as a necessary part of the impedimenta of the stage. Far from decrying the appearance of the candle snuffer on the stage (at a most dramatic moment, perhaps), members of the audience, on seeing certain lights fail, would actually raise a shout for him, and woe betide if he were not soon forthcoming!

THOMAS BETTERTON

The most famous actor in the Restoration theatre was Thomas Betterton, who dominated the scene until the beginning of the eighteenth century. According to most writers of the time, he was excellent in both tragedy and comedy. Some attention devoted here to his life and career will serve to give a general impression of the way in which the actors of the time lived and worked.

There is little information regarding his early life, but Betterton was born in 1635, the son of an under-cook to Charles I. He displayed early tendencies toward reading and study at school, and he was apprenticed as a young man to a bookseller who had some connections with the stage, having at one time been wardrobe keeper and prompter at the Blackfriars Theatre. With him as an apprentice was Edward Kynaston, who also became a well-known actor. The two young men probably started acting during the period of surreptitious private performances when the theatres were closed.

Betterton almost certainly appeared when Davenant decided to reopen the Phoenix after the performances in his own house. In 1660 Betterton signed a contract with Davenant, which is interesting as it showed the method of payment to actors. The total receipts of the house were divided into fifteen parts or shares, of which three went to the management for the house rent, the building of scenery, and costumes and properties. Seven went to Davenant for the maintenance of the women players' costumes and his own personal expenses. The other five shares were divided among the actors. (Mention is made in the contract of the perpetual maintenance of a private box for Thomas Killigrew, which seems to indicate that although the two companies showed outward rivalry, the two managers were on very good terms.)

Betterton played leading parts with Davenant's company. A play seldom ran more than a week at a time in those days, and it was quite common for a play to have only one performance, due no doubt to the limited audience and the fact that there were only two companies permanently in London. From Pepys we read that in 1661 Betterton played *Hamlet:* "To the Opera, and there saw 'Hamlet, Prince of Denmarke,' done with scenes very well, but above all, Betterton did the Prince's part beyond imagination." This was the most successful tragedy for the company for many years, both as regards the money taken and the reputation gained.

THOMAS BETTERTON Here is the famous actor in contemporary dress as Hamlet, played at the Duke's Theatre, London, in 1661. Black was the traditional costume for the role.

About the same year, the company presented another of Davenant's own plays, *Love and Honour,* and in this production we learn of "the King giving Mr. Betterton his Coronation Suit in which he acted the part of Prince Alvaro." The Duke of York and Lord Oxford also lent their coronation clothes to the actors. This indicates the close relationship between the players and the audience of those days, and emphasizes the King's special interest in the theatre.

A link with the theatre of Shakespeare came to light when, in 1664, Betterton played in *Henry VIII.* A writer of the time says, "The part of the King was so right and justly done by Mr. Betterton, he being instructed in it by Sir William, who had it from old Mr. Lowen, that had his instructions from Mr. Shakespeare himself." Mrs. Betterton also appeared in this production.

The constant presentation of new plays and old revivals being such a strain on the actors, and the time being limited, there could have been few rehearsals. Pepys writes of *The Bondman* in 1664: "... it is true for want of practice many of them forgot their parts a little, but Betterton and my poor Ianthe (Mrs. Betterton) outdo all the world."

Betterton wrote three plays himself and played in them with his wife; they were successful and had many revivals. In 1671 he moved with the company to the new theatre in Dorset Garden, and with another leading actor, Harris, formed part of the management with Lady Davenant and her son Charles, who was also acting with the company. Betterton continued with success, and in 1684, when the two companies were united, had available also the new plays of Killigrew's company.

Betterton's chief qualities as an actor were dignity and sincerity, and he seemed to get really under the skin of a part. He was apparently able to give an impression of being natural on the stage, thus contrasting favorably with other actors of those days, whose ranting, "tearing a passion to tatters," was so common at the time. In Pepys and other writers of the time mention is continually made of a successor taking Betterton's part in a play and always proving a disappointment to the audience. A description of Betterton gives him

> . . . a great head, a short thick neck, stoop'd in the shoulders, and . . . fat short arms, . . . his left hand frequently lodg'd in his breast, . . . his actions were few, but just. . . . His aspect was serious, venerable, and majestic. . . . His voice was low and grumbling, yet he could tune it by an artful climax which enforc'd universal attention even from the fops and orange girls.

In 1709 he had a famous benefit night. The play was Congreve's *Love for Love,* in which he played Valentine, and there was a great gathering of distinguished people, who overflowed from pit and gallery onto the stage itself.

Betterton appears to have been a man as highly respected for his moral character as for his dramatic powers. He continued playing intermittently until his death in 1710. He had many friends among the distinguished people of his day, and he was greatly mourned at his funeral in Westminster Abbey, where he was buried.

OTHER LEADING ACTORS

Some of the other important actors of the time were Mohun, who began his career in the time of Charles I, Kynaston, Harris, and Charles Hart. Mountfort was the leading comic actor, and some of his companions were Haines, Nokes, Doggett, and John Lacy.

THE FIRST ENGLISH ACTRESSES

As mentioned previously, the introduction of women on the stage was an innovation in England. On the Continent women had been acting for many years, but in Elizabethan times all the women's parts had been played by boys and young men. Older women's parts were played by the same actors as they grew older.

In 1660 a performance of *Othello* by the King's Players had an actress in the cast. The audience was warned in the prologue, and the epilogue made this inquiry, "And how d'ye like her?" The applause that followed ensured the establishment of the actress as a member of the company.

One of the first women to appear on the stage was a Mrs. Coleman, who played in Davenant's production of his opera, *The Siege of Rhodes*. Now that women were accepted on the stage, the female parts in the plays could be assured of authentic interpretation, and a new interest in the theatre was created for the young gallants of Court and the town.

The most famous of the actresses who graced the Restoration stage was Nell Gwyn, although she played for only a short period, chiefly in comedy parts. Pepys found her a lively and witty creature, although it is probable that she was more important as a personality than as an actress.

A great tragic actress of the time was Mrs. Barry, who often acted with Betterton. Betterton's wife must also have been a very clever actress to have sustained so many roles with her husband. In comedy, Mrs. Mountfort, with her robustness and vivacity, gave ideal interpretations of the parts in the new comedy of manners.

The end of the century saw the rise of the celebrated Mrs. Bracegirdle, an extremely capable actress. She had the vivacity and attack necessary for delivering the prologues and epilogues, which in those days were written for special performances, and she could sing and dance very well. She also appeared in tragic parts, particularly in a play by Mrs. Aphra Behn, who was possibly the first Englishwoman to write for the stage.

BENEFITS

Among the institutions of the stage that survived until the nineteenth century were the benefits. Leading players, and later authors, had a benefit performance during the season for which they received the entire proceeds after certain expenses had been deducted. This system rather tended to reduce their regular salaries, although the stars were always well paid.

COSTUMES FOR JAMES I AND QUEEN ANNE Designs by Inigo Jones show sovereigns in elaborate costumes designed for court masques.

COSTUMES

It is interesting that while vaguely historical costumes were sometimes worn by the male players, the actresses always appeared in the dress of the current vogue, with perhaps just a suggestion of another period when necessary for the plot, such as a plumed headdress or some small concession in the details of the costume. Historical accuracy on the stage was not established until well into the nineteenth century, and until then Shakespeare was usually played in the modern dress of the time.

FOREIGN COMPANIES

From the time of the Restoration, certain foreign companies of players also performed in London. The Royal Court, when in exile in France, had developed a taste for French drama, and companies from France frequently performed and were very popular. Even more popular was the *commedia dell'arte*, which came to London at various times, and in 1683 played at Windsor before the King.

The 18th Century

CHANGES FROM RESTORATION DAYS

From the early years of the eighteenth century onward the theatres began to attract a much larger audience than they had done in Restoration days. Not only did the population of Britain increase from six million in 1650 to ten million in 1800, the rise of the middle class enforced certain changes in the nature of theatrical entertainment. The loose morals and behavior of Restoration Court circles gave way to more polite and respectable standards under Queen Anne, the result of which was that Court interest and influence in the theatre waned. Subsequently, the growing middle class, which had formerly stayed away, began to patronize the theatres.

Whatever may be said of Court circles in the days of Charles II, they certainly appreciated wit and poetry, and they generally had good taste in art. The same could not be said of the stolid, unimaginative middle class, so the comedy of manners gave way to productions with more spectacular and sentimental qualities.

The increase in the theatre-going public meant, of course, the building of new theatres and the enlarging of those already in existence. Many new theatres were built during the century in London and in all the larger towns of England. The fashionable resorts of Bath, Tunbridge Wells, and Brighton also had their theatres, and the provinces generally saw much thriving theatrical activity.

The small select group of the community which formed the audience in Restoration days demanded a constant change of bill and a continual flow of new plays. In Betterton's day plays were usually put on for one or two nights, very rarely running for a week, while in the eighteenth century the larger public created a longer run for the plays, and forty and fifty performances were not uncommon.

Although there was a change in the kind of play necessary to meet the demands of the new type of audiences, the actual mounting and presentation of the plays showed little radical alteration. The design and structure of the playhouses were not altered to any great extent, and the theatre in general underwent a pause in its development. It was a period of expansion rather than of change, and many of the old traditions of the Elizabethan stage were continued throughout the century.

COLLEY CIBBER

Much of our knowledge of the theatre in the first half of the century is derived from Cibber's famous *Apology for the Life of Colley Cibber*. Cibber began acting in 1690 with Betterton, and eventually became the most popular personality in the theatre during the first three decades of the eighteenth century. Cibber had not the qualities of a great actor, but he was a good comedian, he could write successful comedies, and he was an excellent manager.

In 1714, with Sir Richard Steele and three other actors (Wilks, Doggett, and Booth), he took over the management of the Theatre Royal, Drury Lane, of which he had already for some time been virtual manager. The theatre was still operating under the original royal patent, while the other patent operated at the old Lincoln's Inn Theatre, which seceding actors from Betterton's company had taken over in 1695. Among the shareholders of this company was

Christopher Rich, a lawyer who found the theatre a better business proposition than his law practice. Control of the Lincoln's Inn Theatre eventually passed to his son, John Rich.

JOHN RICH AND INNOVATIONS AT THE LINCOLN'S INN THEATRE

Christopher Rich rebuilt the theatre, but it was not completed until shortly after his death in 1714. His son appeared for the first time in a prologue at the opening of the new theatre, which gave as its first play Farquhar's *The Recruiting Officer*. The following year he made his only appearance as a tragedian, but it is his development of pantomime to which his fame is due.

The new theatre began a successful policy of putting on an entirely new form of entertainment composed of music, spectacle, dancing, and mime. It was, of course, not new in its elements, as Davenant in his so-called "operas" had had similar ideas in mind; but the form it took was an innovation. Rich took some of the characters from the *commedia dell'arte*, adapted them to conform with English conventions, and used them in comic scenes which were interwoven with rather dull allegorical plays based on the lives and loves of various gods and goddesses. At first dialogue was used in the allegorical scenes of the production, but gradually music was introduced and recitative and arias found most suitable. The comic part of the operas, which was quite divorced from the rest, was entirely in dumb show, being devoted to the adventures of Harlequin and Columbine, Clown and Pantaloon. Rich himself was Harlequin, and he became famous for his dancing and miming in that role.

It was said that Rich developed his powers of miming because he had no voice, or that his voice was rough and uncultured, but whatever the reason, his actions and gestures were so expressive that he did not need to speak. All writers of that period agree about his extraordinary powers of miming.

Rich also made great strides in the staging of his productions, and used transformation scenes with surprising effect. At the touch of Harlequin's magic bat, huts and cottages would be transformed into palaces and temples and some of the characters changed into animals or articles of furniture, while gods and goddesses were continually descending to earth or being whisked up to the heavens. All of this was accomplished by the ingenious use of the flies and various trapdoors. Sound effects played a great part, and there was much thunder, rainstorms, and roaring of seas, together with fire and lightning, not to mention the gentle fall of paper snow.

It is understandable that all this went down very well with the large, unsophisticated audiences of those days, and Rich had many years of complete success. His success was a constant source of worry to Drury Lane, and Cibber had to put on something similar.

As far back as 1702 Drury Lane had presented an entertainment of dancing and action only, accompanied by music. The production was called *The Cheats of Scapin or the Tavern Bilkers,* and was created by John Weaver, a Shrewsbury dancing master. Although at the time it was considered something of a novelty, the success of Rich's policy at Lincoln's Inn demanded more of Weaver's creations. In 1717 he presented ballets, as we would call them today, on the themes of Mars and Venus, Orpheus and Eurydice and, a little later, Cupid and Bacchus. These productions were in addition to the plays presented on the same program, and Cibber and his co-managers felt the need to apologize for them, which, as he said, "we generally use as crutches to our weakest plays."

THE BEGGAR'S OPERA

Apart from Rich's success as the English Harlequin (under the stage name of Lun, the name of a noted French comedian), he was an enterprising manager, and was responsible in 1728 for the first production of John Gay's *The Beggar's Opera,* which ran at the Lincoln's Inn Theatre with great success for sixty-three nights. Cibber was mortified at this, as he had been offered the "Newgate pastoral," as it was called by Swift, and had declined to produce it.

The receipts from the run of *The Beggar's Opera* were over 11,000 pounds, and with the spread of the news theatre managers put it on throughout the provinces, achieving runs of forty and fifty nights. Rich now began to look about for another house, and plans were made to build a new theatre which would house a much larger audience. The site chosen was in the Covent Garden.

COVENT GARDEN

Rich raised the money required to build the new theatre by public subscription. The fifty subscribers made three payments of 100 pounds, and in return were to receive a rent of two shillings for every performance and, in addition, free seats anywhere in the house except behind the scenes. When one remembers that in Restoration days the public were permitted, on payment of a fee, to go behind the scenes to see the actors, one realizes that this was an important step when even shareholders were confined to the front of the house.

The new theatre opened in 1732 with a well-tried play, Congreve's *Way of the World*. The auditorium had been enlarged in the new theatre; the stage remained the same, actually being made smaller, if anything, by the placing of seats on the apron. With the emphasis on spectacle and dumb show, the actors tended to retire behind the proscenium, their actions and movements being viewed immediately in front of the scenery. In contrast with Betterton's day when the actors performed largely on the apron and the scenery was well in the background, they now became part of the stage picture. Also, the seats on the apron stage, while still further evidence of the need to house more people, brought in half a guinea per seat, more than twice as much as the box seats. The pit remained at half a crown, and there were two galleries at two shillings and one shilling.

Seats were not numbered or reserved in those days, and a notice concerning the seats on the apron stage ran: "Servants will be allowed to keep places on the stage, and the ladies are desired to send them by 3 o'clock." As the performances began at 6 P.M., this indicates that stage seats were very popular, at least with some sections of the audience.

When the doors of the theatre were thrown open, there would

be a concerted rush by the waiting crowd and an excited scramble for the best seats. The seats were backless benches, and since there was no central gangway a wild hurdle race would ensue in which the ladies, with their large hooped skirts, would be at a distinct disadvantage. The ladies would frequently lose their hats, and sometimes their shoes, in the struggle, and once seated would spend quite a time in collecting and rearranging themselves.

The competitive spirit so instilled into the audience put them on their mettle, and the play had to start with a bang or the players were soon greeted with a very noisy reception. The audiences were very lively and knew what they wanted—action and spectacle rather than wit and poetry.

Although the new house proved a success from the beginning, Rich kept on the Lincoln's Inn Theatre, but transferred the patent to Covent Garden. Drury Lane and Covent Garden were now the "legitimate" theatres, with the monopoly of the spoken word. While the other theatres in town were legally allowed to present only pantomime, spectacle, and musical shows, there was at this time no hard-and-fast application of the rule, particularly as even the Drury Lane Theatre was forced to present pantomine instead of Shakespeare.

HENRY FIELDING AND THE HAYMARKET

Of the other theatres, the Haymarket, where Fielding's company played, had acquired a reputation for burlesques, opera, and musical shows. Fielding wrote some brilliantly satirical pieces for the stage, the best-known being *Tom Thumb the Great,* which ridiculed the kind of tragedy that was being continually played at the time, in which all the characters were killed off in the last scene.

As long as he confined his satire to the contemporary stage, Fielding was safe, but when he turned to politics he was on very dangerous ground. It is said that Walpole passed the Licensing Act of 1737, which gave the Lord Chamberlain powers of censorship of all plays performed within the city of Westminster, because of the content of one of Fielding's plays. Fielding soon gave up writing for the stage and devoted his whole time to novel writing.

HANDEL

It was at the Haymarket, which was open only during the summer months when the other theatres were closed, that Handel had his seasons of opera. In addition to writing his own operas, Handel produced Italian operas and scoured the Continent for singers. These seasons proved financially unsuccessful, and Handel went heavily into debt.

On certain nights Rich leased the Covent Garden Theatre to Handel for the presentation of opera, and eventually he had a regular Lenten season for his sacred oratorios. It was here, in 1743, that *The Messiah* had its first London performance. These seasons proved very successful, and became an institution. Handel was able to recoup his past losses, to pay all his debts, and to retire with a comfortable income. After his death the oratorios were continued, and ever since Covent Garden has been linked with the names of some of the greatest singers of the times.

PEG WOFFINGTON

The year 1740 saw the debut at Covent Garden of the celebrated Peg Woffington. She had appeared in London before, at the Haymarket, when at the age of fifteen she performed as a member of the juvenile troupe of the famous Madame Violante. After years of touring the country she eventually settled down in the theatre at Dublin, where she achieved great fame, especially in the part of Sir Harry Wildair in Farquhar's *Constant Couple*.

On coming to London she called at Rich's house nineteen times, without giving her name, and each time she was refused an interview. When Rich finally knew who his persistent caller really was he, being an astute manager, invited her in and acquired her services for Covent Garden at the modest salary of nine pounds per week. Rich was rather an eccentric in private life, and Peg, recording her visit, describes him lounging on a sofa with a cup of tea in one hand, from which he took occasional sips, and a book in the other; he was surrounded by no fewer than twenty-seven cats, which walked all over the sofa, climbed onto his lap and his shoulders, and even sipped his tea.

Peg's debut was in the role of Sylvia in *The Recruiting Officer*, a part in which she appeared for several scenes in male costume. As this suited her sparkling and vivacious personality, following on her success in Dublin as Sir Harry Wildair, she began to play men's roles in other plays. From then onward the "breeches" part was an accepted convention, and most leading actresses were prepared to assume a male role occasionally.

MRS. CIBBER

Some years previously another famous actress began her career at Drury Lane. Susannah Cibber was a sister of the composer Thomas Arne and the wife of Colley Cibber's son Theophilus. She was trained by her father-in-law and played in both comedy and trag- edy. She had such a fine voice that it is said that Handel especially arranged the contralto songs in *The Messiah* for her. There was a good deal of cooperation between the two patent theatres at this time, and actors played at both theatres by mutual arrangement. In 1742 Rich acquired Mrs. Cibber's services, and she played in tragedies with Quin, who was then Rich's leading tragic actor.

DAVID GARRICK

In the previous year an event happened in the theatrical world which shook the management of both theatres: a new star had arisen at the Goodman's Fields Theatre whose advent caused such a sensation that the receipts of both Drury Lane and Covent Garden showed an immediate and precipitate decline. David Gar- rick had arrived; at the age of twenty-four he was playing Richard III, being billed as "a gentleman who never appeared on any stage."

This was not strictly true, as for several years he had gained ex- perience in amateur theatricals and had played under an assumed name in provincial theatres. Half French and half Irish by descent, Garrick was the son of an army captain, and had received a good education (he and his brother had been the first pupils at the private school set up by Dr. Johnson).

DAVID GARRICK   From his sensational debut in "Richard III" in 1741, until his retirement, three years before his death, from the management of the Drury Lane in 1776, Garrick established a very great career as actor-manager.

He was rather short, but extremely handsome. His business sense was apparent in his having acquired the foundations of his art in the provinces under an assumed name, and in making his debut in

GARRICK AND CIBBER David Garrick as Jaffier and Susannah Cibber as Belvidera in Otway's "Venice Preserved,"
presented at the Drury Lane, London, 1762. Contemporary
dress was the costume for most tragic plays of the time.

London he took the town by storm. The secret was, of course, that
he had developed an entirely fresh approach to acting.

The playgoing public, now a little tired with so much spectacle
and with the rather heavy, stilted style of such leading actors as

Wilks, Booth, and Quin, found something quite new in Garrick's approach. The Goodman's Fields Theatre played to such crowded houses that the two patent theatres had to do something quickly in order to stop the fall in their receipts.

After going through the necessary legal formalities they successfully invoked their monopoly rights, with the result that Giffard, the manager of Goodman's Fields, had to cut the season short and close the theatre; whereupon Fleetwood, the wealthy, irresponsible youth who was managing Drury Lane, persuaded Garrick to join his company at the colossal salary (for those days) of six hundred guineas a season.

Garrick seized his opportunity and set forth on a series of roles in Shakespearean and contemporary plays which he interpreted in an entirely fresh manner, although not without some opposition from Macklin, who had until then been the leading actor in the company and whose acting belonged to the old traditional style. Macklin, however, was later to come under Garrick's influence and to revolutionize the portrayal of Shylock by giving him tragic qualities.

Peg Woffington, after having quarreled with Rich, had left Covent Garden and had also joined the Drury Lane company. An attachment was formed with Garrick which eventually blossomed into a love affair. It did not culminate in marriage, unfortunately for Peg, but it possibly had an effect on Garrick's move to Dublin two years later. Fleetwood, ever a bad manager, had got into arrears with the players' salaries, and although Garrick had led the company on strike, matters were not settled satisfactorily.

In 1745 Garrick left the Drury Lane Theatre and accepted an offer of another season in Dublin. Here he was enthusiastically received by Irish audiences and added further to his laurels. In June of the following year he returned to London for a short season with Rich at Covent Garden. For only six performances, five of which were Shakespearean roles—King Lear, Hamlet, Richard III, Othello, and Macbeth—Garrick and Rich each netted 300 pounds.

Drama was back with a vengeance after a period of management chiefly devoted to pantomime and spectacle.

GARRICK VERSUS QUIN

The following season Garrick was naturally re-engaged, and played alternately with Quin. Mrs. Cibber was also in the company, and Garrick began a long and happy partnership with her. On October 20 Quin played Richard III, and on October 31 Garrick played the same part, giving the public the chance to compare the two greatly differing styles. One cannot but admire Rich's showmanship in thus presenting the new and the old in the theatre. Here is a contemporary description of Quin:

> *Quin presented himself upon the rising of the curtain in a green velvet coat, embroidered down the seams, an enormous full-bottom periwig, rolled stockings, and high-heeled, square-toed shoes; with very little variation of cadence, and in deep, full tones, accompanied by a sawing kind of motion which had more of the senate than the stage in it, he rolled out his heroics with an air of dignified indifference that seemed to disdain the plaudits bestowed upon him.*

And of Garrick:

> *When, after long and eager expectation, I first beheld little Garrick, then young and light, and alive in every muscle and in every feature, come bounding on the stage . . . Heavens, what a transition! It seemed as if a whole century had been stepped over in the changing of a single scene—old things were done away, and a new order at once brought forward, light and luminous, and clearly destined to dispel the barbarisms and bigotry of a tasteless age, too long . . . superstitiously devoted to the illusions of imposing declamation.*

Garrick had broken all the rules, upset stage convention, and by his naturalistic acting had won over the public. Quin, although he was a good enough actor in his own style, suffered the humiliation

DAVID GARRICK AS MACBETH
As played at Drury Lane in 1768, the famous actor wears the accepted costume for Macbeth: the fashionable dress of the day.

of seeing receipts on Garrick's nights increase with every performance, while on the nights he played they fell in equivalent proportion. It says a lot for Quin's good nature that he and Garrick got on quite well together, and that throughout the entire season there was no sign of enmity between them. At the end of the season Garrick bought a share in the patent of the Drury Lane Theatre, and in 1747 he assumed management.

GARRICK'S MANAGEMENT OF THE DRURY LANE

Garrick had persuaded Mrs. Cibber to join the Drury Lane company, which also included Peg Woffington, lively Kitty Clive (of whom Dr. Johnson said, "She was a better romp than any I ever saw in nature"), Mrs. Pritchard, Delane, Yates, and Macklin. At thirty, Garrick was leading actor and manager of the most brilliant company of players in the theatre of the time. He ruled the company with an iron hand, and by careful training of the players in his own ways of acting and by the force of his overriding personality, he achieved a unity in the production of plays which has rarely been exceeded in the history of the theatre.

He continued his repertoire of Shakespearean roles with great

QUIN AS CORIOLANUS   The actor is portrayed as he appeared in James Thompson's play, presented at Covent Garden in 1749. The costume is a variation of the semi-classical dress adapted for Roman characters. The plumed helmet, full periwig, and wide skirt are far from historically accurate.

success. He also found time to write over forty plays of his own, few of which proved failures when produced. After many years of public acclaim Garrick suddenly tired of London and set off on a grand tour of France and Italy. This lasted two years, during which he played with his company in most of the principal cities, with continual welcome and success.

In 1765 he returned from his triumphs abroad to Drury Lane, bringing with him a mass of new ideas for revolutionizing the stage. England had always been behind the European theatres with her stage technique, and just as Inigo Jones and Davenant found new ideas in the theatres of France and Italy, so Garrick returned ready to equip the Drury Lane stage with the latest Continental innovations.

GARRICK'S STAGING INNOVATIONS

There had already been some development since the Restoration stage, chiefly because of the need to house more of the public. The apron stage, with its two doors on either side of the proscenium, was diminished to half its former depth, and the two doors were reduced to one. The tendency was for the actors to play more and more behind the proscenium and to be seen against the scenery.

The scenery had by now progressed from Davenant's simple and easily movable flats or shutters, and solid doors and windows were now constructed in the flats. Garrick realized that the new tendency of the actors put them farther away from the audience, so that the finer points of acting were lost, and by his lighting innovations he somewhat counteracted this tendency.

First of all he removed the great hoops of candles, which provided illumination to auditorium and stage alike, and hung them behind the proscenium arch out of sight of the audience. The main result of concealing the chief source of lighting, which hitherto had always been a cause of irritation to the folk in the gallery, was to make the stage easier to see, while incidentally heightening the dramatic effect. He also placed lights behind the wings, on a level with the actors, likewise concealed from the audience.

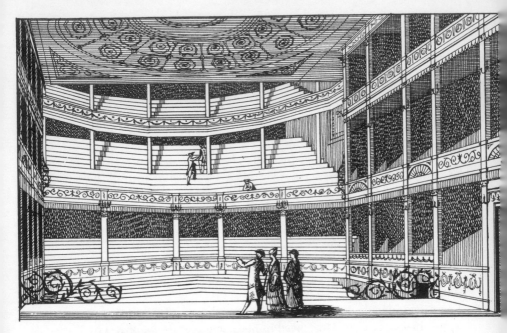

INTERIOR OF THE DRURY LANE   This is how this theatre looked in 1791, a year before its demolition. It was rebuilt in 1794. The proscenium door and the stage boxes are just within view at the right.

"THE SCHOOL FOR SCANDAL" Here is the famous "Screen Scene," as performed at the Drury Lane in 1777. Note the proscenium doors and the stage boxes.

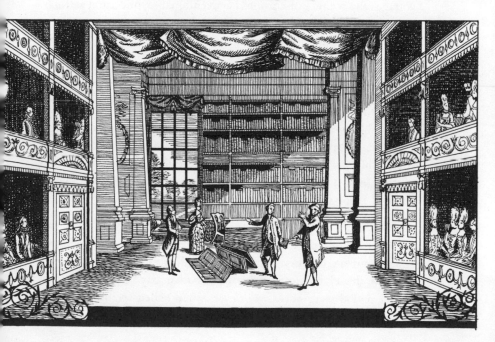

Other innovations were the greater use of oil lamps, and colored transparent silks for producing colored lighting effects. Garrick also made greater use of the footlights, for although they had been introduced in England many years before, their use was not universal, and even in the new Covent Garden Theatre of 1732 they had not been installed. A further introduction was the use of lanterns and wall brackets as an integral part of the setting, which also provided more light on the stage. Briefly, the effect of Garrick's innovations was more light on the actors and less on the audience.

Garrick made many other innovations on the stage itself, which were all intended to further naturalistic representation.

SCENERY: THE BEGINNINGS OF REALISM

Up to the middle of the eighteenth century, scenery had been quite conventional. Wherever the scene of the play took place—in foreign countries, in palace or chamber, in marketplace or humble cottage—the scenic artist painted conventional architectural settings, with no regard for either style or period.

Garrick's influence on stage design was manifest when his scenic artist, De Loutherbourg, took a sketching trip to Derbyshire in order to provide material for what were then regarded as highly realistic settings. Another designer of that time, Capon, produced settings to which some thought had been given regarding historical accuracy. He produced designs in which houses were painted as they might have appeared in the past, and he paid particular attention to the Gothic style of architecture. Here were the tentative beginnings of the great quest for realism on the stage which was ultimately reached at the end of the following century.

COSTUMES

Strangely enough, there was little development in stage costume throughout the century. Garrick played all his great Shakespearean roles in the elaborate costume of his own day. Costumes of an earlier period were never worn even when called for by the action of the play. This may have been due to the demands of the audience,

MACKLIN AS SHYLOCK The play was performed at the Drury Lane, London, in 1741. The actor wears the traditional long, black gaberdine. Macklin restored dignity to a role that had until then been treated as crude farce.

for when Macklin appeared at Covent Garden as *Macbeth* in 1773 clad in correct Scottish costume, he was greeted with boos, hisses, and a storm of disapproval.

Some progress was made in women's costume, which up to 1734 had been strictly à la mode. For a long time no actress would dare wear anything but the very latest fashion, whatever the period of the play. In 1734 a ballet dancer, Mlle. Salle, at Covent Garden, discarded the enormous hooped skirt and the fashionable piled-up coiffure of false hair. She wore her own hair, unpowdered, simply arranged, and without ornament, while she was dressed in a bodice and petticoat over which a simple robe of muslin was carefully draped after the model of a Greek statue. While this freedom was dictated by the needs of dancing, it also met with approval from the audience.

The lighter forms of entertainment, pantomime and ballet, had their special costumes, which were conventional rather than historical, but in tragedy the costume was the current vogue. It was left to Mrs. Siddons, toward the end of the century, to introduce more freedom and variety into women's dress on the stage.

GARRICK'S LAST YEARS

Soon after his return from the Continent, Garrick retired from acting, but remained a very active manager at Drury Lane. The public, however, clamored for his return to the stage, and six months later George III issued a royal command to Garrick to resume acting, which he could not ignore. He continued acting until he finally left the stage in 1776.

Garrick amassed a considerable fortune, and built a large house at Hampton which still stands, together with the delightful little temple he erected in the grounds on the riverbank as a tribute to Shakespeare, to whom he owed so much of his success.

Garrick did much to raise the social status of players, who now began to regard themselves no longer as servants of the aristocracy, but more as equals.

THE GREEN ROOM

The institution of the green room, the salon in which interested members of the upper classes could meet the players during the intervals between their appearances on the stage, had its origin in Restoration days, in the scene-room described by Pepys. It is not known why this particular color was chosen for the room, but green was a very popular color in the theatre during the eighteenth century. Tragedies were always played on a green carpet; the stage curtain itself was green; and the stage attendants, who moved the furniture and changed the scenery, wore green livery.

THE GUARDSMEN

It is chiefly due to Garrick that the theatre banished those snobs of high society from their privileged seats on the stage, which since Shakespeare's day had caused embarrassment to the actors and ill-feeling in the pit. The only persons, apart from the actors, who could be seen on the stage after this reform were the green-liveried stage attendants and the guards who, in the days of riots in the theatre, stood at both sides of the stage as a first line of defense against the pit.

There is a story that one of these guardsmen was so overcome by the strength of Garrick's acting in a certain tragedy that he fell in a faint. Garrick afterward sent for the man and, sympathizing with his embarrassment, presented him with a guinea. The news soon got around, and the following night another guardsman collapsed. Unfortunately for him, he had not realized that this night Garrick was playing in a comedy, so the guinea was not forthcoming.

Guardsmen were also used to keep order outside the doors of the theatre, for in those days, of course, there was no police force to carry out these duties. Today guardsmen are still employed by the theatres, not as custodians of the peace, but as supers in large productions such as operas, when numbers of soldiers are required on the stage. Even in early Victorian times, on the occasion of a royal visit to the theatre, a yeoman of the guard would stand at either side of the stage during the performance.

PLAYS

The first seventy years of the eighteenth century produced few plays of lasting value. Writers had discovered the novel and essay as new forms for their endeavors, and while such writers as Pope and Johnson wrote plays, they were too literary to live as drama.

The Augustan period, as it was called, produced the grand and heroic figures that actors such as Booth, Wilks, and Quin interpreted in heavy, stilted acting. The fresh, romantic approach of Garrick had little counterpart in the writings of the opposing school as exemplified in Shelley's poetry. The best writers generally neglected the theatre, and the whole century produced only three comedies which have acquired universal acclaim—Goldsmith's *She Stoops to Conquer,* and Sheridan's *The Rivals* and *The School for Scandal.*

SHE STOOPS TO CONQUER

Goldsmith's play was first produced at Covent Garden in 1773. The manager, Colman, had accepted the play with misgivings because of the very moderate success of Goldsmith's earlier play, *The Good Natur'd Man,* and had delayed presenting it for over a year. Owing to Dr. Johnson's persistent and enthusiastic influence, Colman at last put the play into rehearsal and, while still seeing no merit in the play, presented it on March 15, 1773.

It was an immediate success, and the press and public were full of acclaim. Besides being a good play, it had humor and the rather sentimental quality of the happy ending, which was much appreciated by the large popular audiences. Poor Goldsmith was unable to enjoy his first real financial success for long, as he died the following year, at the age of forty-six.

RICHARD BRINSLEY SHERIDAN

Richard Brinsley Sheridan was born in 1751, the son of Thomas Sheridan, an actor of the old school who had played at both Covent Garden and Drury Lane, where for a time he was stage manager under Garrick. In 1773 Sheridan married a singer, Elizabeth Linley, who had sung in oratorios at Covent Garden. Her father, Dr. Linley, was a distinguished musician, and his talent was passed on to his children.

The Rivals was produced at Covent Garden for the first time in 1775, and although the first night was not a success, when alterations had been made in the cast and the dialogue speeded up, it immediately rose in public favor.

The following year Garrick retired from Drury Lane, and Sheridan managed to raise the money to buy his share of the patent. He moved in with his whole family—his wife as accounts keeper, his father-in-law as musical director, and Mrs. Linley as wardrobe mistress. His father, old Thomas Sheridan, was installed as stage manager, while his own position was that of supervisor and playwright.

The first season at Drury Lane saw the production of his masterpiece, *The School for Scandal,* which brought Sheridan a large amount of money and an international reputation as a playwright. The same year he wrote *The Duenna,* an opera with music by Dr. Linley, which was produced at Covent Garden. *The Critic,* a comedy based largely on the Duke of Buckingham's farce, *The Rehearsal,* soon followed. As this play burlesques the stage of the earlier days, and in particular the rhyming tragedies of Dryden, it is rarely revived now. *Pizarro,* his only tragedy, is also rarely revived, as it has few lasting qualities, although it achieved popularity at the time it was written.

Sheridan gave up writing for the stage at the age of twenty-eight, and thenceforth confined his activities to management. His sparkling wit and social qualities were not to be lost to the nation, however, for in 1780 he entered Parliament and distinguished himself as an orator and a master of debate, notably at the impeachment of Warren Hastings.

His interest in the theatre declined, and he became a thoroughly bad manager. He dressed and lived in a style totally beyond his means, and played an active part in the theatre only when receipts began to fall and his way of living was in danger. Thus, in 1791, he rebuilt the theatre, making room for 3,600 people instead of 2,000 as previously, and the stage had a proscenium opening of forty-three feet.

In spite of numerous fire precautions, water taps well distributed throughout, and an iron curtain, the theatre caught fire in 1809 and burned to the ground. At the time Sheridan first heard the news he was debating in Parliament on the war in Spain, and it is typical of the man that he stayed on until the House adjourned, returning to find the theatre a smoldering shell.

Sheridan was completely ruined, and he remained bankrupt until his death in 1816—a rather depressing end to a brilliant beginning. In 1812 a new theatre was built on the site by Samuel Whitbread, the brewer, and although considerably altered, it remains there today.

"THE COUNTRY WIFE" An eighteenth century costume for the play, showing the elaborately powdered wig and the hooped skirt of the day's fashion.

MRS. SIDDONS

During Garrick's last years at Drury Lane he was continually on the lookout for fresh talent. Owing to his ill health and declining years, the leading actresses of the company were getting a little out of hand, so he decided to introduce into the theatre a young and beautiful actress who had been playing in the provinces.

He had first heard of Mrs. Siddons when she was playing at a small theatre at Cheltenham. He followed her travels about the country and sent out agents to report her progress for a whole year before deciding to offer her an engagement. Mrs. Siddons, at the age of twenty and already a mother, made her debut at Drury Lane in December, 1775, as Portia in *The Merchant of Venice*.

Although young, she was not without experience. Born of a

theatrical family—the Roger Kembles, who had quite a provincial reputation—she had first appeared on the stage at a very early age. All through her childhood acting with her parents alternated with periods when she was sent away to school. This training gave her an easy facility for remembering lines, a clear and pleasing voice, and a passion for Milton and the classic poets. Her parents naturally encouraged and developed her talents for the stage, and were not a little disappointed when, at the age of eighteen, she married a rather second-rate actor, William Siddons. The young couple left the Kembles and joined another company touring the west of England. It was with this company that Mrs. Siddons was discovered at Cheltenham in the summer of 1774.

When she at last arrived at Drury Lane, Garrick was pleased with her appearance, paid her compliments, and recognized both her promise and her inexperience of large theatres. Although he gave her every encouragement, her debut was doomed to failure. Poor Sarah was in a panic. She walked onto the stage, a tall, slender, and rather gawky figure, and immediately her voice began to fail. Her lines died off in a whisper and, in addition, she became so nervous that she completely forgot her actions and movements. The play dragged on and came to a depressing end. Except for one newspaper, the press confirmed the public reaction to a disappointing first appearance, the solitary exception being written by a friend of Garrick's who had seen her in the provinces.

In spite of the bad beginning, Garrick decided to continue her engagement all through the season, and she played opposite him in one of his own farewell performances toward the end of the season. Garrick spent considerable time giving her instructions, and on her spare evenings she would watch his acting from the special box with which he had provided her. Her misfortune, however, continued throughout the season, and she had no better reception from press or public. When Sheridan took over management at the end of the season her services were not retained.

With a heavy heart she set off with her husband again for the provinces, determined at least to make a success in the flourishing theatres of Birmingham, York, Liverpool, and the other large towns. After periods of local success, illness, and confinement, she finally settled down at Bath, which was then becoming a center of fashion, elegance, and scandal. Her success among this critical public was immediate. She worked hard and gave creditable performances in Shakespearean parts and in contemporary plays.

SARAH SIDDONS   Leading tragedienne of the eighteenth century, she dominated the English stage from her appearance in 1782 at the Drury Lane in "The Fatal Marriage" to her final performance as Lady Macbeth in 1812, the year of her retirement.

She played for four seasons at Bath, and during this time her art slowly matured. Her intellectual powers grew, and with increasing experience and the time to develop her own approach to acting, she acquired a new sense of confidence with the knowledge of her own powers of restraint. In 1780 Thomas Sheridan came to Bath for his health, and on seeing Mrs. Siddons act was so struck with her development that he hastened back to persuade his son to engage her for Drury Lane.

Sarah was a success at Bath and had many friends in the town, so she was not easily persuaded to give up the certainty of a small but regular income for uncertainty in London. No doubt, too, she had thoughts of her previous disappointment. Finally, two years later, she agreed to accept an engagement from Sheridan and said farewell to her enthusiastic audiences in Bath, who were greatly disappointed at her leaving. At her farewell performance she produced on the stage her three "reasons" for accepting the London engagement—her three small children.

Her first reappearance at Drury Lane was in the leading part of Isabella in the play of that name, a version by Garrick of Southerne's *The Fatal Marriage,* in which grief and tears were predominant. On the evening of the first night her father, Roger Kemble, turned up to comfort her and to allay her fears and worries. Although she was inwardly quaking with thoughts of her past experience at the enormous theatre, she walked onto the stage and began to immerse herself completely in the part. It was a role that gave her magnificent opportunities for displaying her pathos and tragic qualities, and with her now well-matured style she gave a great performance. The audience was deeply moved, and before the curtain descended spontaneous applause broke out all over the theatre. Sarah Siddons had returned to triumph.

The press followed public opinion and was full of enthusiastic notices, Sarah being placed even above the great Mrs. Cibber. Her success at Drury Lane now complete and her future assured, she remained there playing leading parts for the next twenty years.

At twenty-seven Mrs. Siddons was tall and slender, though not angular, with graceful movements, while her head was small, with classic features and dark, compelling eyes.

At the close of her first season she went to Dublin, accepting a summer engagement at the Smock Alley Theatre, where she was to meet her eldest brother, John Philip Kemble. Kemble had completed his education in France and then set out to conquer the stage. His first important engagement was in Dublin, and on the strength of his successful seasons there Sheridan booked him for Drury Lane. In the autumn they both returned to London and began a long period of successes. Like his sister, Kemble was tall, handsome, and dignified in appearance, and his style of acting was in a way a reversion from Garrick's easy, naturalistic flexibility to the more classic style of the earlier actors. Both Sarah and John found their greatest successes in tragic roles, particularly in Shakespearean plays, and until the early nineteenth century they remained the undisputed leaders of the stage in England.

Mrs. Siddons made several innovations in women's costume in the theatre. She was the first woman to discard the powdered hair and large hooped skirts of the time. She developed costumes of a simple shape, based on classic models, and designed simply draped headdresses to replace the elaborate, beplumed helmets which were traditional wear with the tragic actresses of the past. Her costumes were in no sense historically accurate, but they were no longer of the latest fashion, and were especially designed for acting and the stage.

THE AUDIENCES AND RIOTS

The audiences were lively and vociferous, and if they took a dislike to anything or anybody, instead of just staying away from the theatre they would pay for admission night after night in order to create a disturbance or start a riot, in which they would try to invade the stage and stop the performances. Indeed, riots were common in the theatres throughout the century. At a trial of the ringleaders of a riot at the Haymarket in 1738, the law declared

MRS. SIDDONS AS ELVIRA In "Pizarro," Sheridan's adaptation of the play by Kotzebue, 1799, the actress wears a semi-classical costume and a simple headdress. She was the first actress to alter the traditional stage dress for women, discarding plumes, powdered hair, and the large hooped skirts of the time.

"that the public had a legal right to manifest their dislike to any play or actor; and that the judicature of the pit had been acquiesced in, time immemorial."

The public were very conscious of their rights, and actors and managers were compelled to bow to their demands. The occasional invasions of the stage by unruly members of the pit made necessary the provision of spiked railings over the orchestra, and such decorative ironware as that on the front of the Drury Lane stage served to hinder their destructive efforts.

One of the most serious disturbances occurred in 1755, when a company of French dancers was being presented by Garrick at the Drury Lane Theatre. At this time England was drifting into war with France, and the audiences in pit and galleries showed their disapproval by six nights of prolonged rioting. Garrick appealed to the better instincts of the gathering, and received support from the fashionable folk in the boxes. This incensed the pit and galleries, and fighting broke out among the two factions. Gallants jumped into the pit from the boxes, swords were drawn, and blood was shed; suddenly all were united in a common purpose to do as much damage as possible. Benches were torn up and scenery demolished, the damage amounting to several thousand pounds.

Even in normal times the audience was hardly well behaved. It was common practice for the galleries to pelt unpopular people in the pit with orange peels or rotten fruit. Quarrels were frequent among people in different parts of the theatre, and there was a continual calling-out and impatient knocking of sticks on the floor until the curtain rose. It follows that under these conditions the actors, whatever their style, had to be good; and it was in acting that the century made its greatest contribution.

CHANGES IN THE THEATRE IN THE EIGHTEENTH CENTURY

The use of the large apron stage declined during the century, and scenery became more realistic, taking up more space on the stage. Acting began to lose the freedom of movement possible on the Restoration stage, and the concentration of light on the actors, well behind the proscenium, also tended to confine acting space.

Many more theatres were built for a growing middle-class public whose tastes unfortunately discouraged great drama, so that few plays of lasting value were written. The demands of the audiences made a long bill necessary, which often included a full five-act tragedy, a comic piece, and a ballet or pantomime, together with interludes of dancing or music and the various prologues and epilogues.

The Early 19th Century

KEMBLE'S MANAGEMENT AT COVENT GARDEN

In the summer of 1802, unable any longer to stand the continual wrangles with Sheridan over payment of their salaries, Kemble and Mrs. Siddons left Drury Lane for good. Kemble managed to raise sufficient money to purchase a sixth share in the Covent Garden patent, which brought with it the chance not only of acting but, as stage manager, of deciding who should play with him. While negotiations were being completed Kemble made a holiday tour of the Continent and Sarah went to Ireland. They both returned to London to commence the 1803 season, Kemble first appearing in *Hamlet* with great success, followed soon after by Mrs. Siddons as Isabella in *The Fatal Marriage*.

As a manager Kemble was tactful and considerate, in spite of the excesses of George Frederick Cooke, an actor with a reputation second only to Kemble's. Cooke had an uncontrollable temper and drank heavily, but when sober and in suitable parts he gave extremely good performances. His passionate and erratic acting was a marked contrast to the studied calm and dignity of Kemble's style. The first season went well. Among the list of plays produced, eleven were by Shakespeare, an indication that public taste was for drama rather than spectacle. Soon the pendulum was to swing back, but for the moment acting was the all-important element in the theatre.

MASTER BETTY

The following season both Mrs. Siddons and Kemble were eclipsed by a brighter, though much smaller, star. A young prodigy known as Master Betty, or "the Young Roscius," had sprung into public notice in the provinces, where he had been appearing with great success. Although only about thirteen years of age, he was playing leading parts with grown actors, and his fame had swept the country. He had come from Belfast, where a year or two earlier he had seen Mrs. Siddons play and had been so struck with her acting that he decided to take up the stage himself.

Kemble engaged him for Covent Garden, where his success with the public was so great that Kemble presented him in all his own great tragic roles. Betty's father seems to have been a keen business-man, for when Betty appeared at Covent Garden he received fifty guineas a night. On alternate nights he played at Drury Lane, where he commanded an even greater salary. London went completely mad about Betty, and the climax came when Pitt adjourned the House of Commons, which then went in a body to see Betty play *Hamlet.*

Betty is said to have been able to portray changing emotions well, and his action was good; but his face showed little or no expression and his lines were delivered in a singsong fashion, a style which had been popular early in the eighteenth century. It was probably the novelty of seeing a tiny, slender figure in place of the usual stalwart tragedian rather than Betty's qualities as an actor, clever little boy though he must have been, which attracted the audience.

His success lasted until the end of the following season, when the

JOSEPH GRIMALDI The greatest low comedian of the eighteenth century is pictured as the clown in the English pantomime, "Mother Goose." His stylized make-up established the custom for all future clowns.

public grew tired of the little hero, and although he played a year or two longer in the provinces he soon vanished quietly from the scene.

JOE GRIMALDI AND *MOTHER GOOSE*

A year or so later Covent Garden produced its most successful pantomime, *Mother Goose,* in which Joe Grimaldi established his reputation as the greatest low comedian of the day. Grimaldi's father

had been employed by Garrick at Drury Lane, and young Joe, being brought up in the theatre, was already a highly accomplished
and experienced actor by the time he was in his middle twenties.
He had played at Drury Lane and Sadler's Wells and minor theatres, chiefly in pantomime.

In *Mother Goose* the principal character was not, as in the pantomime of Rich's day, Harlequin, but Clown, and Grimaldi portrayed this character with all the skill of byplay, dumb show, and
subtle gesticulation. He was responsible for the curious costume
and makeup which has been adapted and imitated by all subsequent clowns—nowadays to be seen only at the circus or variety
show. Grimaldi's subtlety of action and movement was ·such that
even Kemble took private lessons from him, as did certain gentlemen of the Court.

Mother Goose was only part of the evening's program, usually
being preceded by a full-length tragedy and a comic ballet. The
popularity of the pantomime enabled it to run for ninety-two performances, during which period the accompanying pieces were
changed many times. There thus began a tendency to spend much
more money on scenery, costumes, and properties for pantomime
than for tragedy, in which the personality and skill of the actor
were held to be sufficient attraction. The long bill led to the practice of admitting the public at half-price midway through the evening's entertainment. Thus, those members of the public who
wished to see only the pantomime could do so at a lower charge
and be encouraged to see it not merely once but several times.

THE FIRE AT COVENT GARDEN

In 1808 Kemble's subsequent misfortunes began when the firing
of a gun on the stage set some scenery smoldering which burst into
flame early in the morning. The fire consumed the entire building
with great rapidity. All the contents of the theatre were destroyed,
including the valuable scenery, costumes, and properties, Kemble's
extensive library of books and manuscripts, and a vast collection of

music by Handel, Arne, and other musicians who had been associated with the theatre in the past. Gone too was Handel's great organ that he had bequeathed to Rich after a long and happy collaboration. Mrs. Siddons lost her entire collection of stage jewelry and costumes.

THE NEW THEATRE

Evidence of public concern and esteem for the two great stars was soon forthcoming, however, and public subscriptions for the rebuilding of the theatre poured in. The company moved to the King's Theatre in the Haymarket while money was being raised for the new building. Insurance claims brought in about half the

THE NEW COVENT GARDEN Rebuilt in 1809, the galleries of this famous theatre were semi-circular in shape. The apron was considerably foreshortened. One proscenium door with a stage box above it was placed in the proscenium arch.

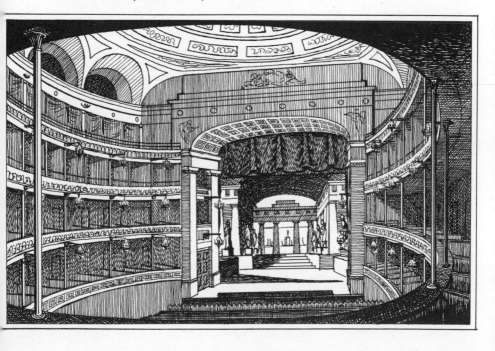

necessary capital, and within a year the new theatre was actually completed.

The new building was designed in the prevailing classic architecture, fronted by a huge Doric portico. The row of dwelling houses that had originally screened the theatre in Bow Street having also been burnt down, the extra space available was used to enlarge the interior, and grand anterooms and salons were added for "the comfort and convenience" of the public. There were three tiers of boxes as well as the two galleries, and two central gangways made the pit more easily accessible. The third tier was made up of twenty-three "private" boxes, each with its own anteroom and furnished with chairs, the latter a great innovation in those days, as hitherto the seating accommodations, even in the boxes, had consisted of rows of backless benches.

The house was illuminated by forty glass chandeliers, each holding many candles. Not only was the auditorium made much grander, the stage was considerably enlarged, the proscenium opening being about forty feet wide and the depth of the stage from the footlights to the back wall increased to nearly seventy feet. The theatre, when full, held an audience of nearly three thousand, and the entire cost of rebuilding and furnishing amounted to over 300,000 pounds.

As less than half the money had been raised, the new theatre began its life under a heavy burden of debt, and this led to an increase in the admission prices which was to provoke a storm of public disapproval and Kemble's subsequent eclipse in the favor of the public.

THE O.P. RIOTS

The theatre opened on Septemebr 18, 1809, with *Macbeth*, followed by a musical farce called *The Quaker*. No sooner had Kemble appeared on the stage to make the customary opening address than pandemonium broke out. Many members of the audience produced handbells, watchmen's rattles, and all kinds of noisy instruments, proving that the action was premeditated. Placards were

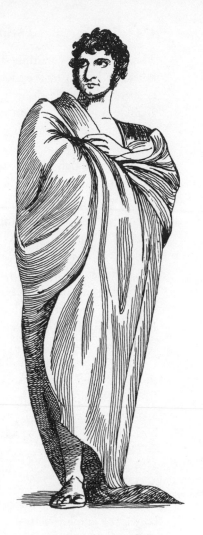

KEMBLE AS CORIOLANUS The actor is garbed in classical Roman costume. His appearance as Hamlet in historical costume in 1783 abolished contemporary dress in Shakespeare.

produced declaring their demand for "Old Prices" or "Kemble, Tremble," and the audience kept up a continual chant of "O.P.," accompanied by a regular beat of stamping feet or blows on the floor.

The demonstration was chiefly directed against Kemble and Mrs. Siddons. The company went on with the performance of the play with admirable self-control, although they were quite inaudible.

The disturbances continued night after night. Kemble, determined not to be beaten by the mob, had Bow Street runners in the house to arrest the ringleaders. In spite of this the riots continued, and Kemble was forced to put on a program composed entirely of dumb show. The demonstrations went on throughout the season, even the introduction of prizefighters hired by Kemble failing to put an end to them, although a temporary lull was effected by the appearance of the darling of the public, Grimaldi.

The press was divided on the issue, taking both sides, and many were the cartoons and prints published satirizing the whole affair. Kemble submitted his books to an impartial committee of influential persons, including the Solicitor-General and the Governor of the Bank of England, to prove how speculative theatre management really was and that he was justified in raising the prices of admission. The committee published its report, completely confirming Kemble's action, but all to no purpose, for the nightly cry of "O.P." continued.

Finally, Kemble had to bow to public demand, and on meeting three hundred of the rioters at a dinner at the Crown and Anchor Tavern he signed a paper agreeing to their demands. The public apology that followed from the stage was greeted with a placard hoisted in the pit on which was written, "We are satisfied."

The disturbances were not entirely due to the increase in prices, as the two galleries had remained at the old price. From the ranks of the pit the leaders of the riots gave vent to their disapproval not only of the increased prices but also of the innovation of "private" boxes, the employment of a foreign singer, and later, of course, of the strongarm methods used to counter the rioters by means of pugilists. The galleries followed the lead of the pit, but they had an additional complaint in their poor view of the stage due to the increased height of the galleries, which was necessitated by the extra tier of "private" boxes.

SPECTACLES AT COVENT GARDEN

The "private" boxes were let for the season, and brought in about

10,000 pounds a year. As Kemble was forced to abolish them, the loss of this considerable income had to be made up somehow, and he inevitably turned to what we today call the "box-office draw."

The fact that pantomime, burlesque, and the lighter forms of entertainment were becoming increasingly popular, that the minor theatres were booming, together with the success of Astley's Amphitheatre where horses and other animals provided the entertainment, all supplied the reasons for Kemble's production of *Bluebeard* in 1811, complete with sixteen horses. The following year an elephant appeared on the stage in another pantomime at the theatre. Although this greatly appealed to the public, the stage mechanic of Drury Lane, making a comment on the inevitable triumph of art over nature, said that he would be sorry if he could not design and construct a moving animal greatly superior in every degree.

MRS. SIDDONS' RETIREMENT

In the same year Mrs. Siddons retired from the stage, at the age of fifty-six. After over forty years of acting she had attained a unique position in the history of the theatre. In the "grand manner," which she had established with her brother, she remained unsurpassed, and she was the first notable actress to lead a blameless and normal life.

Her final performance was as Lady Macbeth. In accordance with the custom of that time the play was stopped immediately after her final exit in the sleepwalking scene, when the audience, as a compliment to the great actress, insisted that the performance come to an end. Mrs. Siddons reappeared, after changing her costume, to make a farewell speech especially written for her in verse by her nephew, Horace Twiss.

She retired with a comfortable income to enjoy her last years in peace and quiet. Even in retirement, however, the stage still attracted her, and she made occasional appearances, chiefly at benefit performances for other actors, appearing in the popular tragedy *Douglas* as late as 1819. She died in 1831.

KEMBLE'S CONTRIBUTIONS AS ACTOR AND MANAGER

Kemble never recaptured his popularity after the "O.P." riots, and although he continued acting, he was an aging and disappointed man. He retired in 1817, receiving an ovation as great as his sister's, and died in 1823.

Kemble as an actor had a stately and picturesque appearance, although he possessed a rather husky voice. He represented on the stage the pseudo-classical interest that was so greatly influencing architecture and painting at the time. His deportment and pose were modeled on Roman sculpture rather than on Roman life.

As a manager his reputation rests on his presentation of Shakespeare's plays. He tried to dress the players in costumes of varying periods, and he spent considerable care and time in making the settings appropriate. Garrick had played Shakespeare in modern costume and had spent more money on his pantomimes, preferring to rely on his acting alone to draw the crowds to Shakespeare. Garrick restored Shakespeare to his former importance in the theatre, and Kemble and Mrs. Siddons continued to keep the great tragedies before the public.

The Victorians

NEW AUDIENCES FOR THE THEATRE

In 1800 there were only ten theatres in London; by 1840 there were twenty-two. Although this was partly due to the increase in the population of London, then growing rapidly, it was also due to the theatre's increasing attraction for a rather different class of audience.

We have seen how, in the early eighteenth century, the Court influence declined in the theatre, being succeeded by that of the upper middle class, until eventually this section of the community also lost interest in the theatre. By the early years of the nineteenth century, polite society generally stayed away from the theatres, which now, much enlarged, housed great numbers of the working classes.

"GIVING OUT"

As evidenced by Kemble's experience at Covent Garden, the audiences were emphatic in their likes and dislikes, and this had no little effect on drama at the time. The custom of "giving out" after the play, although traditional and dating back to Restoration days, was in a way the managers' safeguard against the tyranny of the audience. At the close of the play a representative of the management, often the stage manager, would announce the repetition of the performance on subsequent nights. The nature of his reception from the very vociferous audience usually decided the fate of the production. Several great writers of the time, including Dickens and Browning, were to hear the hissing and booing that marked the reception of their plays and, naturally, decide to confine their activities to the much safer practice of publication.

PLAY "PIRATING"

On the other hand, there were plenty of hack writers in the theatre successfully writing melodramas, burlesques, and other forms of light entertainment. Much of the work was adapted from French comedies and farces, and there was a great deal of "pirating" of plays written in England.

Until the Authors Act was passed by Parliament in 1832, there were no acting rights, and when an author presented a new play to a manager he received only an agreed sum. Authors had no claim on other managers who might send their servants to make a copy of the play from the performances at the theatre and might later present it in a rather mangled form at their own theatres. There was no serious writing for the English stage for about the first forty years of the century, partly for these reasons, but also because of theatrical monopoly.

MONOPOLY BY THE PATENT THEATRES

Those ghosts of the Restoration theatre, the Killigrew and Davenant patents, still persisted, and the managers of Drury Lane and Covent Garden held the exclusive rights to present spoken drama. Apart from the Haymarket, which was open only in the summer when the patent theatres were closed, all the other so-called minor theatres in London were obliged to present only "illegitimate" drama, or entertainment in which any dialogue spoken had to be accompanied by music. The minor theatres were continually at odds with the two patent theatres, which in turn did all they could to enforce their monopoly.

Two Acts of Parliament were passed during the eighteenth century which, although not defining the position very clearly, in practice enabled the monopoly conditions to continue. The Licensing Act of 1737 gave the Crown, through the Lord Chamberlain, unlimited powers in license and censorship of plays within the confines of the City of Westminster. Each succeeding Lord Chamberlain interpreted the Act·differently, some reading it literally and licensing "illegitimate" houses, others sustaining the patent theatres to the exclusion of all rivals. A second Act, passed in 1752, extended its scope to all places of amusement in Westminster and elsewhere and gave local magistrates authority to grant licenses at their quarter sessions. There was only a vague understanding between the magistrates and the Lord Chamberlain concerning the restriction of licensed theatres to "illegitimate" drama. No real definition existed as to how far these theatres were confined to pantomime, music, and dancing.

A further Act of 1832 merely confirmed previous enactments and extended the powers of local magistrates to license "legitimate" theatres outside the twenty-mile limit of London. This third Act greatly increased the number of theatres in the provinces, for although in the larger cities theatres already existed under royal patent, magistrates could now license performances of serious drama in any town or city, and companies unable to work in London because of the monopoly conditions found new scope for their activities.

One of the minor theatres had defied these monopoly conditions in 1787 by putting on *As You Like It*, with the result that the patent theatres immediately had the unfortunate manager charged with vagrancy under the original Licensing Act, which revived the vagrancy law under which actors performing without a license were termed "vagrants and sturdy beggars."

THE BURLETTA

With the rights of the patent theatres upheld, the minor theatres were confined to presenting dancing, pantomime, and what came to be known as the *burletta*. Originally, the burletta was a burlesque type of musical piece without a word of dialogue. When the plot required some explanation too difficult to portray by mime alone, large pieces of cloth were lowered from the flies on which the story was told in letters big enough for all to read.

The development of the burletta is, in effect, the story of the rise of the minor theatres and the eventual defeat of monopoly. When melodrama was introduced from France early in the century, it was given a form similar to that of the burletta, and in the eyes of the law was subject to the same conditions. Elliston was the first manager of the minor theatres to develop the possibilities arising from the vagueness of the law in defining "illegitimate" drama. He rented the Royal Circus (later known as the Surrey Theatre) which, like Astley's, had been giving equestrian displays. Under the title of "burletta" he presented *Macbeth* and other well-known classics. In order to conform with the law and to escape the wrath of the patent theatres, Elliston largely rewrote the plays in doggerel verse and arranged a continuous piano accompaniment.

This advance on the completely dumb-show kind of entertainment continued, and the important question now arose of how much music should accompany the speaking of the verse. As time went on, the piano accompaniment dwindled until it existed only as a few almost inaudible chords. When Dibdin, the songwriter, succeeded Elliston at the Surrey he presented *The Vicar of Wakefield*, which was highly praised, although one writer regretted that "the good old Vicar is forced to sing in order to evade the watchfulness of the proprietors of the two patent theatres."

By this time (in 1819) the definition of *burletta* came to include prose comedy, provided it had five songs to each act. The minor theatres usually gave more care and attention to the scenery and costumes than did the patent theatres which, in order to attract full houses, were nevertheless forced to concentrate more on spectacle than on the legitimate drama in which they held the monopoly.

Indeed, in 1831, as *The Observer* pointed out, Drury Lane was showing *Timor the Tartar* and the horses; at Covent Garden *The Life and Death of Buonaparte* was showing as a mere spectacle with horses. On the other hand, the minors were presenting: at Sadler's Wells, *Romeo and Juliet* and *Katherine and Petruchio;* at the Surrey, *Richard III* and other Shakespearean plays; and at the new City Theatre, *The Merchant of Venice.* These productions of Shakespeare were arranged to conform with the burletta definition, but their success emphasized the futility of the prevailing conditions.

THE END OF THEATRE MONOPOLY

In 1832 a group of writers for the stage met under the chairmanship of Bulwer-Lytton, and a petition to Parliament followed. The same year a Bill was presented to Parliament which was intended to free the minors from the monopoly and so once more make conditions possible for creative writing for the theatre. The Bill passed the Commons, but was rejected by the Lords, chiefly because of a fanatical speech by the Bishop of London attacking theatres in general as hotbeds of vice and immorality.

Fortunately for the minors, the Lord Chamberlain at the time, Lord Conyngham, sympathized with them and interpreted the Licensing Act as a means for extending the interests of the theatre. He granted many licenses to new theatres and extended the seasons of the Adelphi and the Olympic. He also insisted that the patent theatres limit their performances to spoken dialogue and made them close during Lent, although the minors were allowed to remain open.

The patent theatres were now running at a loss because of the restrictions on their monopoly, and serious drama soon dwindled in their programs, eventually disappearing completely. Finally, in 1843, the Theatre Regulations Act was passed. The minors at last acquired their freedom, and theatre monopoly passed into history.

EDMUND KEAN

By this time there had been considerable development in the presentation of plays, chiefly due to the activities of the actor-managers,

EDMUND KEAN AS GLOUCESTER IN "RICHARD III" Presented at the Drury Lane in 1814, Richard was Kean's most famous role. Overnight, Kean's passionate style of acting made the declamatory style of the Kembles out-of-date.

who now dominated the scene. Acting developed greatly under new styles created by the leading actors who succeeded Kemble.

The first of the new stars was Edmund Kean, who grew up in the theatre and at an early age was a strolling player in the provinces. Making his debut at Drury Lane in 1814 as Shylock, he thrilled the audience with a new style of interpretation, highly emotional and passionate, acting rather by inspiration than in the calm, studied, classical manner of Kemble. His success was immediate, and with a rapidly increasing salary he played all the great tragic roles—Hamlet, Othello, Macbeth, Lear, and Richard III. He acquired a fortune in his first years in London, but lived rather recklessly, became involved in a scandal, and left England to tour in America.

In the rapidly growing Eastern cities, theatres were springing up and English actors, proving very popular, were finding an attractive new field for further increasing their fortunes. Kean, however, was not satisfied with the success he found in America, and eventually returned to London, appearing at Drury Lane. The public appeared to distinguish the actor from the man, and his reception was as warm as in his most popular days before the scandal. His way of life, however, still estranged him from polite society and exacted its toll. When he died in 1833 at forty-six, he was an exhausted and prematurely aged man.

WILLIAM CHARLES MACREADY

Two years after Edmund Kean made his Drury Lane debut, William Charles Macready first appeared at Covent Garden, then in the last year of Kemble's management. Macready had not the immediate success of Edmund Kean, but proved in the long run to be of more solid worth.

Macready's style was largely in the Kemble tradition, but was blended with some of Kean's passion and a touch of the easy, polished acting of the French players he had seen on trips to Paris. Macready was a man of considerable intelligence, and he attracted the company of the great writers of the time. He played in contemporary plays, provided they were written in the traditional form of comedy or tragedy; but he had his greatest successes in Shakespearean parts.

A man of good taste, Macready achieved much in raising the standard of production of serious plays. For the first time since Garrick's day plays received adequate rehearsal. Previously, actors had merely read their lines and were allowed to interpret their parts as they wished at the actual performance, provided the interpretation was within the bounds of the accepted traditions. Under these conditions, a play of Shakespeare's with Edmund Kean resolved itself into the solo performance of the star surrounded by a host of supernumeraries.

Macready, when he was in management, ensured that rehearsals

WILLIAM MACREADY AS HAMLET The play was performed with notable success during his thirteen-year stay at the Drury Lane, commencing in 1823.

were thorough, that all parts were equally well played, and that the whole production aimed at a unified effect. To attain this end he cast aside the rather mangled forms of Shakespeare's plays that were universally used at the time and went back to the original text. To ensure that his scenery and costumes were harmonious and correct, he employed J. R. Planche who, apart from being an accomplished writer of the lighter forms of entertainment, was an expert on historical costumes. Planche had collaborated in 1823 with Charles Kemble (who had succeeded his brother John as manager at Covent Garden) in a production of *King John* in which, for the first time in the history of the theatre, costumes of the past were reproduced with reasonable accuracy.

Macready had financially unsuccessful periods of management at both the patent theatres during the monopoly period. He also played at many of the minor theatres and had many successful tours, including those to America. He retired from the stage in 1851, and died in 1873.

CHARLES KEAN

Charles Kean, the son of Edmund, began acting in 1827, much against his father's wish. A limited success started him on a life of touring the provinces and, for some years, America. Having achieved some reputation in America, he returned to London at a convenient time, when Macready was about to retire, and making full use of the opportunity, soon became the leading tragedian of the day.

Queen Victoria who, unlike other monarchs of the preceding hundred years, took an interest in the theatre, saw him in 1849 and was so delighted with his performance that she inaugurated a series of "theatricals" at Windsor Castle, with Kean as "Master of the Revels." The Queen's regular attendance at the theatre, together with the more scholarly and tasteful productions of Macready and Kean, had the effect of bringing the upper classes back into the auditorium.

Charles Kean had not the brilliant (though erratic) genius of his father, and was generally considered to be a lesser actor. As a manager, however, he saw to it that he was surrounded by a first-rate cast and that his productions were mounted with taste and splendor. He continued with Macready's ideas of using historically accurate costumes and working out the production in detail so that the leading actor no longer monopolized the stage and by over-emphasis distorted the true intent of the play.

Kean took over management of the Princess's Theatre in 1850 and enjoyed continuous success for nine years, after which he played in the provinces and undertook extensive tours of America and Australia. This small theatre made the long run possible. Previously, only the spectacular afterpieces and pantomimes ever enjoyed runs of several weeks. Plays were continued only as long as

CHARLES KEAN AS HENRY V A typical example of Kean's high regard for authentic costume.

the public would attend, and during the first half of the century a fortnight was the usual length of run for serious drama, although the production could, of course, be judiciously revived from time to time. Kean's productions at the Princess's usually ran for a hundred nights. Apart from his Shakespearean successes, Kean was responsible for the introduction of contemporary French dramas on the London stage.

MADAME VESTRIS

What Charles Kean and Macready did for the production of serious drama, Lucia Vestris and C. J. Mathews did for comedy and burlesque. Vestris, a charming and delightful creature possessed of a rich contralto voice, married a famous ballet master, Armand Vestris, only to be separated a few years later. Although she was by profession a dancer, her first London appearance in 1815 was as an opera singer. She subsequently appeared at the patent theatres as singer, dancer, and actress, acquiring great popularity as a personality.

It is her achievements as a manager, however, which make her position important in the early Victorian theatre. In 1831 she acquired the management of the small Olympic Theatre, at which she intended to present "legitimate" drama, but in accordance with the current monopoly conditions. The little theatre was redecorated in the prevailing excellent taste and made much more comfortable than the large patent theatres. In many ways the Olympic was the forerunner of the small intimate theatres which are to be found in London today. It presented comedies and burlesques by J. R. Planche and others, and achieved a quiet revolution in the manner of presentation.

For some years previously, characters in comedies had always worn eccentric costumes, and comic acting was broad and extravagant. Madame Vestris introduced the use of contemporary costume, and when we consider that the period from 1830 to 1850 was probably the most charming from the point of view of costume in the whole century, it can well be imagined that the productions reached new heights of taste and elegance. Her company was a small one and chosen with care. None of her productions required a large cast, and consequently a high standard of acting was achieved in all the parts.

By this time stalls were being introduced in the pit, and the fashionable element of society gradually began to frequent the theatres again. The intimate atmosphere of the Olympic appealed to them, particularly when they could be assured of a refined and tasteful production. Madame Vestris introduced the innovation of concluding the evening's program by about eleven o'clock. Before this, the theatres rarely concluded their performances before midnight; when the bill was particularly long, they went on until the small hours of the morning.

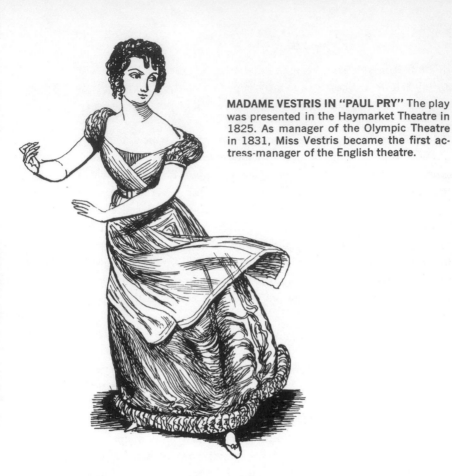

MADAME VESTRIS IN "PAUL PRY" The play was presented in the Haymarket Theatre in 1825. As manager of the Olympic Theatre in 1831, Miss Vestris became the first actress-manager of the English theatre.

MATHEWS-VESTRIS MANAGEMENT

Charles Mathews the younger joined the company in 1835, and rapidly became the leading light comedian of the day. His father, the elder Charles Mathews, had been a famous comic actor known chiefly for his monologues and character studies. Mathews was sympathetic to the policy of his manager, and developed a style of acting based on the observation of contemporary manners. He soon succumbed to the charms of Madame Vestris, and married her three years later.

CHARLES JAMES MATHEWS The nineteenth-century actor-manager is portrayed as George Rattleton in his own play, "The Humpbacked Lover," presented at the Olympic Theatre in London in 1835.

Not long after their marriage, they gave up the Olympic and spent a year touring in America. On their return to London they took over management of Covent Garden, but because of the general monopoly conditions they were not very successful. During their management there, however, a further milestone was passed in the great trend toward realism which was the century's contribution to theatrical art.

In 1841 a play by Dion Boucicault called *London Assurance* was produced. Boucicault was an actor and writer with a thorough knowledge of both French and English stage traditions. While chiefly engaged in adapting French pieces for the English stage, he was feeling his way in quest of a more realistic contemporary drama. He later developed a more melodramatic style.

In spite of some excellent productions of Shakespeare's comedies, the Vestris-Mathews management at Covent Garden ceased in 1842. After a few years of various managements, they acquired control of the Lyceum, where they went back to burlesque and light comedy. This was their last management together. Madame Vestris retired in 1854 and died two years later. Mathews continued acting for another twenty years.

SAMUEL PHELPS'S MANAGEMENT AT SADLER'S WELLS

Contemporaneous with Charles Kean's management of the Princess's Theatre was Samuel Phelps's management of Sadler's Wells. Phelps, who had received his training under Macready, took over management of the theatre in 1844. Previously, Sadler's Wells had confined its activities to melodrama. Making use of its watery surroundings, it had a large tank on the stage for aquatic displays.

Sadler's Wells had generally a low reputation as a rendezvous for the rougher elements in the town. Yet Phelps played Shakespeare there successfully for eighteen years during which most of Shakespeare's plays were produced, in addition to other classic dramas of the past. His own acting was in the Macready style, and he shone particularly as Falstaff and Malvolio.

In contrast with Charles Kean, Phelps stressed good acting, settings and costumes having less importance in his productions. His great success was possibly partly because this was the first time serious drama had been given at this theatre, which had hitherto suffered from a surfeit of spectacle and watery melodrama.

SCENERY

By the middle of the century there had been considerable develop-

SAMUEL PHELPS AS FALSTAFF   As actor-manager of Sadlers Wells in 1843, he presented a record of 34 of Shakespeare's plays, unbroken until 1923 by the Old Vic, with a fidelity to the texts unmatched before his time.

ment in the theatre since Kemble's time. The early years of the monopoly period were great times for the scenic artist. Settings of romantic grandeur played an important part in burletta and melodrama, and artists designed not only interiors but whole landscapes.

The scenery became more solid and built-up, and the constant change of scene that was required demanded some development in stage machinery. As settings became more elaborate the stage roof was heightened to permit the scenery to be hoisted out of sight of the audience.

Devices such as the diorama were evolved. The diorama was a landscape painted on a continuous backcloth which, mounted on rollers and turned mechanically, gave the audience some illusion of movement in plays where exciting journeys or races took place.

The use of the apron stage, when there was one, declined as the action of the play was developed behind the proscenium. The cumbersome scenery now confined the acting space still further.

Although Kean had developed historical accuracy in costume and setting, scenery was still artificial in the sense that it was chiefly painted scenery and not three-dimensional. Interiors, for instance, were still represented by a painted backcloth and several sets of wings; while the ceiling was represented by a hanging border.

LIGHTING

Gas lighting had been introduced early in the century, being used originally to light the auditorium. It was gradually developed for stage purposes. The great advantage of gas lighting was in its control. The days of the "invisible" candle snuffer now belonged to history; with the movement of a lever, a stage mechanic could subdue or increase the lighting at will.

In 1860 the first use was made of limelight, which produced a strong, incandescent light and became the chief means of emphasizing a character or portion of a scene. The limelight led to the use of incandescent gas lighting, which greatly increased its effectiveness.

CHARLES FECHTER The actor is shown as he appeared in his highly acclaimed portrayal of Hamlet, at the Princess Theatre, London, 1861. Though clad in traditional black, his realistic interpretation led him to wear a blond wig.

CHANGES IN THE THEATRES

By this time a great change had come about in the auditorium of the theatre. Upholstered seats were now provided in the boxes and stalls, which were gradually ousting the pit to the rear of the theatre. The crudely printed playbills—a foot or more long, printed in ink that smeared at a touch—had given way to smaller, better-printed programs, much the same as those we know today. Following the interest of the Queen, polite society was back in the theatres. These factors, together with the fact that the novelty of the new technical advances on the stage had been played out, combined to bring about a desire for the development of drama in some new direction.

CHARLES FECHTER

A step in this new direction was achieved under the management of Charles Fechter, a well-known French actor who had first appeared in London acting at the St. James's Theatre in French plays, French companies had always made periodic visits to London, usually playing at the Queen's, the Lyceum, or the St. James's. Mlle. Rachel had acted at the St. James's and had attracted the fashionable world much as Sarah Bernhardt was to do later.

In 1860 Fechter appeared at the Princess's in *Ruy Blas*, and later as Hamlet, playing in English. It was in *Hamlet* that Fechter created a sensation, not only in acting but also in production. In contrast with the traditional English style of tragic acting, he played the role in a comparatively realistic manner, interpreting the play as a refined melodrama.

Fechter was the innovator of the box set, an interior setting with the appearance of solid walls and with a realistic ceiling. He also used a sinking stage, so that all the solidly built scenery could be changed in the basement.

THE BANCROFTS AND TOM ROBERTSON

Five years later, a new management made its contribution to the rapidly changing methods of stage representation. Marie Wilton, who had succeeded Vestris as queen of burlesque, went into partnership with H. J. Byron, a writer of light pieces, at the old Prince of Wales's Theatre (the site of which is now occupied by the Scala). It soon became noted for its production of a new kind of play by a rising young dramatist, Tom Robertson. He had already won recognition with *David Garrick* at the Haymarket, in which the famous E. A. Sothern had appeared with great success. Robertson's subsequent plays—*Society, Ours, Caste, M. P., Play,* and *School*— were all comedy-dramas based on contemporary life, with flesh-and-blood characters drawn from observation of the life of the times.

Marie Wilton acted in these plays with Squire Bancroft (whom she soon married) and John Hare. The Bancrofts further developed the realistic method of production which had begun with Fechter and which Robertson had visualized for his plays. Scenery became thoroughly realistic, much of the painted architectural detail of interior sets giving way to solid cornices and pillars. Furniture acquired a new dramatic significance, and the Bancrofts spent much time and trouble creating a realistic atmosphere in general detail. In *Money*, by Lord Lytton, an exact reproduction was made on the stage of a card room in a famous West End club.

Robertson had been an actor, and he knew the problems of the stage. His realism was, of course, only comparative; today his plays seem stagey and melodramatic. But at the time they were written they gave the public a new representation of mid-Victorian life with all its social and economic significance. His work made possible the portrayal of social problems on the stage, which was further developed by Pinero, Henry Arthur Jones, and later by Galsworthy. In Pinero's *Trelawney of the Wells* the character of Tom Wrench is supposed to be Robertson in his early days. The play is also interesting for its portrayal of stage life and the changing conditions of the times.

The Bancrofts had twenty years of unbroken success, having finally moved to the Haymarket in 1879. They were responsible for many innovations in management: notably, the restriction of the program to one play, the raising of the status of the small-part player, and the introduction of the matinee performance.

MUSIC HALLS

At the time of the Bancrofts' management, the music halls reached new heights of importance. Originally the halls were special saloons attached to a tavern, where musical entertainment as well as refreshment were provided. With the passage of the Theatre Regulations Act of 1843 and the abolition of monopoly, plays could be given at any licensed house, although no smoking or drinking was allowed in the auditorium. This was permitted, however, at the music halls, and by 1870 there were over twenty of them in London. Some were quite large theatres, such as the Alhambra, and many palatial new theatres were built in the eighties, including the Empire and the New Tivoli.

The audiences consisted chiefly of the working class and the male section of the middle class, and the fare provided was fashioned to suit their demands. The artists had only to amuse and entertain, with no pretensions to art. They knew what their audiences wanted, and if they could provide it well enough they were assured of success. The best of them assumed set characters in which they invariably appeared, usually with a rather eccentric costume and makeup. Their brief turn on the stage was made up of song, dance, and comic patter. Acrobats, jugglers, and contortionists also found their place on the program. The stars were able to play at several theatres during the evening, repeating their short turn at each and driving off to the next theatre.

The music hall songs still live today (that is, the tunes are still heard, but the words usually seem either vulgar or trite). The songs were especially written for the working-class audiences of those times, and often reflected their social and economic discontent.

Such stars as Jenny Hill, Dan Leno, Alfred Glanville Vance, George Leybourne, Herbert Campbell, Albert Chevalier, Gus Elen, Vesta Tilley, and Marie Lloyd were immensely popular and attracted crowded houses to the music halls, or the variety theatres as they came to be called.

The rougher elements of the town, who in the past made the "O. P." riots possible, largely deserted the theatres in favor of the variety houses, and the theatres became almost the sole domain of the middle class. However, theatres such as the Drury Lane, with their thousands of seats to be filled, could not afford to ignore the drawing power of the variety stars, and therefore engaged them to fill the chief parts in their annual pantomimes. Whatever the pantomime was, the stars had little to do apart from their normal music hall turns. The Christmas pantomime today still makes use of variety stars to fill the chief parts, although in the last few years players from the legitimate stage have been included.

TECHNICAL ADVANCES

From the time of the Bancrofts' production of Robertson's plays onward, the tendency of stage presentation became increasingly realistic. With the introduction of electric lighting at the Savoy in 1880, a great step forward had been made. The great flexibility and control of electricity made all kinds of realistic effects possible for the first time. It was now possible to reproduce the effect of sunlight and make outside settings more realistic, while a subdued lighting effect was just as simple to create. Stage equipment and machinery were improved to permit an easier change of scene.

From Germany, where the technical improvements of the stage were chiefly developed, came the sliding and sinking stages which enabled whole settings to be moved out of sight and replaced with an entirely complete scene, the cyclorama, the revolving stage, and many electrical devices for controlling lighting.

The cyclorama was developed in Germany as a plaster half-dome covering the back of the stage, on which light could be thrown to represent the sky. Since it had no shadows it gave a great illusion of depth, particularly if a blue light were used. The cyclorama reached England in a different form—as a skycloth of canvas hung in a large semicircular arc, which could be drawn to one side if necessary.

The large stages of Covent Garden and Drury Lane were reconstructed in sections, each of which could be raised or lowered at will, enabling built-up scenic effects to be quickly changed.

HENRY IRVING

Actors, too, were developing their technique, throwing aside many traditional habits of stagey presentation. The greatest figure of the last thirty years of the century was Henry Irving. Like many actors before him, he served his apprenticeship in his art in the provincial theatres of Dublin, Liverpool, Manchester, and other big cities. By the time he made his London debut in 1866 he was an experienced and accomplished actor.

Irving's performance as Hamlet in 1874 established his reputation as the leading actor on the English stage. By comparison with the tragic actors of the past, he gave a fresh and naturalistic interpretation. His use of the new improvements in the theatre as they became available ensured his continuing success. One of his innovations was the stage blackout, during which scenery was changed.

Irving had a wonderful sense of the pictorial effect of a scene. He managed to interest some of the leading painters in designing for the stage, and persuaded Burne-Jones, Alma-Tadema, Ford Madox Brown, and Gustave Doré to work for him. Some of his productions tended toward overelaboration, as he was in the habit of introducing considerable stage business not in the script.

Apart from Shakespeare, Irving preferred to use rather inferior plays and adaptations as vehicles for his art. It seems a pity that great acting should be remembered chiefly by the production of quite second-rate plays. He economized on authors in this way, and was able to spend more on production. In spite of this economy, Irving failed financially after long periods of management at the Lyceum, and the management was taken over by a syndicate in 1899.

As an actor, a personality, and a man, Irving was always respected, and he did much to raise the status of the acting profession. He was the first actor to receive the honor of a knighthood. He played in melodrama, and is particularly remembered for his performance in the horror play, *The Bells*. He possessed enormous personal magnetism, and held audiences spellbound by the mastery of his acting. His style was not a passionate one, but by superb timing his long speeches moved the audiences much as they had been moved by Garrick. His popularity was also great in America, where he made many tours. His last tour was begun in England in 1905, and he died in Bradford a few days after. He was buried in Westminster Abbey.

ELLEN TERRY

Ellen Terry was the leading actress during the last quarter of the century. She was born of parents who were well-known provincial actors and close friends of Charles Kean. She first appeared on the stage in 1856 at an early age as the boy, Mamillius, in *The Win-*

SIR HENRY IRVING The actor is portrayed as he appeared as Mathias in "The Bells," a melodrama shown at the Lyceum Theatre, London, 1871. The role brought him immediate acclaim. He is the first great star to have been knighted.

ter's Tale at the Princess's Theatre. In 1867 she played with Irving
as Katherine to his Petruchio in *The Taming of the Shrew*.

For some years after this, she retired from the stage, returning in
1875, when she played Portia under the Bancrofts' management at
the old Prince of Wales's Theatre. After this she rejoined Irving,
and a long and happy partnership ensued in which she played all
Shakespeare's great heroines. Later she also appeared in some of the
early Shaw plays. Most critics of the time write of the freshness and
vitality of her acting. Even in her old age she could convincingly
portray the feeling of youth.

LILY LANGTRY

Lily Langtry was more famed for her beauty and personality than
for her acting. She was painted by Millais and Burne-Jones. She
appeared chiefly in modern plays, and achieved tremendous popularity. Oscar Wilde wrote *Lady Windermere's Fan* as a vehicle for
her.

MRS. PATRICK CAMPBELL

The dynamic personality and temperament of Mrs. Patrick Campbell accounted for her being much sought after as a leading lady.
She achieved great success in 1893 in Pinero's very popular *The
Second Mrs. Tanqueray*. She is particularly remembered as the
original Eliza Doolittle in Shaw's *Pygmalion*.

THE ACTOR-MANAGERS

The last years of the century were dominated by the actor-manager,
who led his company on the numerous tours that were necessary to
ensure a regular living. Each company had its repertoire of plays,
to which it was constantly adding, and when playing for a week at
a certain town could easily present a fresh play each evening.

For the younger actors who were employed for the tour the variety of parts to be played, which often entailed doubling during the
evening, gave good groundwork for developing the powers of acting, and there was no time for their work to become dull and lifeless. The actor-manager usually played the leading roles himself,

but he also kept an eye on the performances of the youngsters and gave them their chance when they were ready for it.

GEORGE ALEXANDER

Most of the managers of the West End theatres in London had been actors at one time and understood the stage. George Alexander, who had acted with Irving, was a typical example. He managed the St. James's Theatre and presented a series of well-produced modern plays by H. A. Jones, Pinero, and Oscar Wilde, with a distinguished company that included Mrs. Patrick Campbell, Irene Vanbrugh, Marie Tempest, and Henry Ainley.

HERBERT BEERBOHM TREE

Herbert Beerbohm Tree was known chiefly for his melodramatic and character parts, Falstaff and Hamlet being his most successful roles. In his productions of Shakespeare he was greatly influenced by Irving's elaboration of the stage picture. He also produced and acted in dramas by Ibsen, Wilde, and Maeterlinck. He founded a school for acting and was prominent in furthering the interests of the theatre. He built Her Majesty's Theatre in 1897.

FRANK BENSON

Frank Benson led a company which included most of Shakespeare's plays in its repertoire. They traveled all over the country, and as far as Canada and South Africa. For many years Benson organized the annual festivals at Stratford-on-Avon. His organization of a regular touring company was superb, and he had considerable influence on his contemporaries. His company were almost as well known for their cricket prowess as for their acting, and it is said that he recruited the men of his company with more thought for their skill at the wicket than their ability on the boards.

JOHNSTON FORBES-ROBERTSON

Johnston Forbes-Robertson served his apprenticeship with Samuel Phelps. He played under the Bancrofts' management, and at various times with Irving. He took up management at the Lyceum in 1895.

His distinguished appearance and romantic temperament suited his best roles—Romeo, Hamlet, and Macbeth.

OTHER ACTOR-MANAGERS

Other actor-managers of the period who achieved distinction in their work were Charles Wyndham, Wilson Barrett, John Martin-Harvey, Cyril Maude, Charles Hawtrey, and Arthur Bourchier.

BRIDGE FROM THE PAST

The Victorians bequeathed to the theatre considerable technical development in lighting, settings, greater realism in scenery, and in acting, which was freed from a conventional style and also became more realistic. Drama for the first time began to deal with day-to-day life. The era saw the end of the patent theatre monopoly, and thus the building of many new theatres in London and in other large cities. Extensive tours were undertaken by companies throughout England and to other countries. The advent of the actor-managers brought productions of greater distinction, with more care given to rehearsals and the details of production. The theatre began to resemble the stage we recognize today. The Victorians were, in many respects, the link with the modern theatre.

Early American

EARLY PURITAN OPPOSITION

Few records have survived of early theatrical performances in America, and it is quite clear that the professional stage was very slow in establishing itself. The main obstacle in those early days was the strong Puritan prejudice against all forms of show and pretense. The Pilgrim Fathers who landed at Plymouth Rock in 1620, although themselves the victims of intolerance, brought with them a hatred of all those aspects of English life associated with the somewhat loose living of the aristocracy of the times. This association must also have extended to the licentious atmosphere of Bankside and the companies of players whose very existence depended on the patronage of the great lords. There is no doubt that this prejudice against the theatre was very deeply rooted, for during the whole of the seventeenth century only a few spasmodic performances of plays are recorded, and during the following century when strolling players began to arrive from England, the population of the growing towns was still sharply divided almost equally between those descendants of the early Puritan settlers and others of a more liberal attitude toward the living arts.

EARLY PERFORMANCES

In the South, in Virginia, where the original settlers were generally of the established Church of England, there was greater tolerance, and here, at Charleston in 1703, an English actor, poet, and gentleman, one Anthony Aston, put on a play he had written about the country with the help of some of the younger citizens. He later moved on to New York, joining forces with an old friend from London, and gave some performances during the following year. After this he returned to England where he resumed his acting career with his own company at Oxford. Perhaps he sensed that the time was not ripe for the development of the theatre in New York, as the Governor's Council in 1709 forbade "play-acting and prize fighting."

At Williamsburg, at that time the capital of Virginia, a contract was signed in 1716 between William Levingston, Merchant, and Charles and Mary Stagg to build a theatre; but although the building is recorded nothing is known of the performances. Presumably Mr. and Mrs. Stagg were strolling players with a small company from England who moved on after some performances.

Gradually, as the population increased, amateur performances were given, usually in courthouses or other buildings which could be made to house a makeshift stage and with sufficient seating space to allow a tolerable audience. In 1736 the students of William and Mary College, whose first productions dated back to the beginning of the century, performed the tragedy of *Cato,* which was followed on successive days by productions with other amateur players— "ladies and gentlemen of the country"—of *The Busybody, The Recruiting Officer,* and *The Beaux' Stratagem.* This indicates a knowledge of the fashionable London stage of the time, for these were favorite vehicles for London actors, with many rich parts, and were often played by the English professionals who followed during the subsequent years of the century.

Cato became one of the most popular tragic plays in America during the eighteenth century. Written by Joseph Addison in the early years of the century when England herself was threatened by political tyranny, its noble Roman philosopher, whose patriotism and love of liberty transcended even life itself, became for the American colonies a symbolic representation of their own struggle for political freedom.

ENGLISH TOURING COMPANIES

The most important factor in the growth of the theatre in the eighteenth century was the willingness of companies of English players to tour the country, then regarded in England as a western wilderness. They took things as they found them, playing in converted storehouses or even building themselves a theatre where they could expect a good reception, and avoiding towns where the Puritan attitude continued to prevail. The plays they brought with them were those currently in favor on the London stage, and with their great skill and ability acquired in the arduous conditions of constant, even nightly, change of bill, made such an impact on their American audiences that their successes encouraged many of them to settle permanently in the country. With the general growth of the population in the towns by the middle of the century, theatres were established in Charleston, Philadelphia, New York, and Baltimore, which opened for occasional seasons by visiting companies.

EARLY THEATRE IN CHARLESTON

At Charleston, it is recorded that in 1735 Otway's *The Orphan,* with a pantomime as an afterpiece (*The Adventures of Harlequin and Scaramouche,* an English version of Italian comedy), were staged in the courthouse. This must have been the performance of professional players. The following month an opera was given entitled *Flora or Hob in the Well,* which may have been the very first musical piece on the American stage. At the end of March that year the final performance of the season was a benefit for the leading lady of Dryden's *The Spanish Fryar.* She was known as Monimia after a character which she played with great success in *The Orphan.*

So successful was this short season by these unknown players that a subscription campaign was started soon after for a second season and the construction of a playhouse. Charleston's founders were noblemen with a charter from Charles II (1670). The early settlers were by no means prejudiced against the theatre, and by this time there was a lively social life with occasional concerts, balls, and other activities. The construction of a playhouse therefore went ahead without opposition, and early in the following year the New Theatre in Dock Street opened with *The Recruiting Officer* and later a revival of *The Orphan* with the popular Monimia. *The London Merchant* and a ballad opera, *The Devil to Pay*, were the other productions of the season.

The following winter another season was given, with revivals of the earlier productions, but nothing is known of the company after this. The theatre, perhaps being used occasionally for concerts and balls, burned down in 1740.

THE MURRAY-KEAN COMPANY

Charleston was without a theatre until 1751, when a new theatre was built by subscription for "the company of comedians from New York." This was the company of Walter Murray and Thomas Kean, who had performed *Cato* and other plays in Philadelphia in 1749, probably beginning as amateurs. In New York they had converted a storehouse in Nassau Street and played *Richard III, Love for Love, The Orphan,* and *George Barnwell*. They opened in Charleston in late October, 1751, in *Richard III* with an augmented company. Although little is known of their season there, they played the following year at Williamsburg and Annapolis.

The composition of the company and the standards of their performances remain unknown, but they created an interest in the theatre and prepared the ground for the very able and talented players of William and Lewis Hallam, the first important company to sail from England about whom we know a good deal.

THE HALLAM COMPANY

Lewis Hallam sailed early in May, 1752, with a complete company, properties, costumes, scenery, and a repertoire of no less than twenty-four plays and their accompanying afterpieces. The afterpiece of this time was a short farce or pantomime with which it was customary to conclude the evening's performance. This gave the audience time to regain their spirits if they had previously witnessed a somewhat heavy, tragic play. It also gave the lesser actors a chance to shine.

William Hallam had been the manager of the Goodman's Fields Theatre in London, taking over after the departure of Garrick and his manager Giffard to the Theatre Royal, Drury Lane, where Garrick was to rise to the great heights of his career. Although receiving some reflection of glory from its departed star, Goodman's Fields Theatre became a difficult house to operate financially, and in a few years Hallam became bankrupt. His failure was for a comparatively small sum and he settled his affairs in such a reasonable manner that his creditors allowed him to retain his scenery, costumes, and sufficient capital to start again. With this, he formed a small company to send to the American colonies.

His brother Lewis had been the chief low comedian in the company at Goodman's Fields, while Mrs. Lewis, who was related to Rich of Covent Garden, played the leading women's parts in both tragedy and comedy. The new company was thus led by players of a stature used to competing with the patent theatres. The rest of the company was composed of efficient and useful players, all willing to leave the country for an indefinite period.

The repertoire of plays was prepared and cast at the house of William Hallam, who was to remain at home as directing manager. Mr. Rigby was to play the leads in tragedy and comedy. Mrs. Rigby, Mr. and Mrs. Clarkson, Miss Palmer, and Messrs. Singleton, Herbert, Winnell, Adcock, and Malone made up the rest of the company. Three of the four children of Lewis Hallam were to accompany their parents, later to perform with the company:

Lewis, junior, then a boy of twelve; a younger son, Adam; and an older daughter, eventually introduced on the stage as Miss Hallam.

Of the plays prepared, all tried and successful pieces on the London stage, four were by Shakespeare, five by Farquhar, two by Cibber, two by Nicolas Rowe, and others by Bishop Hoadley, Lillo, Lee, Bullock, Sir Richard Steele, and Sir Robert Howard. Three of the farces were by Garrick, and there was one pantomime.

The following list is incomplete, but it indicates the range of the repertoire: *The Merchant of Venice, Hamlet, Othello, Richard III* (Shakespeare); *The Recruiting Officer, The Constant Couple, The Beaux' Stratagem, The Twin Rivals, The Inconstant* (George Farquhar); *The Careless Husband, The Provoked Husband* (Colley Cibber); *Jane Shore, Tamerlaine* (Nicolas Rowe); *The Suspicious Husband* (Bishop Hoadley); *George Barnwell* (Lillo); *Theodosius* (Nathaniel Lee); *Woman's a Riddle* (Christopher Bullock); *The Conscious Lovers* (Sir Richard Steele); *The Committee* (Sir Robert Howard); *Lethe, The Lying Valet, Miss in Her Teens* (Garrick); *The Mock Doctor, The Devil to Pay, Hob in the Well, Damon and Phillida, The Anatomist, Harlequin Collector or the Miller Deceived.*

These plays were thoroughly rehearsed and prepared for production during the six-week voyage of the *Charming Sally* on which the company sailed, much to the delight of Captain Lee and his crew. Disembarking at Yorktown, the company set off for Williamsburg where application had been made to the Governor for an official license to perform. On being favorably received, Lewis Hallam set about converting an unused storehouse on the outskirts of the town, fitting it with a stage, pit, gallery, and boxes—complete as a "regular Theatre, fit for the Reception of Ladies and Gentlemen."

The opening performance took place on September 5, 1752, with *The Merchant of Venice,* preceded by a prologue written by Mr. Singleton in which he eulogized the practice of watching plays in which the art of the players transported the audience through the action and unfolding of the story, emphasizing the high moral tone of what they were about to witness, at the same time reminding them that the players had come from England as their humble servants. Among the audience was probably the young Lieutenant George Washington, who had developed a taste for theatricals in the West Indies. Certainly he was to see the younger Lewis Hallam in many of his performances in later years.

No records exist of the reactions of the townspeople of Williamsburg to the company's first long season, but it would be fair to conclude that they were a great success and were made very welcome. How often they played then is not known, but later custom was to play on Monday, Wednesday, and Friday of each week.

To the townspeople it must have been a delight of a fine evening to walk to the playhouse on the edge of the woods, to see and hear great stories played out and emotions aroused with all the skill and sophistication of the players. The accent was on taste and refinement, and the makeshift building was made to appear as much as possible like a small London theatre. The ability of the company and the general good behavior of the actors was confirmed by a testimonial which Hallam obtained from the Governor at the close of the season. This was to be used as a passport to good relations with the elders of other towns in which they might give performances.

From Williamsburg the company journeyed to Annapolis, where another theatre had been erected early in 1752. Two of Hallam's company, Winnell and Herbert, had performed there with a scratch company before opening in Williamsburg. After a short season in Annapolis, the company continued their journey northward, playing at other places of consequence in Maryland and eventually arriving in New York where they settled in a theatre in Nassau Street which had been converted by the Murray and Kean company from Philadelphia. This is the company which had played at Charleston the previous year.

A year after their first performance in Williamsburg, the Hallam Company opened at Nassau Street with *The Conscious Lovers*,

followed by *Damon and Phillida*. The company had been enlarged
by the addition of other players, including a Mr. Hewlett whom
William Hallam had sent out from England where he had been at
Goodman's Fields as a dancer and violinist. Playing with great success, they continued with performances on Mondays, Wednesdays,
and Fridays throughout the following six months, ending their season with a special performance of Congreve's *Love for Love* to a
packed house for the benefit of the poor of the city. During this
season both Lewis Hallam, Jr., and Miss Hallam appeared as regular members of the company.

During the months in New York Hallam considered his next
move and decided that the only city large enough to support his
company for another season was Philadelphia. But there was a
large Quaker element in the city from whom he could certainly expect an attempt to prevent his giving performances. He decided to
send one of his company, Malone—a man of engaging manners and
great powers of persuasion—to the city to make application to the
Governor for permission to play for a few performances. In this he
could count on some support from a number of Philadelphia gentlemen who had seen the company in New York. Malone's reward for
this diplomatic mission was to be the parts of Falstaff and Don
Lewis, which must ordinarily have been taken by Hallam himself.
But an actor is always ready to attempt untried roles if they offer
scope for his particular talents, and at this time the custom was that
once success in a role was confirmed by management and audience,
it became the actor's own property and while he was a member of
the company no other player would have the opportunity to perform it.

However, Malone found the opposition to the players beyond his
powers to overcome and Hallam, following him to the City of
Brotherly Love, found the citizens divided almost equally into two
opposing factions. The Quaker element organized a petition to the
Governor for the prohibition of "lewd and profane stage-plays,"
and their opponents busily collected signatures for a counterpeti-

tion. Eventually, Governor Hamilton decided for the players and gave them permission for twenty-four performances on condition that they offered nothing indecent and immoral and performed one night for the benefit of the poor of the city.

This resistance to the players by a large portion of the population was repeated in many towns during the second half of the century. In many cases the opposition carried the day, the Governor's Council passing an edict prohibiting performances of plays. This did not always stop the players, as their supporters would address themselves to the government in London, which would always repeal the edict. In some ways this was unfortunate, as among many Americans the theatre began to appear as a weapon of political propaganda for the British government. It is therefore understandable that the first Congress of 1774, even among all the preparations for war against Britain, found time to pass a law prohibiting stage performances (for which Washington, although conceding, must have personally felt no little compunction).

Hallam found a convenient storehouse above Pine Street and after the necessary conversion opened with *The Fair Penitent* by Rowe with Garrick's *Miss in Her Teens* as the afterpiece. Needless to say, with all the excitement of the two petitions, the house was packed—even, it is recorded, with certain of the opposing faction. The company performed with their accustomed skill, duly receiving the plaudits of their supporters. So successfully did they carry the house and ultimately the town that the Governor granted them an extra six nights, allowing them ten weeks in all, playing the usual Mondays, Wednesdays, and Fridays.

After the season in Philadelphia, Hallam and his company sailed for the West Indies, but not before they received a visit from William Hallam. It is probable that a settlement was reached over the future of the company and that Lewis purchased his brother's share in the management, as William returned to England shortly after and little further is heard of him.

Lewis must have felt confident for the future as sole proprietor

and manager of a thriving and successful company which had sur-
mounted the difficulties of breaking into new territory. No doubt
the intention was to prepare new plays for another tour of the
mainland and to give some performances in the main ports of the
West Indies. However, he did not live long enough to carry out
this program, as soon after arriving he fell ill and died.

Nothing is known of the company's movements for a few years
after this. No doubt Mrs. Hallam endeavored to hold the company
together, perhaps playing occasionally at the main ports where the
garrisons, the merchants' establishments, and the constantly changing ships' companies would provide a likely audience. But theatrical enterprises are always dependent on strong leadership and personality, and without Lewis Hallam in command the company
gradually drifted apart.

DAVID DOUGLASS AND THE AMERICAN COMPANY

The figure of David Douglass now appears on the scene. Little is
known of his early days except that he was by descent and education a gentleman. He acted with a company in the West Indies,
where he met Mrs. Hallam. The meeting blossomed into marriage
and Douglass began to form a new company which was to be
known as the American Company.

In 1758 he brought Mrs. Hallam, her children, and some members of his original company to New York, where a temporary theatre was erected on Cruger's Wharf, the old Nassau Street theatre
having been demolished. On application to the authorities for the
customary license to perform, however, he was met with a blank
refusal. Although he appealed to the public through the press, he
was forced to use the theatre as an "histrionic academy" in which
he gave dissertations on subjects which were "moral, instructive and
entertaining." This lasted for a short period, and when a further
appeal was made to the authorities, the city fathers relented to the
extent of permitting thirteen performances.

The American Company opened with *Jane Shore* with Lewis
Hallam, Jr., now a handsome youth of eighteen, delivering Single-

ton's former prologue. The success of this short season established the reputation of the new company and Douglass continued with a long series of tours to Philadelphia, Newport, Williamsburg, and Annapolis, returning eventually to New York. He proved to be a very efficient manager—building new theatres, dealing with the authorities, always giving a special performance at the close of a season for the benefit of the poor, and obtaining a testimonial from the authorities as to the character and ability of the players.

Through the following years the American Company prospered. Lewis Hallam eventually succeeded to leading parts; Mrs. Hallam, Miss Hallam, and the younger brother (billed as Master A. Hallam) performed as regular members. The company was further strengthened by the addition of John Henry, an Irishman who had made his debut in London under the elder Sheridan.

The first plays by American authors were performed, including Thomas Godfrey's *The Prince of Parthia* and Colonel Thomas Forrest's *The Disappointment, or The Force of Credulity,* but these works were generally not successful and the latest plays from London remained the main draw.

In spite of all difficulties, the company had firmly established the theatre in America. Mrs. Douglass died in 1773 and Douglass played a last season at Charleston in 1774, then returned to New York to prepare for a new season there. Meanwhile, Lewis Hallam and his sister sailed to England to recruit more players to strengthen the company. Among them was their cousin, Thomas Wignell, destined soon to act leading parts. But in October of that year Congress passed a resolution forbidding all public amusements, so the company packed their trunks and sailed for the more loyal West Indies. Here they stayed throughout the years of the Revolutionary War. Douglass eventually retired from management and became a judge. The company was then led by Hallam and Henry.

THE REVOLUTIONARY WAR

During the long years of war there was not a complete cessation of theatrical activities, as the troops on both sides felt the need for the relaxation offered by the stage and both sides provided some the-atrical enterprises. General Burgoyne's occupation of Boston was enlivened by many stage performances in the city. He was himself the author of more than one piece and is reputed to have acted on the stage during this time. The performance of his farce, *The Block-ade of Boston,* which was intended to ridicule the Yankee troops who had bottled up the British in the narrow stretch of land outside the city, was interrupted by a sergeant who came on the stage with the news that "the rebels have attacked the lines." He was ap-plauded for his very natural acting, and it was only after some time that it was discovered that he was in fact no actor and that he brought the very real news of the beginning of the triumphal action that led to Burgoyne's surrender on the field of Saratoga. "Gentle-manly Johnny's" philosophical attitude to the various merits of art and war have been well characterized in Shaw's *The Devil's Disciple.*

British troops under General Howe in New York in 1777 also found time to perform a number of plays at the John Street Theatre (renamed the Theatre Royal). Major Williams of the Artillery sup-ported the chief tragic roles, playing Richard, Macbeth, and other tragic parts, and the scenery was painted by Captain Delancey, who also acted as manager. Major André also acted in various parts. André was later to become notorious as a spy behind the American lines, eventually being captured and executed. Captain William Loftus, Captain Edward Bradden, Captain Phipps, Captain Stanley, and Lieutenant Pennefeather also performed at the time, as did a civilian, William Hewlett, who had been sent out by William Hallam to join the Hallam Company years before (1753). The bills advertised that the performances were given for charity, for widows and orphans of fallen soldiers.

During this period, in January, 1778, the military company gave the first performance of Horne's *Douglas,* which was received with great applause. Cumberland's *West Indian* was also given in Amer-ica for the first time. In March of that year Major Moncrieff played Othello, and was eminent in the part. He was reported to have played it before with the American Company under Douglass some years earlier in the city. A good deal of money was spent on costumes and properties. Although at first the female parts were taken by men, after some time the officers' ladies were persuaded to appear in the roles. Among the plays produced were *Tom Thumb*, *Othello, Douglas,* and *The Rivals.* The performances were open to the public of the city, and among the audience was the young William Dunlap, later to become a playwright and manager of the American Company. He was also to become the first historian of the American stage.

During the long wait at Valley Forge, Washington's troops performed the inevitable *Cato,* but little is known of the players or its reception. The theatre had the advantage of the assistance of the military bands in forming a theatre orchestra, and the productions were excellent in many ways. Generally, the scenery was considered poor, but the costumes were elegant, and lively if unskilled performances ensured a sympathetic reception.

When the British occupied Philadelphia they took over the Southwark Street Theatre, with André and Delancey in command of the stage. Gradually the playacting enthusiasm of the military slackened, and after 1781 no more performances were given.

THE POSTWAR PERIOD

After the surrender of the British in 1783, the professional players returned to the theatres, but not immediately. Philadelphia was chosen by Hallam for their opening in 1785, but the full company was not used. This was in a way a trial to test the feeling of the townspeople. They were successful during a short season and performed the customary benefit for the poor of the city.

Soon after this the Legislature of Pennsylvania discussed the possibility of closing the theatre as being a source of vice and immorality but, with many arguments for and against, they eventually decided to allow the theatre to remain open.

Hallam was sufficiently encouraged to open with the full company in New York, led by himself and his partner, John Henry. The company now included Wignell, Harper, Morris, Biddle,

Woolls, Lake, and Durang; the ladies were Mrs. Morris, Mrs. Harper, Miss Tuke, Miss Durang, and Miss Storer (soon to become Mrs. Hallam).

On January 16, 1786, Hallam played Hamlet, which is probably the first time it was performed in America. The reception was polite, more for the pleasure of seeing a favorite actor again than for the play. Hamlet was generally considered at this time a difficult role to sustain, and although in England Betterton was great in the part and Garrick (in his more realistic rendering) made a great impression, it was rarely attempted. Hallam may have seen such a performance on his visit to London in 1774 for, although old and declining, Garrick continued playing until 1776. While in London Hallam himself attempted the role at Covent Garden, but with no great success.

During this season, Sheridan's *The School for Scandal* and *The Duenna* were also played for the first time in America. Wignell took Joseph Surface and Henry, Sir Peter Teazle. O'Keefe also received production of his farces and light operas, the most successful of which were *The Poor Soldier* and *Wild Oats*.

Hallam and Henry, during this first New York season, also built a theatre in Baltimore, now a rapidly growing city, and opened it in 1786. The company played there with great success for two months and then moved to Richmond, now the leading city of Virginia. They then returned to Philadelphia and finally New York.

The company experienced difficulties in Philadelphia, where the Quakers were still petitioning strongly for the closure of the theatre. Greater reliance was placed on musical pieces and pantomime. The old Southwark Street Theatre was renamed the Opera House. The plays produced were disguised under the description of "moral lectures." The billing for *She Stoops to Conquer,* for instance, was "Lecture on the Disadvantages of Improper Education, Exemplified in the History of Tony Lumpkin." Eventually the more liberal members of the population prevailed on the Legislature to permit the theatre to be opened "by Authority."

There followed a slack period in the development of the theatre in America. Although the American Company continued its various seasons, in some cases they were able to play only two evenings a week; benefits were correspondingly lower.

AMERICAN PLAYWRIGHTS

During this period, American authors were tried out by the Company. In 1786 a comedy by Royall Tyler, *The Contrast,* was performed in New York with some success. This encouraged the management to accept a farce by the author, entitled *Mayday or New York in an Uproar,* for Wignell's benefit. Wignell was now the most popular comedian of the company and was able to play in what Dunlap termed a "Yankee dialect." His popularity was perhaps partly due to the general feeling of the public for the home product. Generally, however, this did not extend to the home-written play, and these pieces, although occasionally performed, were not often repeated. A tragedy in blank verse by Barnaby Bidwell entitled *The Mercenary Match,* performed by students of Yale, was greeted with roars of laughter, which must have been most unexpected to the author.

WILLIAM DUNLAP'S PLAYS

William Dunlap's first play was written soon after his return from London in 1787. His taste for the theatre, which had been created by seeing the military performers in New York during the war, had been further strengthened by a three-year sojourn in London, where his father sent him in 1784 to study painting under Benjamin West. He spent much of his time in the theatres and saw the performances of most of the leading players of the time, including John Philip Kemble and Mrs. Siddons as Isabella, Lady Macbeth, Desdemona, and the Grecian Daughter. Some of the players he saw were later persuaded to join the American Company after he entered management.

Dunlap's first literary effort was a comedy in five acts with the title of *The Modest Soldier, or Love in New York.* The author read it to Hallam and Henry, who accepted it. It failed to achieve immediate production, however, as there were no suitable parts for either Henry or Mrs. Henry, and the main parts were intended for Wignell and Mrs. Morris. The acceptance of his play and anticipation of its eventual appearance on the stage (a hope in fact never to be fulfilled) encouraged Dunlap to write another comedy with parts suited to both Henry and his wife. This was *The Father of an Only Child,* and it received its first performance in September, 1789. The performance was well received and the piece was played for six further performances. Hallam, Henry, and Mrs. Henry were excellent in the serious or pathetic parts, and Wignell added to his reputation as a comedian in the part of Tattle, the family physician.

Another occasion for Wignell's triumph was his benefit in November of that year for which Dunlap provided him with a comic sketch, *Darby's Return,* based on a popular character in O'Keefe's *The Poor Soldier.* Dunlap had included some references to topical matters, and President Washington, who was in the audience, was well pleased with the complimentary allusions to his inauguration.

REORGANIZATION OF THE AMERICAN COMPANY

At the close of the season in 1791 Wignell seceded from the old American Company, due to the continued hostility of Henry, and took some of the company with him. Joining forces with Alexander Reinagle, a prominent musician, he formed a company and set about raising funds for the erection of a new theatre in Chestnut Street. In the meantime, he sailed to England to recruit more experienced players. Henry had sailed earlier in the year on a similar mission. During this time the old American Company was joined by a troupe of dancers and pantomimists led by Mr. and Mrs. Placide from France, who had begun their performances at Charleston and later moved to New York. This reflects the inevitable weakening of the company by the loss of its mainstays and the desire to shift the attention from the quality of the acting to spectacle. Some competition was also felt from a smaller company, the New American Company, which played in New York at a small wooden theatre in Front Street, led by Mr. and Mrs. Kenna, formerly members of the

Hallam and Henry Company.

The following year the company was completely reorganized and many of the older performers, such as Harper and Woolls, left to seek their fortunes elsewhere. The new players brought by Henry from England greatly strengthened and revitalized the company. The chief acquisition was John Hodgkinson, a brilliant actor of twenty-six whom Henry had seen in Bath. He was extremely versatile, with such a wide range that he eventually became known as the "provincial Garrick." He was described by Dunlap as some five feet, ten inches tall and rather thick set (eventually becoming corpulent), with a lively theatrical manner, his hair worn in the old fashion—powdered, with side curls ending in a black queue.

Hodgkinson's wife was an excellent actress, particularly good in comedy, playing hoydenish girls and romps with great spirit; even in tragedy, as in Ophelia, she was very moving. She had the advantage of having been trained as a singer by her father, Brett, a performer at both Covent Garden and the Haymarket. Dunlap records her speaking and singing voice as being powerful and sweet.

Other new members of the company included John Martin, an American-born actor who had made his debut in Philadelphia, and Miss Prigmore, King, West, and Mrs. Pownall (previously known as Mrs. Wrighton on the London stage) from England.

The new company made its debut in Philadelphia at the end of September in 1792, and enjoyed a successful short season before returning to New York for the New Year. In the following years Hodgkinson became a performer of increasing popularity, while the performances of Henry and Hallam enjoyed less appeal. This led to much ill feeling, and to downright hostility from Henry when Hodgkinson claimed a share in the management, to which he felt entitled as he was now supporting the leading roles in both comedy and tragedy. Hallam avoided open conflict, but tended to support Hodgkinson.

THE FEDERAL STREET THEATRE IN BOSTON

About the same time, attempts were made to found a theatre in

Boston. A number of actors from England, together with the two former members of the American Company, Harper and Woolls, gained the support of some prominent citizens and started a subscription fund for the erection of a theatre. Much opposition was met with from other sections of the community, but a temporary theatre was built in 1792 and called the New Exhibition Room. It was opened in August of that year with a mixed entertainment of music, ballets, and pantomimes performed by the Placide troupe. By the end of September the management was emboldened enough to present standard plays. This was done until the law was invoked by the opposition on December 5, when a sheriff interrupted the performance and, although with loud protest from the audience, arrested Harper, then acting as manager.

The theatre was permanently closed, but a good many citizens had enjoyed the performances and developed a taste for the drama. When Harper was released the following day, an association of interested parties was formed to establish the theatre by a repeal of the law. This was achieved the following year. Plans for a first-class theatre were made and Powell, one of the leading players, departed for England to recruit further members for the company.

In 1794 the Federal Street Theatre was built and became firmly established, surviving a disastrous fire in 1798. It was rebuilt and continued to be the leading theatre in Boston for the next thirty years. Another playhouse, the Haymarket, was built in 1796 and for some years offered alternative fare before finally being closed in 1803 because of its failure in opposition to the Federal Street Theatre.

WIGNELL AND REINAGLE'S COMPANY IN PHILADELPHIA

In Philadelphia, Wignell and Reinagle built a fine new theatre in Chestnut Street, based largely on the design of the Theatre Royal at Bath. The auditorium was semicircular, with two rows of boxes and with side boxes higher up in line with a gallery. Among those brought by Wignell from England was Milbourne, an excellent scene painter, who decorated the house and produced stage settings better than anything previously seen in America. The new company included Mrs. Oldmixon, the celebrated singer from Covent Garden and the Haymarket, who was to play the leading roles in light opera and also appeared in straight plays. The other members were able and experienced players of the first rank. For many years the company eclipsed the American Company in the standard of its productions.

DUNLAP'S MANAGEMENT OF THE AMERICAN COMPANY

The American Company was now led by Hodgkinson, Henry having died in 1795. William Dunlap entered management the following year. Hallam was no longer a partner, but a salaried actor. Dunlap found a success in his play, *André*, based on those wartime incidents already touched on. Hodgkinson played the main part of Major André and Cooper played the character of Bland, the young American officer André befriended while the latter was a prisoner of war.

After this season Hodgkinson retired from management and Dunlap continued on his own. He produced a large number of his own plays, based on or adapted from foreign originals. His first important success in this field was with *The Stranger,* a comedy adapted from a play originally known as *Menschenhass und Reue,* by Kotzebue, the German dramatist.

At this time Kotzebue was turning out play after play and submitting them to most of the leading playhouses of Europe. A letter from the playwright to Dunlap offered several of his plays for use, payment to depend on what the house would take. At the same time he pointed out that the manager of Covent Garden had paid him £100 for each play accepted. Sheridan himself adapted one which was subsequently very popular as *Pizarro.* Kotzebue's works were of little lasting merit, and were generally sensationally melodramatic, but they provided many excellent acting parts. He also had a very good idea of what would be popular with the audiences of his day and supplied it wholesale. Hodgkinson had continual success appearing in the Kotzebue plays, the best of which, according to Dunlap,

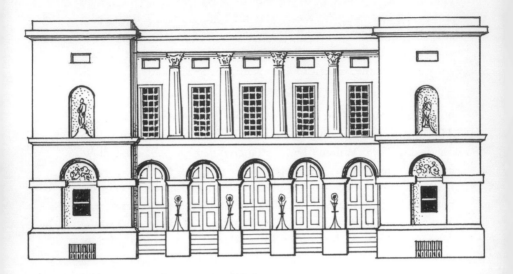

CHESTNUT STREET THEATRE   Modelled after the Theatre Royal at Bath
opened on February 17, 1794, this lavish structure plus a superior
acting company (largely recruited from England), immediately established the Chestnut Street Theatre as the leading house in America, a
position it was to retain for a quarter of a century. Its raked stage, deep
apron, proscenium doors, and proscenium boxes, familiar features in
English theatre, were then still unknown in America.

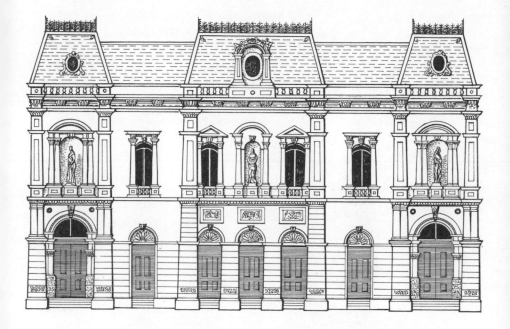

BOOTH'S THEATRE   Built by Edwin Booth and Richard A. Robertson, a Boston businessman, at a cost of $1,000,000, Booth's Theatre opened on February 3, 1869, with a sumptuous production of "Romeo and Juliet." This theatre made important technical innovations in theatre design. It was the first theatre to have a "loft" above the stage in which to house scenery for quick changes.

were *The Stranger, False Shame, Lovers' Vows, The Force of Cal-umny,* and *The Death of Rolla,* from which Sheridan had adapted *Pizarro.*

Hodgkinson had strengthened the company with the addition of Mrs. Melmoth, who was remembered for her great success in tragic roles in Dublin and Edinburgh; Mrs. Merry from Covent Garden; and Mrs. Pownall, who was celebrated in London for her roles in comedy and opera.

MRS. MELMOTH   She is costumed for her appearance in "The Rival Queens."

At the new theatre greater attention was paid to the quality of the scenery, and the company acquired the valuable services of Charles Ciceri as scene painter and machinist. He had received his early training in France and London and was particularly good at architectural effects and detail. Hitherto little attention had been paid to settings, and many early critics of the theatre in America had made references to the poor "dirty canvas" scenes. The staging was the normal backcloth and side wings of the time; the backcloth unrolled to depict an interior or exterior scene, while the side wings ran in grooves and could be changed accordingly. The actors made their entrances and exits either through the stage doors on either side of the front of the stage or through the wings. As with the new theatre at Philadelphia, more curtains were used in furnishing and elaborate chandeliers gave illumination to a more elegant house.

THOMAS ABTHORPE COOPER

Thomas Abthorpe Cooper, who was brought from England by Wignell, first appeared at the Park Theatre as Hamlet, and achieved immediate success. The son of a surgeon, he was trained by Stephen Kemble, a member of the famous theatrical family, and made his debut at Edinburgh in 1792. Three years later, at the early age of twenty, he had played leading roles at Covent Garden, including Hamlet and Macbeth. He was a handsome young man with a fine, eloquent voice and great dignity. He was soon to become the most popular tragedian in America.

After quarreling with Wignell, Cooper joined the American Company, then established in New York at the New Park Theatre. However, the inevitable quarrel with the management over salary led to his return to England, where he enjoyed a brilliant triumph playing Othello with George Frederick Cooke and Charles Kemble at Drury Lane. This acclaim aided his return to America, where he was immediately re-engaged by Dunlap at a much-increased salary.

After Dunlap's failure and bankruptcy in 1802, Cooper took over management of the Park Theatre with Stephen Price, employing Dunlap as stage manager. Cooper appeared in most of the tragic parts in Shakespeare, his Macbeth being particularly notable. He also appeared in such popular roles as Jaffierin in *Venice Preserved*. He was generally considered the finest actor to have settled permanently in America.

In 1815 the partnership with Price was dissolved, and Cooper took to touring the country. Thus began a tendency which was to become common practice. The touring star, not always with adequate support, was to mean the theatre to many of the smaller towns in the early years of the nineteenth century.

THOMAS A. COOPER   He was the leading actor on the American stage from 1797 until the advent of Forrest in 1826. As manager of the Park Theatre, he introduced the guest star system with the importation of George Frederick Cooke in 1810.

GEORGE FREDERICK COOKE IN AMERICA

Price was responsible for the importation of great stars, a practice begun by Cooper with such as the brilliant though erratic George Frederick Cooke, who spent the last two years of his life in America. Cooke's greatest role was as Richard III. He was a powerful actor, generally playing villainous parts. He had acted in Dublin for many years before coming to play with Mrs. Siddons and John Kemble at

GEORGE FREDERICK COOKE In this costume, he appeared as Iago at the Covent Garden in 1800. Brought to America in 1810 by Cooper and Price, he was the first true guest star.

Covent Garden, where he remained for ten years. His lack of grace or nobility was no great disability when he played, with great passion, the villainous roles of Richard III, Iago, Stukely, and Sir Pertinax MacSycophant. His strong, dark appearance, long hooked nose, and a powerful voice of great depth added to his characterizations. He was, however, dissipated with drink and his appearances were somewhat uncertain.

The success he enjoyed at the Park Theatre during the first season dwindled during the second, when his appearances became increasingly uncertain. Although he was able to play by intuition when drunk, the audience at times reacted strongly against him. He did create a sensation by his powerful acting in Boston, Philadelphia, Baltimore, and at Providence, where he last performed. He died in New York later in 1811 and was buried in St. Paul's Church. Edmund Kean was later to erect a monument to him in the churchyard.

THE EARLY NINETEENTH CENTURY

The first half of the nineteenth century saw a much greater development of the theatre in America. The main capitals of the drama were New York, Philadelphia, Boston, and Charleston. These cities began to build new theatres. The secondary circuit was Baltimore, Washington, Richmond, Savannah, and many towns of the Atlantic Seaboard which had erected theatres. Later the frontier towns further west offered other opportunities for touring companies. The old stock theatres with their permanent companies and repertory of standard plays found it necessary to support the performances of visiting players of great fame and reputation in order to draw full houses.

Generally, the plays presented were familiar, and the audiences went to see vivid performances and new interpretations of well-known parts. New plays were infrequent and few were of lasting merit. It was a period of great acting and of great partisanship among the audience. It was not the play which was discussed among theatregoers, but the comparison of one performance with another. At a time when the theatres in England were being rebuilt to house vast audiences (and were thus becoming increasingly difficult to fill), an American tour was looked upon by actors as a means of adding to their reputations and as a happy relief from the search for new attractions at home. But similar tendencies in time overtook the American theatre, and the English stars were not always successful in filling American theatres.

AMERICA'S FIRST ACTING FAMILIES

There were a number of English actors who settled permanently in America and in some cases founded families of players. Such a one was Junius Brutus Booth, whose successful debut at the newly rebuilt Park Theatre in New York in 1821 in the role of Richard III (played with great success at Covent Garden in 1817) led to a long and popular career in America. His three sons—Edwin, eventually to become America's greatest tragedian of the age; Junius Brutus, Jr., a popular supporting player and manager; and John Wilkes, later to achieve notoriety as the assassinator of Lincoln—were to appear throughout the middle of the century.

Two other actor families were established in America, those of William Warren and Joseph Jefferson, who joined the American Company in New York in 1796. William Warren, after some success there, eventually became manager of the rival Chestnut Street Theatre in Philadelphia after the death of Wignell in 1803, marrying his widow (the former Mrs. Merry) in 1806. With another of the company, William B. Wood, as co-manager, the company was strengthened by William Twaits and Joseph Jefferson, who became one of its leading players. Warren and Wood were in control of no less than four theatres: in Philadelphia and Baltimore, with short summer seasons at theatres in Alexandria and Washington.

Another family to be established was that of the Wallacks. James William Wallack was recruited from England for the Park Theatre, making his debut in *Macbeth* in 1818. His brother, Henry John, made his debut in America the following year. They were to become two of America's leading actor-managers. James's son, Lester, and various nephews and nieces continued to keep the name prominent in the theatre for the rest of the century.

EXPANSION OF THE THEATRE IN AMERICA

Theatrical companies also explored the hitherto untried territories. Luke Usher and Noah M. Ludlow went up the Allegheny River to Pittsburgh and established the theatre there. They then pushed on to Frankfort on the Ohio River, traveling partly by wagon and partly by boat. Ludlow and his company went down the Mississippi to Nashville and Cincinnati and eventually founded the first English-speaking theatre in New Orleans, where there was already a French theatre giving performances of Racine, Molière, and Beaumarchais. Other theatres were founded in Alabama and St. Louis.

American actors were also beginning to make star reputations. John Howard Payne, who was to make his name as playwright and composer as well as actor, and James Henry Hackett achieved positions which enabled them to reverse the usual process and play in leading roles in England.

THEATRE FIRES

The theatre suffered some reverses during this period when three of the leading playhouses were inexplicably burned to the ground. The first big disaster was at Richmond in 1811 when, during a play produced by the Placide Company, the scenery caught fire and the fire spread to the auditorium. The ensuing panic was largely responsible for the deaths of seventy-one members of the audience. The Richmond authorities' reaction to this disaster was to prohibit stage plays and amusements of any kind for four years. The news of the Richmond fire spread throughout the country and must have had a deleterious effect on the theatre by frightening away some of the audiences.

In 1820, on the night of May 24, the Park Theatre, long the most fashionable and popular of the several theatres now established in New York, burned to the ground, fortunately after the audience had left. In April of the same year, the Chestnut Street Theatre in Philadelphia was also destroyed by fire, together with its scenery, costumes, properties, library, and a new gas works which had introduced gas lighting to the theatre in 1816. A few days later the theatre of Warren and Wood in Washington was also destroyed by fire. In spite of these setbacks, the public interest in theatregoing continued, and ensured new and enlarged theatres immediately springing up in place of the smoldering ruins.

EDMUND KEAN IN AMERICA

During the period after the fire, before the Park Theatre was rebuilt and when the company was temporarily established at the small Anthony Street Theatre, a most notable event occurred—the guest appearance of Drury Lane's leading star, Edmund Kean. Hitherto, George Frederick Cooke had been the greatest attraction to come from England. Now his oft-remembered performances, erratic, unavailing, or brilliant as they may have been, were completely overshadowed by the greatest actor of the new passionate and emotional Romantic style.

Kean made his American debut, for which he received a guaranteed sum of £50 per performance plus a share of the profits, in *Richard III*. His successive performances were in *Hamlet, Othello, Merchant of Venice*, and Payne's *Brutus*. The reception of his short season was enthusiastic and his audiences responded to his brilliant highlighting of the parts, in which he built emotional effects by acting somewhat beyond the actual script of the play (which, though sacred in our day, was commonly expanded or cut as required by the leading players of those times).

Kean continued his triumphal tour to Philadelphia and Boston, meeting with great success, and then returned to New York. An ill-judged attempt at a return engagement soon afterward in Boston was rewarded by poor houses, because May was too late in the season to attract large audiences. On the third night, seeing only about twenty in the audience, Kean walked out of the theatre and refused to play. This enraged the people of Boston, the newspapers published disparaging notices of the incident, and his reputation suffered as the news spread to other theatres. Although Kean courageously issued a public apology and tried to make good his relations with the townspeople, he was never forgiven or allowed to play in Boston again. Before returning to England, he erected a memorial to George Frederick Cooke in St. Paul's churchyard, an act which, although a typical spontaneous gesture, did little to improve his relations with the public.

Kean made another American tour in 1825 after his conduct in London and the legal action which ensued (brought about by Alderman Cox) had turned his audiences there against him. His appearance at the Park Theatre in November 24 in *Richard III* was greeted with such abuse and showering of the stage with missiles that nothing of his performance could be heard. He refused to retire, however, and the performance was completed entirely by miming. After another contrite public apology, Kean was allowed to give eight more performances in different roles and to some extent regained the favor of his audiences. His attempts to play again in Boston were, however, completely shattered by a mob outside the playhouse breaking the doors and windows of the theatre and causing the audience to riot. Kean managed to escape and left the town immediately (it was said, in tears). The theatre was badly damaged but no one was hurt.

IRA ALDRIDGE   He is shown here in the traditional costume of Othello.

IRA ALDRIDGE

During Kean's first tour of America he had as a valet a young Negro named Ira Aldridge, a native of Bel Air, Maryland, who was inspired by his employer to essay the stage. He traveled to England with Kean, and in 1826 made a successful debut as Othello at the Royalty Theatre in London. Known as the African Roscius, he went on tour with a good company and at one time had Charles Kean as his Iago.

The favorable reception accorded him as Othello led Aldridge to play Lear, Macbeth, and many other roles, including the West Indian slave, Merugo, in the comedy *The Padlock*. He eventually came to be regarded as one of the leading actors of his time. He settled in England, became naturalized, and extended his tours to the Continent, where he was even more popular. He played in Russia and in Germany, where he played in English while the supporting cast played in German. He continued acting in England and on the Continent until his death in 1867.

WILLIAM CHARLES MACREADY IN AMERICA

Another great actor from England first appeared in America at the Park Theatre in October, 1826. William Charles Macready was a great success in several of the roles for which he was famous—Virginius, Macbeth, Lear, and Hamlet. He was admired for his consistent, intelligent performances, giving more time to rehearsals than was customary. In Shakespeare he discarded the versions of Nahum Tate and others, which were universally played at that time, and went back to the original texts. He was to make further appearances in America in 1843, 1848, and 1849, when he was caught up in the regrettable feud with Edwin Forrest which culminated in the Astor Place riot in New York.

THE SUPPORTING CASTS

The supporting players in these "guest" performances were the members of the theatres' permanent companies. Many were recruits from the London stage, and although efficient enough, they must have seemed quite second rate by comparison with the visiting stars. There was no question of ensemble playing. Rehearsals were perfunctory, and the whole success of the play's performance was dependent on individual acting. That the individual star reached great heights and moved his audience deeply is implicit in the violent passions aroused in the partisanship which split audiences into rival groups and made attendance at the theatre an occasion for bitter warfare.

EDWIN FORREST

Edwin Forrest, perhaps the finest American actor of the first half of the nineteenth century, made his debut in November, 1820, at the Walnut Street Theatre in Philadelphia, then the rival of the Chestnut Street Theatre. Success did not come easily to him, and in his early days he suffered much hardship and difficulty. But his ambition carried him along and he gradually matured his own style, influenced perhaps by Cooke and Cooper. He also benefited from seeing some of the performances of Edmund Kean.

Forrest was a slow-moving, ponderous giant of a man with a magnificent voice which he used to its full extent. He gave an impression of immense strength subdued under a dignity which was much admired. His repose was contrasted with flashes of fierce emotion accompanied by snorts and groans and roaring which led critics in his early days to accuse him of ranting; but his performances were always remarkably effective and sometimes reached the heights of greatness. In the physical aspects of the characters he portrayed he was unequaled, although perhaps weaker in his expression of the spiritual or poetic parts.

Although he appeared in the standard tragic roles of Othello, Lear, Macbeth, and Richelieu, it was in the creation of the character of Spartacus in the play *The Gladiator,* which he inspired Montgomery Bird to write, that he was to achieve his greatest success. It was through his encouragement that several other Philadelphia writers began to write plays, including Richard Penn Smith, Robert T. Conrad, and G. H. Miles. John Augustus Stone was awarded a

prize by Forrest for the best tragedy in five acts in which the hero
or principal character was an American. This was *Metamora*, in
which Forrest appeared for many years with success, although he
subsequently commissioned Bird to rewrite it.

Forrest visited London in 1836, appearing as Spartacus. Although
the *Times* noted his spirited acting, his reception was very mixed.

On this first tour to England, Forrest also played Othello with great success at Drury Lane just after Macready had played the part at Covent Garden. Macready had met Forrest on his first visit to New York in 1826 when he played at the Park. Forrest was playing at the large new Bowery Theatre which, although never to achieve the fashionable popularity of the Park, was nevertheless playing to large popular audiences of solid citizens. Forrest was then only twenty-one and played Mark Antony in *Julius Caesar*. Macready's reaction was encouraging, although he remained doubtful of the young player's powers of self discipline—so necessary in a first-class actor.

Although the two actors met off the stage with friendliness, the press tended to whip up a rivalry between them that neithr desired. On the later tour of America in 1843, Macready renewed the acquaintance on friendly terms and witnessed Forrest's Lear in Philadelphia, which he felt was powerful in rage but lacking in grandeur and pathos. Both actors, however, were capable of displaying almost ungovernable tempers when upset.

THE FORREST–MACREADY FEUD AND THE ASTOR PLACE RIOT

It was not until Forrest's further tour of Britain in 1846, in which he met with much opposition from the critics, that the trouble between the two really began. Forrest believed that Macready's influence with the press was responsible for his bad notices. Macready was playing *Hamlet* in Edinburgh when, during the action just before the Play scene, some extravagant business which he had introduced with a handkerchief was met with a long sustained hiss from a member of the audience in the upper side box. The audience turned to the interrupter with some anger and the somber dark figure of Edwin Forrest was seen sitting motionless with arms folded. He glared at the audience and then got up and left. Much was made of this by the press, and a few days later Forrest justified himself by a statement that he sometimes applauded actors and had an equal right to hiss them.

In 1848 Macready set out on another American tour. Although

successful in New York, he found the old feud worked up in Philadelphia, where Forrest fanned the flames with a denunciation of Macready's supposed intrigues with the press in London to obtain harsh notices of his performances.

After successful seasons at Charleston and New Orleans, Macready returned to New York the following year. He was to appear at the Astor Place Opera House on May 7 as Macbeth. As soon as he appeared on the stage pandemonium began. One section of the audience was obviously set on breaking up the performance, while another group applauded him with cheers. Macready walked forward to address the audience, but such a howl went up that he was inaudible. Rotten eggs and other missiles were pelted at the stage. He was determined to continue, and *Macbeth* was played out in dumb show with increasingly angry attacks from the audience until the third act, when chairs were flung from the gallery. At this, without showing fear or bravado, Macready bowed to the audience, withdrew, and left the theatre. There was a great crowd outside the main doors with the police holding them back.

On the same evening Forrest also played Macbeth at the Broadway Theatre and was received with great enthusiasm. Macready had contracted to play again three days later and, much against advice, decided to appear. This time the police were in the theatre and although there was opposition as before, the first three scenes were played through without any danger. During the fourth scene, however, the police closed in on the rioters and bundled a number of them from the body of the pit to the outside. There they joined with a crowd which had gathered in anticipation of trouble. As the road was unluckily under repair, with many loose paving stones, the windows of the theatre were immediately smashed. The missiles then began to fall inside the theatre. The roar increased and the players began to lose their nerve. Macready refused to give up and the performance dragged on to the last act, when he was cheered by his faithful followers and howled down by others of the much-depleted audience who were sheltering where they could.

The mob outside increased and began to storm the theatre. The police had sent for the military in anticipation of trouble, and more than two hundred troops were brought before the theatre. This incensed the mob, now increased to many thousands. Stones and brickbats flew, and the troops were ordered to fire above the heads of the crowd. In the confusion and noise, some of the soldiers misheard the order and fired into the crowd. The mob, thinking the troops were using blanks, pressed forward. Then they received the full force of a second round of musket fire; several men fell. Another charge by the mob was met with further fire, causing many casualties, but only the appearance of two brass cannon loaded with grapeshot broke up the crowd.

Macready only escaped from the mob by disguising himself and mixing with remnants of the audience as they left the theatre through the main doors. He dared not return to his hotel as a crowd awaited him there, so he spent some hours at the house of a friend and left New York for good in a covered phaeton at four in the morning on the first stage of his journey home.

Seventeen people had been killed in the riot and many others injured, but at the inquest the authorities were vindicated, although it was pronounced that more police instead of the military might have prevented the loss of life.

The aftermath of the affair reacted on Forrest, who lost many supporters among the thinking, sober citizens. Although he remained the idol of the masses, he experienced failure and bitterness in his later years. He was to encounter the rise of the young Edwin Booth. The inevitable comparison of their performances, to Forrest's detriment, clouded the last years of his life. His last appearance was in Boston in 1872 in the role of Richelieu. He died the same year.

CHARLOTTE CUSHMAN

The first great actress to arise in America was Charlotte Cushman, who began her career at the age of nineteen in opera as Countess Almaviva in *The Marriage of Figaro* in Boston in 1835. Losing her

CHARLOTTE CUSHMAN AND SUSAN CUSHMAN Here
the sisters are playing Viola and Olivia in "Twelfth Night."
America's first great tragedienne, Charlotte Cushman, was
noted for her emotional power.

fine contralto voice, she turned to the legitimate stage and appeared
at the Bowery Theatre as Lady Macbeth the following year. Her
success was immediate and she embarked on a long and brilliant
career in America and England. She played with both Forrest and
Macready, and was universally admired both for her brilliant performances and for her warm and charitable disposition.

A tall and commanding figure, Charlotte had a strong and definite style, imparting to her roles a grandeur which no one could resist. Her performances were uniform and coherent, and when the part called for passionate feeling and dramatic effect she rose to the occasion and made it superb. Her expressive features, although not of classical mold, were full of strength and character.

Her Lady Macbeth was unequaled in her time, but the sympathetic qualities of the role of Queen Katherine in *Henry VIII* made it her favorite. Her third great characterization was her most popular, that of Meg Merrilees in a dramatization of Scott's *Guy Mannering*. In this role, which she first created at the age of twenty-one, she let loose an imaginative power of romance, pathos, and experience of grief that was touching and moving beyond belief. She had a power to stir audiences, to embrace their sympathy, and to compel their applause that was, at supreme moments, the equal of the great tragic actors. Some critics wrote that she lacked femininity, so it is hardly surprising that she also essayed breeches parts and played not only Romeo to her sister Susan's Juliet, but also Hamlet, Claude Melnotte in Bulwer-Lytton's *The Lady of Lyons*, and (almost unimaginably) Cardinal Wolsey.

In her last years, although she acted occasionally, she devoted much of her time to very successful readings of Shakespeare. Among her other great parts were Oberon, Rosalind, Viola, Beatrice, Bianca, Phèdre, Nancy Sikes in a dramatization of *Oliver Twist*, and Lady Gay Spanker in the first American production of *London Assurance*.

MINSTREL SHOWS

One of the products of the American native theatre which deserves notice is the creation of the Negro minstrel. This introduction of the lively, bubbling humor and the rhythmic folk songs of the American Negro was popularized on the stage by Thomas D. Rice. He first appeared in the blackface part of Jim Crow as an interlude between the acts of a play at Louisville, Kentucky, singing and dancing in the manner of the southern Negro. This turn so caught the fancy of the audience that he immediately became popular and was in much demand all over the United States. In Washington, on his benefit night, he appeared carrying a sack which he carefully placed on the stage while he went through his act. At the conclusion he opened the sack and out rolled the four-year-old Joseph Jefferson, in a similar costume and makeup, who proceeded to sing and dance with him as a finale, to the great delight of the audience. This is related in the memoirs of one of America's best-loved players, a grandson of the original Joseph Jefferson who joined the American Company toward the end of the eighteenth century. He was to become universally acclaimed years later for his creation of the part of Rip Van Winkle.

Rice was so popular as a solo turn that he was often more highly paid than the leading player of the drama. Audiences at the Bowery Theatre would not let him go, and he appeared in several shows especially written to perpetuate the character. His *Bone Squash* and *The Virginia Mummy* were perhaps the forerunners of the Negro minstrel shows which swept the United States and England in the 1840's and have continued spasmodically until the present day.

The first regular minstrel troupe consisted of a quartet led by Daniel Emmett, the composer of "Dixie," and appeared on the stage in 1843. Wearing bright gala costumes, with faces blacked with burnt cork, they performed with fiddle, banjo, bones, and tambourine, telling jokes, singing songs, and ending with a final dance and walkround. Very soon larger troupes were formed, and the basic pattern of the performances was established. The Kentucky Minstrels and The Original Christy Minstrels were the best known of the troupes. Stephen Foster wrote many of his best-loved songs for the latter.

The curtain rose on a semicircle of the blackfaced company, with a single whitefaced man in the center who was known as Mr. Interlocutor. Always dignified and correct, he played the feed to the two end men, the chief comedians, who were known as Mr. Bones and Mr. Tambo. Quips and conundrums, jokes and wisecracks, interpolated with comic and sentimental songs by various members of the company, comprised the first part of the show, which concluded with a chorus song and parade. The second part was chiefly individual variety—dances, instrumental music, and songs—concluding with a "breakdown" in which all joined. The show concluded with a burlesque or farce much in the nature of an afterpiece, finishing again with a parade of all the troupe.

The Minstrel Show provided a means of developing on the stage the appeal of simple humor and catchphrase, the popular song and dance of the time. In the hands of expert performers it could never fail to attract an appreciative audience. Even today, although in a form far removed from its original pattern, "The Black and White Minstrels Show" has run in London for over four years, after becoming a great success on television.

UNCLE TOM'S CABIN

Rice also appeared in a dramatization of Harriet Beecher Stowe's *Uncle Tom's Cabin*. The immediate success of the book made its translation to the stage inevitable, although Mrs. Stowe's religious beliefs forbade her to be connected in any way with the theatre. Within six months of the first appearance of the book, two versions were presented in the New York theatre, and it soon swept the country. Many touring companies were formed, and soon every little town was visited by the "Tom Show" as it was known in stage circles. It is claimed that the play was performed continuously without a break until the early 1930's and has appeared in various forms since then.

Even in England its popularity was immense. In 1878 no less than five London theatres were presenting it concurrently. The best-known version was by George L. Aiken, who infused more sentimentality into the story and gave the part of Topsy a quality borrowed from the minstrel shows, as were the chorus songs and breakdown dances. The staging of Eliza crossing the ice became a theatrical sensation. Large, fierce hounds were especially bred and trained to appear in the shows and contributed much to the spectacle.

Many first-rate American actors received their apprenticeship in the theatre by joining one of the many road companies. Because of the lack of copyright laws, Mrs. Stowe failed to benefit from the immense sums taken in by these performances, although they no doubt contributed to the popular success of her books.

GROWTH OF THE AMERICAN THEATRE

The rapid growth of the theatre from the middle of the nineteenth century followed the opening of new frontiers and the remarkable growth of the main cities. By 1850 New York was a city of half a million inhabitants and could support no less than six theatres for the legitimate drama—the Park, the Broadway, Burton's, the Bowery, the National, and Brougham's Lyceum (later known as Wallack's)—and several other houses which did plays occasionally although the general fare was opera, concerts, ballet, and variety shows. These were Barnum's American Museum, the Astor Place Opera House, Niblo's Garden, Castle Garden, and Tripler's. The Gold Rush of 1849 established theatres on the Pacific Coast at San Francisco, Stockton, Sacramento, and elsewhere. The floating theatre, or Showboat, was born in this era.

SETTINGS AND LIGHTING

The theatres were also much bigger; the Bowery, for instance, had a capacity of four thousand. With such large houses, the emphasis was on spectacle, and much greater attention was devoted to making the settings more effective, with much greater realism. The stage retreated somewhat behind the proscenium and actors rarely used the forestage, which gradually dwindled. The stage picture and illusion were given more importance than previously. The box set, an innovation when used for Dion Boucicault's new comedy, *London Assurance,* at the Park Theatre in 1841, became established. Actors no longer made their entrances and exits from open wings, but used practical doors and windows conceived in architectural unity with the apparently solid walls and ceilings.

By now most theatres were using gas lighting which, by the ease of its control, enabled various effects to be rapidly or gradually brought on as needed. The larger theatres required more light on the stage, and this was achieved by gas battens concealed by borders at various positions over the stage, side wings in which the burners were arranged like rungs of a ladder, footlights or floats which had replaced the old oil lamps, and by the use of flexible tubing and temporary pieces of apparatus which could be moved wherever extra lighting was required. The control of all the lighting was arranged at the prompter's desk, where a number of handles were affixed which affected the lights on various parts of the stage. A complete blackout was made possible with one switch, and every burner could be instantly relit with the aid of an electric button.

In addition to gas lighting, the limelight perfected by Drummond in 1816 gave a brilliant white light which was much used in realistic effects of sunlight or moonlight beams directed through windows and doors. It was also used for spotlighting and following actors about on the stage.

Thus, in the larger theatres, while the action had retreated behind the proscenium in the stage picture and the players were much farther from the audience than they had ever been, this disadvantage was somewhat offset by the much greater brilliance of lighting and its easy control in helping to create the change of mood or atmosphere which might be necessary to the play.

The electric arc lamp never completely replaced the limelight because, although it was much more brilliant, its noise of operation and its occasional flickering limited its use. Electricity as a complete method of lighting the stage had to await the perfection of the filament lamp, an event associated with the name of Thomas Alva Edison, who personally supervised the installation of overhead stage lighting for Steele MacKaye in 1879 at the Madison Square Theatre.

THE NEW PARK THEATRE   Opened in September, 1821, this house was built on the site of its predecessor which was destroyed by fire the previous year. The new theatre still had proscenium doors, but proscenium boxes were eliminated, and the stage apron was much more shallow.

DION BOUCICAULT

One of the most important figures of the American theatre during the third quarter of the century was the actor-dramatist Dion Boucicault. Of Irish parentage, he achieved an instant hit with his first play, *London Assurance,* which received its premiere in London with Charles Mathews, Madame Vestris, and William Warren at Covent Garden in 1841. He was then only nineteen years old. His subsequent plays, although of no great literary merit, provided many good acting parts and were very popular among the stars of his time. Four years spent in France acquainted him with the French drama and provided him with many originals from which he translated and adapted his own versions.

Boucicault acted in many of his own plays, as did his supposed second wife, Agnes Robertson, the adopted daughter of Charles Kean. They first came to America in 1853 and appeared together with many of the leading companies. His first outstanding play written in America was *Grimaldi, or the Life of an Actress,* produced in New Orleans in 1855, in which society was satirized for its opinion of women taking up the stage as a career. He turned to domestic drama in *The Sidewalks of New York,* and to low life in *Ten Nights in a Bar Room.* But his most successful plays at this time were aimed at the large Irish immigrant population—*The Colleen Bawn, Arragh-na-Pogue,* and *The Shaughraun,* in which he and Miss Robertson were deservedly popular.

In 1859 he went into management in New York, taking over Burton's Theatre, now known as the Winter Garden. The opening play was his version of a French piece which was originally based on Dickens's *The Cricket on the Hearth,* unknown to him. When he discovered the original source he rewrote the play under the title *Dot.* The same year he wrote *The Octoroon, or Life in Louisiana,* a strong treatment of the subject of slavery.

At a time when the pirating of plays was very common, Boucicault joined brother dramatists and helped to get the law changed which, although it did not do all he had hoped, limited the plagiarism to some extent.

As a manager he was responsible for organizing the road shows, which were complete companies sent out to tour with his plays. His touring companies spread his work throughout the country.

He appeared with Laura Keene's company, and Miss Robertson achieved great popularity as Jeanie Deans in a dramatization of *The Heart of Midlothian*. As an actor, Boucicault was best in comedy and character parts. As a producer, he introduced many ingenious stage effects. His plays were generally a mixture of naturalistic domestic scenes heightened with occasional melodramatic passages.

JOSEPH JEFFERSON

Boucicault rewrote *Rip Van Winkle* for Joseph Jefferson, who had already been successful in his own version of Washington Irving's popular story, but still thought the play was weak.

Joseph Jefferson had also appeared in Boucicault's *Dot* at the Winter Garden, where he created the part of Caleb Plummer. Essentially a comedian, Jefferson was persuaded to attempt the more serious character role much against his own belief in his powers to sustain it. He insisted that he should appear in a farcical afterpiece in which he could display his talent for comedy. The success of *Dot* and of Jefferson as Caleb Plummer on the first night (much to his surprise) made the farce an anticlimax, so it was immediately dropped.

Jefferson was something of a painter, with an eye for visual effects. He built up his great part of Rip with a host of small details, and his acting of a long silent passage in the play was much enjoyed by the audience and regarded by his fellow actors with great respect. He did not aspire to a wide range of parts, but he was also notable as Dr. Panglos in *Heir at Law,* Bob Acres in *The Rivals,* and as Salem Scudder in *The Octoroon*. His work typified the growing tendency toward naturalistic acting and the greater realism in the theatre of the time.

JOSEPH JEFFERSON III Here is how the actor appeared in his immortal role of Rip Van Winkle which he played intermittently for 40 years.

LAURA KEENE'S COMPANY

Laura Keene was one of the leading actresses in America during this period, playing at her best in light comedy roles. She had received her early training at the London Lyceum and was subsequently a member of the stock company at Wallack's Theatre.

She entered management, and it was under her direction that Tom Taylor's *Our American Cousin* was first produced in America. It was in this play that E. A. Sothern created the character of Lord Dundreary. At rehearsals of the play Sothern was disappointed in what he considered a very dull part and at first could make little

248

of it. Jefferson, who was also in the play as Asa Trenchard, recalls that after playing a week or so Sothern, in desperation, introduced some extravagant business—skipping about the stage, sneezing, stammering, and generally behaving in an odd manner. To the surprise of the rest of the cast the audience received this with delight, and by gradually building up the character, Sothern, by the end of the month, was the play. He was to play this part many times, achieving a record run of five months in New York and taking it on to London with great success. It was this play, also, that Laura Keene's company gave at Ford's Theatre, Washington, on the fateful night of April 14, 1865, when Lincoln, while watching the performance, was shot dead by John Wilkes Booth.

JUNIUS BRUTUS BOOTH

The Booths were perhaps the most important family in the American theatre for much of the nineteenth century. Junius Brutus Booth was the first member of his family to take to the stage. An erratic and temperamental disposition with a hint of mental instability drove him from his father's law office after he had received a sound classical education. His father, Richard, was a great republican in his youth and tried to join the American forces during the Revolutionary War. His revolutionary beliefs, coupled with a classical education, were responsible for the unusual names he gave his son.

Junius joined a small stock theatre at Deptford, then a suburb of London, making his debut in 1813. Within a few years he was playing leading roles. After touring the provinces, he deputized for Edmund Kean as Sir Giles Overreach and was then invited to appear at Covent Garden as Richard III. At this time Kean was at Drury Lane.

Although his style was somewhat based on that of Kean (indeed one of the critics noted the resemblance as "surely one of nature's duplicates"), Booth began to offer such serious competition that the Drury Lane management approached him with a contract at a much greater salary than Covent Garden was paying him. Accepting with great alacrity, he joined the rival house and then found that he was playing Iago to Kean's Othello and, further to his dismay, that he would not be able to play any part that Kean might wish to perform. In great dudgeon he returned to Covent Garden, where audiences received him badly, thinking he was part of a conspiracy against Kean. So he once again returned to touring the provinces.

Junius first came to America in 1821 at the age of twenty-five, making his debut in Richmond as Richard III. His passionate emotional acting ensured him a continued popularity which was to last for thirty years or more, although his occasional erratic behavior and the gradual increase in bouts of heavy drinking clouded his later years.

Booth bought some farming land near Baltimore and a log cabin on another property. He moved the cabin across the fields on rollers to be set up as a permanent home. Here his large family were born and grew up in a completely free environment. Junius was a strict vegetarian on humanitarian grounds, and was intensely moved at the death of his pony Peacock, whom he desired to be buried with the attendance of the clergy. Richard Booth, Junius' father, joined them from England to farm the land.

Edwin Booth was the fourth son (named after Edwin Forrest with whom Junius had played and who was a great friend) and from his early days displayed a close and sympathetic attachment to his father, which was reciprocated. Often when Junius was called upon to tour he would take Edwin with him, and as the boy grew up he acquired a knowledge of the theatre and its actors which took the place of a very irregular attendance at school. He served as dresser to his father and eventually appeared in small parts in the plays in which his father was performing. This first occurred at the Boston Museum on September 10, 1849, when Edwin appeared as Tyrell in *Richard III*. For the next years he played in similar minor parts, always traveling with his father.

The eldest son, Junius Brutus, Jr., had also entered the theatre

JUNIUS BRUTUS BOOTH The founder of the famous American acting family is seen here as Sir Giles Overreach in Massinger's "A New Way to Play Old Debts." Failing to outshine Edmund Kean, Booth emigrated to the United States and opened as Richard III at the Park Theatre in 1821.

but, being of a more reliable and settled temperament, was attracted more to the management side. The third son, also to become an actor, was John Wilkes, a wild and unstable character who was to bring the family only tears and disgrace.

After the Gold Rush and the opening of the Pacific Coast, Junius

Brutus, Jr., arranged in 1852 to take over management of one of the theatres in San Francisco for a season with his father and his brother Edwin in standard plays. This proving financially successful, they moved on to Sacramento where they failed and lost most of what they had gained in San Francisco. After this Junius decided to return home alone to Baltimore, and on the long journey, while aboard a Mississippi steamer, he fell ill and died.

EDWIN BOOTH

Junius Brutus, Jr., continued in management at the small theatre in San Francisco, where he presented burlesques and farces with his brother Edwin playing a host of small roles, even a blackface part in *Dandy Cox*, a Negro farce. Here in the West Edwin consoli-

EDWIN BOOTH AT THE AGE OF 20 America's leading tragedian developed his great talent touring throughout the West in minor roles with his father, Junius Brutus.

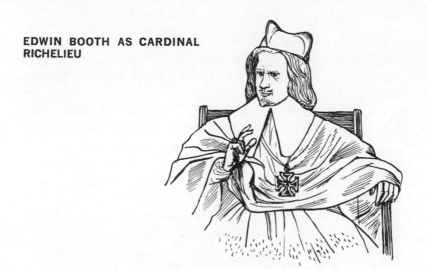

EDWIN BOOTH AS CARDINAL RICHELIEU

dated his training for the theatre, acquiring a perfect mastery of acting technique.

Under his brother's management, he first played Petruchio and then Richard III. The favorable reception he received moved Junius to advise his appearance in other great Shakespearean parts. Shylock and Macbeth followed and, for his benefit, Hamlet for the first time. All met with great success.

In 1854 Edwin undertook a tour of Australia under the management of Laura Keene, and achieved a great success with Shylock in Sydney. His reception in Melbourne was not as good, however, and he decided to part company with the management and took ship for San Francisco. On the way back the ship stopped at Honolulu and he stayed there for two months, taking over the island's only theatre and playing *Richard III* and *The Lady of Lyons,* with his companion, Roe, playing the female role of Pauline.

Arriving back in San Francisco Edwin was immediately offered the part of Benedick in *Much Ado About Nothing* at the Metropolitan Theatre. The success there led to tours to Sacramento and the neighboring country. He returned to San Francisco to play Lear for the first time in 1856.

By now he had sufficient experience and reputation to return to the East. Successful tours of Baltimore, Washington, Richmond, New Orleans, Mobile, and Memphis led to his brilliant triumphs in Boston and New York.

Edwin was described at this time as a young man of extraordinary personal grace with a magnetic personality, full of the fire of youthful genius, vigorous but without the overpowering robustness of Forrest, and a more sensitive and imaginative interpreter of Shakespeare than had yet appeared in America. He was of slight build, of medium height, with an extremely mobile and expressive face, luminous dark eyes, and clean-cut mouth. His voice had great beauty, his elocutionary skill was remarkable, and he was able to impart psychological depths to the characters he played beyond what was apparent in the actual dialogue.

In contrast to Forrest, who built up his roles by external effects and technique, Edwin Booth penetrated below the surface of the character and, using his intelligence and matchless theatrical skill, brought new light to the familiar tragedies of Shakespeare. Some critics thought him greater in the more melodramatic parts such as Overreach and Richelieu, but this might have been the greater distinction he brought to the interpretation of otherwise familiar vehicles. In 1861 he went to England where he stayed for two years, appearing successfully as Shylock, Overreach, and Richelieu.

In America now torn by the strife of war, the theatres continued to operate, although with much more difficulty than normal, what with selecting their offerings as relaxation for their more concerned audiences and the shortage of actors caused by their flocking to the colors in large numbers.

Edwin Booth returned to New York in 1862, and in March of the same year his brother John Wilkes appeared with success in a season at Wallack's old theatre playing Richard III, Hamlet, and Macbeth. Inevitably the critics made comparisons between John and his father and his brother Edwin, but they found his Richard a notable performance.

The following year Edwin entered management at the Winter Garden Theatre which for a time was occupied with such pieces as *East Lynne,* a successful dramatization of the popular novel with Lucille Westen, and *The Ticket of Leave Man,* a new play by Tom Taylor in which Mr. and Mrs. W. J. Florence were a great hit.

On November 25, 1864, an event occurred in the theatre which perhaps would have given the elder Booth some satisfaction: his three sons played in a benefit performance of *Julius Caesar* for the purpose of commemorating the tercentenary of Shakespeare by erecting a memorial statue in Central Park. Junius Brutus, Jr., played Cassius, Edwin played Brutus, and John Wilkes was Mark Antony. This was the only occasion on which the three Booths appeared together.

Edwin followed, the next evening, with *Hamlet,* a production which ran for one hundred nights, the longest run ever achieved in America in the nineteenth century. Edwin reached new heights in this role, and the critics were universal in their praise, the performance being described as one of the noblest pieces of dramatic art ever seen, performed by an actor who had no living equal.

On the fateful night of April 14, 1865, John Wilkes Booth walked casually into the stage door of Ford's Theatre in Washington, where he was well known, having played there frequently. He walked through the wings behind the stage where Laura Keene's company was giving *Our American Cousin,* went through the pass door to the auditorium, slipped quietly into the first box, drew a revolver, and shot President Lincoln point blank in the back of the head. He then climbed over the front of the box and jumped onto the stage. In so doing he misjudged the jutting cornice and broke his leg. He landed on his feet, however, on the stage. With such an entrance he could not resist uttering a quotation from *Julius Caesar,* "Liberty! Freedom! Tyranny is dead!" He then ran through the wings and out of the theatre and disappeared into the night.

By mutual agreement the theatres of New York remained closed for two weeks in mourning. Edwin Booth, intensely shocked on

EDWIN BOOTH AT THE AGE OF 31
He is shown here in his historic portrayal of Hamlet which opened at the Winter Garden on November 26, 1865. This production enjoyed the longest run of any Shakespearean play up to that time.

learning of his brother's dastardly crime, went into retirement from the stage immediately. The brooding introspection of this period was not lessened by the news of the discovery of his brother's body in a Virginia barn on April 26. John Wilkes Booth died by a shot through the head, probably self-inflicted. Edwin's constant thought must have been fear of the incipient strain of mental instability which had been observed at times in both his father and his grandfather and now was made so clear in the actions of his younger brother.

The following months must have been a private hell which affected him for the rest of his life. But time passes, and a faithful following persuaded him to return to the stage early in 1866. He opened at the Winter Garden in *Hamlet*, then in *Ruy Blas*, followed by a long run in *Richelieu*.

The next years saw many lavish and beautiful productions. Booth was acknowledged by all as the leading actor in America. When the Winter Garden burned down in 1868 he built his own theatre on Sixth Avenue. Booth's Theatre was large and impressive and provided with the last word in stage equipment, hydraulic lifts for moving entire settings from below, and a great stage loft for flying solid backdrops and other scenery. There was no forestage and no proscenium doors, and the side boxes were sited in the auditorium. The withdrawal of the actor within the stage picture was now complete.

Although Edwin Booth continued to remain popular as an actor and with a fine company presented many distinguished productions, he failed financially as a manager, gave up his theatre, and in 1873 embarked on a long series of road tours throughout America with his friend Lawrence Barrett, building a new reputation. He traveled to England in 1880 and 1882 and also to Germany, with continued success. He appeared at the Lyceum in London with Irving in *Othello* and by agreement they alternated the parts of Othello and Iago. Many critics considered Iago his finest characterization, in which he revealed depths of a subtle, malignant evil beneath the outward show of friendliness which had hitherto rarely been approached.

NEW THEATRICAL DEVELOPMENTS

The last thirty years of the nineteenth century brought many developments in the theatre. The increase in travel made possible by the building of new railways, continued improvement in education, the growth of the main centers, immigration, and the doubling of the total population of the country were all important factors. It became an era in which entertainment was paramount, and to provide it in the theatre a new group of individuals rose to importance.

The old actor-manager who played the chief roles and governed his company, whether centered on a metropolitan theatre or on tour, was generally unable to cope with the greatly increased financial risk incurred in running the new large theatres and organizing the extensive touring companies. There was a vast amount of money to be gained or lost in theatrical enterprises, and the business manager now became the important figure. He treated the stage as any other business, and was concerned with capital investment, running costs, and returns. He chose his plays with great care, used the developing arts of publicity to advertise them, and created the star system. The most successful controlled several theatres, organized circuits for touring their productions, contracted prominent actors exclusively to their own organizations, and employed playwrights to write for them. Their organizations covered the whole country, and some spread their interests to England, taking over management of London theatres.

REALISM

While the great actors of England and the Continent were frequently seen in America, it was the native product who developed chiefly in this period. New plays by American writers, more of whom were writing for the stage, were being performed by American actors whose skill and ability were adeptly suited to the tempo and climate of the age. Audiences were now responding to plays dealing with themes and experiences reflecting the richness and variety of American life. The greater realism in the theatre, with its new technical machinery and lighting, brought new emphasis to the part the actor played in presenting "a mirror up to nature." As was to be expected, the new plays were chiefly domestic dramas, sometimes perhaps rather melodramatic, but often the action would be overshadowed by great events of a nationwide significance.

The realism did not extend to the complete overthrow of the long tradition of stage technique which actors had acquired assiduously over the years. They still behaved in a theatrical manner and did not achieve the complete synthesis of stage realism until the present century. Playwrights too, although their themes were drawn from life, were still dependent on the soliloquy (the stage aside directed to the audience) and other traditional methods of ensuring a continuity of plot.

America saw many fine actors from Europe during this period. Tommaso Salvini and Adelaide Ristori from Italy; Réjane, Bernhardt, and Coquelin from Paris; Henry Irving, Ellen Terry, William and Madge Kendall, and many others from the London stage were all welcomed with the warmth traditionally shown distinguished visitors. America's own leading players undoubtedly gained much from their superb technique, but they developed along the lines already inherent in the changing importance of presentation and tended to concentrate on particular types of roles.

THE "ROYAL FAMILY OF BROADWAY"

Mrs. John Drew, for over thirty years an indefatigable manageress of the Arch Street Theatre in Philadelphia, founded the "Royal Family of Broadway" when her daughter Georgiana married Maurice Barrymore and had three gifted and talented children—Lionel, Ethel, and John—each to make his own contribution to the theatre in the present century. Her son John Drew became one of the best romantic actors of light comedy, particularly excelling in *Pendennis,* a dramatization of Thackeray's novel, and Pinero's *Trelawney of the Wells.*

LEADING PERFORMERS

Among other leading actors were Otis Skinner, who appeared in many Shakespearean roles from Romeo to Falstaff, but is best remembered for his performances in contemporary plays; Edward Hugh Sothern, the talented son of E. A. "Dundreary" Sothern, who also played much in Shakespeare with Julia Marlowe, but was immensely popular as a romantic hero in such plays as *The Prisoner of Zenda;* and Richard Mansfield, a fine actor who appeared in many historical pieces such as *Cyrano de Bergerac* and *Monsieur Beaucaire,* and in Clyde Fitch's *Beau Brummell,* and also first introduced the plays of Bernard Shaw to America, appearing with success in *Arms and the Man* and *The Devil's Disciple.* Henry

Miller, later to enter management (continued by his son Gilbert), and James O'Neill, the father of Eugene, America's greatest dramatist of the twentieth century, were other leading actors of the time.

Of the many actresses to become prominent, Helen Modjeska, Annie Russell, Lillian Russell, Ada Rehan, Julia Marlowe, Maude Adams, Fanny Davenport, Lotta, Rose Coghlan, Clara Morris, and Minnie Fiske were particularly successful, many of them playing leading roles well into the twentieth century.

AUGUSTIN DALY

The new trends in the American theatre were well exemplified in the presentations of Augustin Daly, one of the most successful managers of the period. His somewhat lurid melodrama, *Under the Gaslight*, produced at the New York Theatre in 1867, had the sensational climax of the chief character's being bound hand and foot to a railway line in the path of a thundering locomotive, being rescued just in time by the heroine—a situation later much employed in the first movies. For this production Daly devised many ingenious stage effects which he was able to patent.

Daly made many adaptations from successful English novels by Wilkie Collins, Trollope, and Florence Marryat; from the French writers, Sardou, Dumas, Meilhac, and Halévy; and from the contemporary German writings of Gustav von Moser and Julius Rosen. But he also encouraged American writers to write for the stage, including Bronson Howard, who became one of the most important dramatists of the period.

For the rest of the century Daly operated one or more theatres in New York and organized touring companies with steady success. In 1879 he took over Wood's Museum and renamed it Daly's Theatre, where he gathered some of the most brilliant actors of the time, including James Lewis, Mrs. Gilbert, Clara Morris, Fanny Davenport, Ada Rehan, and John Drew. He concentrated on comedy, producing many of Shakespeare's, with occasional farces and melodramas.

In 1884 he took a company to England and the Continent. It received such a warm reception in London that he decided to establish himself there, and in 1893, with George Edwardes, opened his own theatre, also known as Daly's.

Some of his outstanding successes were *Frou-Frou* from Meilhac and Halévy and *Our Boys,* with Maurice Barrymore and Fanny Davenport, who also enjoyed a success in *Pique,* in which Georgiana Drew first appeared. Daly also had successes with productions of *The Taming of the Shrew, The Merry Wives of Windsor,* and *A Midsummer Night's Dream,* Colley Cibber's *She Would and She Would Not;* and Garrick's expurgated version of Wycherley's *The Country Wife,* in which Ada Rehan and John Drew were very popular.

Ada Rehan was very successful in Daly's Shakespearean productions, playing Viola, Rosalind, and in particular Katherine in *The Taming of the Shrew.* In the latter Daly went back to the original text, ignoring Garrick's edited version which had hitherto been widely used. This may have contributed to Ada Rehan's memorable performance in the role.

Daly exercised close control over his productions, setting a high standard of presentation, with skillful, elegant acting. He did occasionally produce native works, including Bronson Howard's satirical comedy, *Saratoga* and his own play, *Horizon,* a frontier drama of great realism.

LESTER WALLACK

Lester Wallack, the son of James William Wallack, the English actor, who had made his debut at the Park Theatre in 1818, was a survival of the old actor-manager regime who operated a fine stock company for over twenty years. He acted himself in brilliant comedy presentations such as *The School for Scandal* and in such romantic pieces as Boucicault's *The Shaughraun.* He also employed some of the finest actors, including E. L. Davenport, Charles and Rose Coghlan, Maurice Barrymore, John Brougham, Steele MacKaye, and H. G. Montague. His long career in the theatre was crowned by a magnificent production of *Hamlet* with Edwin Booth and Helen Modjeska as Hamlet and Ophelia, John Gilbert as Polonius, Joseph Jefferson and W. J. Florence as the gravediggers, and many other notable stars walking on in small parts and as supers.

STEELE MAC KAYE

Steele MacKaye was another manager who had entered the theatre through becoming interested in acting in Paris, where he had originally studied painting. He was much influenced in theories of acting and studied under François Delsarte and Regnier of the Comédie Française. He was somewhat erratic, but versatile and inventive.

He began his career with a season of management at the St. James Theatre, New York, in 1872. This was a failure, so he returned to France. He acted Hamlet in French in both Paris and London. In 1874 he returned to America where he devoted himself for some years to writing plays, inventing new stage effects and machinery, occasionally acting or stage managing, and giving lectures. The following year he wrote *Rose Michel*, adapted from the French, which was produced at the Union Square Theatre by the manager, A. M. Palmer. Although it was not a great success, he was encouraged to continue writing and working out his own ideas of production.

In 1879 he obtained control of the Madison Square Theatre and rebuilt the stage with elevators and fitted overhead lighting by electricity. He also remodeled the auditorium, installing folding seats and a modern system of ventilation. The following year it opened with his own play, *Hazel Kirke*, a domestic drama, realistically presented, which achieved the great success of a record run of 486 performances. A duplicate cast took the play on tour at the same time. In 1885 he joined the Frohmans and installed the new equipment in the Lyceum. He was to pass on to their management many of his new ideas, which were gradually assimilated into general theatrical practice. The importance of technique was a relevant factor in the building of star reputations, so significant in the later years of the century.

MacKaye's ideas of a vast auditorium seating 10,000, with a cyclorama and sliding stages moved by electricity was projected for the Chicago World's Fair of 1893. It never materialized because of failure of the finances, but he built a small theatre in 1894, incorporating many of his ideas. He died shortly after its completion. His career exemplifies the emergence of a new figure in the theatre— the director, whose knowledge of acting and stage technique became much more important in the twentieth century.

BRONSON HOWARD

The playwright Bronson Howard's biggest success was probably *Shenandoah,* a drama of life during the Civil War in which the war itself was the impelling background but against which the love stories and play of characters in various circumstances was skillfully interwoven. Howard's other plays which attained great success were *The Young Mrs. Winthrop,* a social drama, and *Henrietta,* a satirical play especially written for Stuart Robson and William H. Crane, actors of the Union Square Company. The latter was produced in 1887 and ran for over a year.

Howard was instrumental in getting the copyright laws amended to protect playwrights from much piracy. He elevated the profession of play writing in America, and made it more profitable by founding the American Dramatists' Club in 1891. It eventually became the Dramatists' Guild, which exists today to protect playwrights from exploitation.

THE FROHMANS

Daniel and Charles Frohman were each an example of the new type of business manager who was not trained as an actor but began in the theatre on the management side and was highly successful through having a flair for anticipation of the public's taste. Daniel worked for Steele MacKaye for a time at the Lyceum in New York, and in 1886 became its sole manager. A strong stock company had been established there with E. H. Sothern, Frank Mayo, Henry Miller, James K. Hackett, Mrs. Whiffen, Effie Shannon, and May

Robson. Charles Frohman began his career as a touring manager, also for Steele MacKaye, particularly with the play *Hazel Kirke*. He took over the Star Theatre in New York and produced Bronson Howard's *Shenandoah* which, although it had failed when first produced in Boston, became a great success and ran for several months.

Charles Frohman operated five theatres in New York and one in London at the height of his career. He also controlled the bookings of many theatres throughout America. He made stars of Maude Adams, Ethel Barrymore, May Robson, Arthur Byron, Margaret Anglia, Henry Miller, John Drew, William Gillette, Julia Marlowe, Blanche Bates, and William Faversham. He was the first manager to regard the theatre as big business. He produced popular plays by the American writers David Belasco, William Gillette, Henry C. de Mille, and Clyde Fitch, particularly at the Twenty-third Street Theatre and his new playhouse, the Empire Theatre. He may not have contributed much to the artistic presentation of plays, but he organized and rationalized much theatre practice.

DAVID BELASCO

David Belasco, born in San Francisco of a father who had been a clown in London, had a long life in the theatre, first performing at the age of twelve. At fourteen he played in the Charles Kean production of *Richard III* at Victoria, British Columbia. During the 1870's he continually acted in California and Nevada, meeting most of the important figures in the theatre of the time. He became assistant to Dion Boucicault, who taught him stage management and the difficult art of play writing. By 1882 he felt confident enough to tackle New York, having had a vast experience in the theatre acting, adapting or writing plays, and directing. He eventually became stage manager or director and staff playwright to Charles Frohman.

Belasco contributed much to the popular successes of such pieces as *The Wife, Lord Chumley, The Charity Ball,* and *Men and Women,* collaborating with Henry C. de Mille. His plays possess no great literary merit, but were efficient vehicles for the stars, with fine acting parts, simple themes, and strong dramatic climaxes. He made a star of Mrs. Leslie Carter, a divorcée from Chicago society who had charm, looks, but no stage training. He wrote for her *The Heart of Maryland,* in which she was a success, although after a modest beginning. This was followed in 1899 by *ZaZa,* adapted from the French of Berton and Simon, and in 1904 by *Andrea,* a romantic tragedy of Roman times in which she achieved her greatest success.

Belasco directed his productions with great attention to detail and invented many realistic stage effects which were much admired. He also made many improvements in the practical matters of scenery construction and in an imaginative use of stage lighting.

He later collaborated with John Luther Long in writing a one-act play, *Madame Butterfly,* in which Blanche Bates appeared. This was later used by Puccini as the scenario for his well-known opera, as was *The Girl of the Golden West,* produced as a starring vehicle for Blanche Bates in 1905. In 1910 it was presented as an opera at the Metropolitan Opera House with Caruso and Emmy Destinn.

Belasco also made a star of David Warfield, a Jewish comedian from vaudeville, presenting him in a number of dramatic roles in *The Auctioneer, The Music Master, A Grand Army Man, The Return of Peter Grimm,* and *The Merchant of Venice.* Other stars he made were Henrietta Crosman, Frances Starr, and Beth Merrill. Many of his leading players eventually also became stars of the movies: George Arliss, Lillian Gish, Mary Pickford, and Henry Hull all appeared in his productions before starting their film careers.

In 1890 he left the Frohmans and became an independent producer, putting on his own plays. In 1902 he took over the Republic Theatre in New York (which he renamed the Belasco), as he found difficulties getting his productions launched because of opposition from the monopoly created by the Frohmans and other theatre managers and booking agents in New York and Philadelphia. He continued in opposition to this syndicate, building the Stuyvesant

Theatre (the present Belasco), and in 1907 opening with David Warfield in *A Grand Army Man*. Many of the leading actors supported him in his fight against the syndicate and eventually the monopoly was broken by a rival organization of theatre managers run by the three Shubert brothers, who in time became the leading producing and booking company throughout America.

Belasco did much in his sympathetic handling of players and got the most out of them in his productions, often training young actresses from scratch and building their reputations by increasingly important and dramatic roles. His advances in technique, although in the main toward realism on the stage, also involved an imaginative and artistic sensibility. He had a sure grasp of what the public wanted and rarely experienced anything but financial success, producing plays successfully until well into the 1920's.

LATE NINETEENTH CENTURY PLAYWRIGHTS

Apart from Belasco, Bronson Howard, and Steele MacKaye, the chief American playwrights of the late nineteenth century were Edward Harrigan, William Dean Howells, James A. Herne, William Gillette, Charles Hoyt, Augustus Thomas, and the prolific Clyde Fitch. They wrote plays mostly based on themes taken from American life. Although perhaps not reaching the stature of European work of the time, they laid the foundation of American drama, which was to blossom so profusely in the second quarter of the twentieth century.

EDWARD HARRIGAN

Edward Harrigan, originally an actor, wrote short sketches for himself and a partner in which he characterized the immigrant types in farcical situations in their new life in New York. While the Irish were his most popular characterizations in such sketches as the Mulligan Guard series, he also introduced German, Italian, and Negro types into his shrewdly observed and good-humored pieces.

WILLIAM DEAN HOWELLS

William Dean Howells was a literary figure of some importance in the late nineteenth and early twentieth centuries. An editor of the *Atlantic Monthly* and a regular contributor to *Harper's Magazine*, he imposed a strong influence on American literature of the time both as a novelist and as a critic. He wrote many short one-act plays in the form of "polite" comedy and, although they were rarely produced in the professional theatre, they were published and were much in demand among amateur players. Two of these short plays were professionally produced in London and received a good reception, including a favorable notice from Bernard Shaw. None of his full-length plays was successful in the professional theatre, although the most notable were *A Counterfeit Presentment*, produced by Lawrence Barrett in 1877, and *The American Claimant*, written in collaboration with Mark Twain.

JAMES A. HERNE

James A. Herne began as an actor and toured the country. He learned much about play writing by early collaboration with David Belasco. His early attempts were adaptations from English originals, *Marriage by Moonlight* and *Chums*. The latter was retitled *Hearts of Oak* and became a hit in Chicago and New York. Herne and his wife toured in it for many years with great success. This was later renamed yet again *Sag Harbor*.

His first original works were *The Minute Men of 1774/5*, *Drifting Apart*, a drama woven around the lives of fishermen, followed by *Shore Acres*, a simple melodrama of farm life with excellent characterization, which brought him recognition and fortune when it ran for a whole season at Daly's in 1893. Herne and his wife played in it for many years on tour and in stock with constant success. Attempts to write plays outside the milieu of the simple working man—*Margaret Fleming*, a social drama, and *The Reverend Griffith Davenport*, with its Civil War background and its principal character, a Southerner who opposed slavery—ended in failure and considerable financial loss. His characterizations of the simple life were sentimental, perhaps, but written with a profound understanding of his subjects.

WILLIAM GILLETTE

William Gillette was another actor who turned to the writing of plays, many of which he appeared in with great acclaim. His first play was *The Professor,* a light comedy in which he took the title role at the Madison Square Theatre in 1881, where it had a fair success. His second was an adaptation from a story by Frances Hodgson Burnett, *Esmeralda,* which ran for a whole year at the same theatre. He then turned to melodrama, and it was the action, which Gillette presented realistically and effectively on the stage, which was to make his name. *Held by the Enemy,* a Civil War melodrama with conflicts and heroism behind the lines, also enjoyed a long run in 1886 at the Madison Square. He was unsuccessful in his *The Legal Wreck* and an adaptation of *She* by Rider Haggard, but regained his popularity with three farces, all based on foreign sources: *All the Comforts of Home, Mr. Wilkinson's Widows,* and *Too Much Johnson,* in the last of which he appeared with great popularity as a philandering plantation owner.

He wrote many other plays, but his last two great successes were *Secret Service* (1895) and *Sherlock Holmes* (1899). The former was again about the Civil War and the spy theme, and the chief character was played so admirably by Gillette that it was rarely attempted by other actors. He also played the title role in *Sherlock Holmes,* which was based on the Conan Doyle stories, but with much original material. In this part he was enthusiastically received in both America and England for over twenty years. Although the success of the play was partly a reflection of the popularity of the immortal character, Gillette was the first actor to achieve its complete embodiment on the stage.

AUGUSTUS THOMAS

Augustus Thomas was born of theatrical parents and grew up in the theatre his father managed in New Orleans. He began writing in his teens, and by his early twenties was touring the Midwest with farces. An early curtain raiser was expanded to a full-length piece, *The Burglar,* and was produced in Boston and New York in

1889. The favorable reception of this piece encouraged him to continue writing plays, and during the next thirty years or so he produced about fifty plays. They were mostly serious pieces based on American themes, and he explored many controversial subjects hitherto unknown to the stage. He was particularly interested in introducing regional or local characteristics as a background in which an individual might struggle for freedom against economic, political, or social pressures. In many ways he explored ground which was to be firmly trod by many of our present-day authors.

His plays set in particular states were received with great interest. *Alabama,* produced by A. H. Palmer at the Madison Square Theatre in 1891, touched on the aftermath of the Civil War at a time when the bitterness of the South was still persistent. *In Mizzoura, Arizona,* and *Colorado,* although not all successful, were further essays in local color. His last plays were more concerned with personal and individual problems and dealt imaginatively with such things as telepathy, in *The Witching Hour,* and the problem of mental adjustment in *As a Man Thinks.*

CHARLES HOYT

Charles Hoyt was a writer of well-constructed farces who was also adept at the creation of character roles. A keen sense of lively fun imbued his popular pieces, the first of note being *A Bunch of Keys,* produced in 1882. *The Texas Steer* of 1890 was a tilt at the antics of Congressmen in Washington. The following year his greatest success, *A Trip to Chinatown,* set in San Francisco, ran for 650 performances. It was revived in 1894 with an even longer run and later had a favorable reception in London. He became a producer and wrote many other farces, although with less success.

CLYDE FITCH

One of the most prolific writers of this period was Clyde Fitch. A graduate of Amherst College, Fitch went to New York with an ambition to write for the stage. He was successful in being commissioned in 1889 by Richard. Mansfield to write a play suited to

Mansfield's own talents. This piece, *Beau Brummell*, was successfully produced at the Madison Square Theatre in 1890. It was subsequently played by Richard Mansfield throughout his career.

This first success encouraged Fitch to settle down in earnest as a playwright, and during the rest of his life he wrote with facility over forty plays. While some of these were adaptations, they cover a wide range of style—from an essay in the comedy of manners, *His Grace of Grammont*, in which Otis Skinner appeared as Charles II, to dramas based on American history such as *Nathan Hale* and *Barbara Frietchie* (for Julia Marlowe). Two melodramas, *The Moth and the Flame* and *The Cowboy and the Lady*, brought Fitch further success in 1898 and 1899. In 1901 came *The Climbers*, an acidly written social satire of New York society which enjoyed a long run, and *Captain Jinks of the Horse Marines*, in which the young Ethel Barrymore became a star under Charles Frohman's management. During this time *The Last of the Dandies* was produced by Beerbohm Tree in London. Two comedies, *The Stubbornness of Geraldine* and *The Girl with the Green Eyes*, were produced in 1902, and the following year Fitch wrote *Major André*, his version of the spy drama, which remained his particular favorite.

Many of his plays were written for particular stars, in the prevailing fashion of the time, and because of this his excellent characterization of contemporary life was somewhat weakened by an awareness of what the public wanted. His work therefore never quite reached the fulfillment of his promise, although his comedy, *The Truth* (1906), a study of a congenital liar, received international acclaim. Although a failure when it opened in New York in 1907, it was produced in London the same year, starring Marie Tempest, with great success. Subsequently it returned to America and had many successful tours and revivals.

His last play (written in 1909, the year of his death), *The City*, was an excellent study of a small-town family suffering under the stresses of life in a big city. His characters were drawn with understanding and sympathy, and it is for this that he is best remembered. Without doubt his plays were excellent acting vehicles and his work as a serious dramatist might have reached greater heights had he been less successful in providing works of the moment.

WILLIAM VAUGHAN MOODY

A greater step forward in American drama was made by William Vaughan Moody. A scholar, teacher, and poet, his early verse plays did not receive production in the professional theatre, but he wrote one play which, although opinion is divided on its intrinsic merits, became a popular success in 1906 through its production by Henry Miller with himself and Margaret Anglia in the leading parts. *The Great Divide* had as its main theme the marriage and eventual love of a sensitive girl from the East and a crude character from the Rocky Mountains who had violated her after a gambling match with his two companions. This strong drama, well written and excellently constructed, dealt with fundamental matters in an honest and dignified manner. It was to point the way to that exploration of psychological and social problems which American playwrights of our present age have exploited so notably.

Moody wrote only one other play before his early death in 1910, *The Faith Healer,* which was not a great success, lacking as it did the popular appeal of his earlier play.

THE THEATRE BOOM

During the early years of the twentieth century, many new theatres were built, audiences increased their support and following of their own stars, while managers, actors, and playwrights made fortunes. In spite of occasional failures, there were always opportunities for new ventures, and the economic expansion of the country was reflected in an unprecedented boom in the theatre, alas never to be repeated in our own troubled times.

The Russian Theatre

THE FOUNDING OF THE MOSCOW ART THEATRE

In Russia, as in other European countries at the end of the nine-teenth century, there was a feeling of revolt in the arts. This was manifested in the theatre at first by much talk and theorizing.

In 1897, two men met at a restaurant in Moscow to discuss the formation of a new theatre. They were Vladimir Nemirovich-Danchenko and Constantin Stanislavsky. Danchenko at forty was playwright, critic, and producer, and at that time was also director of the Philharmonic, one of the two dramatic academies in Moscow. Stanislavsky was a well-to-do merchant of thirty-six, who some years previously had formed a group of actors, all amateurs, in order to pro-duce interesting and unusual plays. Both men were dissatisfied with conditions in the theatres at that time, both had ideas about the way in which plays should be produced, and with Danchenko's students and Stanislavsky's amateurs, they had the nucleus of a permanent company.

When they had finally agreed on the organization of the theatre, they set about raising the necessary funds. This was difficult until an eccentric millionaire merchant named Morozov provided them with the greater part of the money required. They acquired a small theatre in Moscow and called it the Moscow Art Theatre. Stanislavsky was to have charge of the artistic policy and actual direction of the productions, while Danchenko was to choose the plays and control the administration of the theatre. A whole year was spent in preparation for the opening, in welding the two groups together, and in rehearsing a repertoire of several plays.

The policy of the new theatre was to produce plays of distinction by Russian and foreign writers, to subordinate individual acting to the idea of the play itself, to pay great attention to detail and characterization, and to avoid completely the conventional staginess current in the other theatres of the time.

Stanislavsky was a good actor himself, and he appeared in many leading parts; he was also a great director, with a will of iron. With infinite patience, he worked at rehearsals throughout the summer of 1898, the rehearsals being held in a barn in the country just outside Moscow.

INNOVATIONS AT THE MOSCOW ART THEATRE

The method of rehearsal of plays had hitherto been a summary one. The actors would arrive on the stage, be presented with a copy of their parts, and would immediately begin to read their lines and walk about the stage, taking up various "effective" positions. The whole play would be gone through at each rehearsal until the actors were word-perfect, when the play was considered ready for the first performance. The producer suggested the actors' moves on the stage which, if found convenient, were adopted without thought of the dramatic significance of those moves. Often the stars would disagree with the producer, whose authority was little higher than that of a stage manager. On these occasions he would have to give way.

Stanislavsky's methods were quite different. In the first place, there were no stars in the Art Theatre, and all the players were submitted to the most rigid discipline from the director. Rehearsals of a new play would begin, not on the stage, but in the comfort of a private room. This would take the form of a discussion of the play

CONSTANTIN STANISLAVSKY AND NEMIROVICH-DAN-CHENKO These men were the co-founders of the Moscow Art Theatre in 1898.

in which the director and the whole cast would thrash out their ideas of the play and how the various parts should be played. Sometimes the discussion would take place with the author present to explain his ideas of the play. Not until the play had been read and thoroughly understood by all the cast did actual rehearsals begin.

Stanislavsky rehearsed only a small part of the play at one rehearsal—perhaps only one scene, which would be gone over several times until the actors had found the right cadence of voice or the right movements which Stanislavsky had pictured for the characterization. So by rehearsing a scene (or a fragment of a scene) at a time, the whole play would be built up by a concentration of effort on minute detail and by the help of the underlying conception of how the characters would act in real life.

In the other theatres of the time a dress rehearsal was not considered necessary. The players had their own wardrobes and wore what they pleased, often without even consulting the director. The actresses decided what gowns to wear by mutual arrangement so that there should not be a clash of color. Stanislavsky held five or six dress rehearsals of the entire play, and many more of fragments of the play, with leading actors in costume and makeup and with the appropriate scenery. These dress rehearsals of parts of the play took place two months before the final dress rehearsals.

Another principle of the Art Theatre was that each play should
have its own setting, especially designed to suit the theme and mood
of the play. This does not seem an outrageous demand today, but
in those times the theatres usually had a stock of scenery—a draw-
ing-room set, a woods set, and so on—and whatever the setting of
the play this scenery was used. The management of these theatres
having never conceived the idea of attracting artists into the theatre to design the settings, the scenery was painted by a decorator,
a kind of superior stagehand.

A painter of the Russian realistic school, Simov, was brought in
to design the settings. He entered into the task with great enthusiasm, which was matched only by his achievements. Danchenko,
in his book *My Life in the Russian Theatre,* writes of a child in the
audience at a performance of *The Seagull* who turned to its parent
and said, "Mother, let's go into the garden for a walk."

The Art Theatre developed a more naturalistic method of lighting, using much greater variation than was usually thought possible, at times even having so little light on the actors that they were
hardly discernible.

THE DEBUT OF THE MOSCOW ART THEATRE

The first production at the opening of the theatre in October, 1898,
was Tolstoy's *Tsar Feodor,* which was followed by Shakespeare's
Merchant of Venice, two plays by Goldoni, a modern Russian play
by Pisemsky, *The Sunken Bell* by Hauptmann, *Antigone* by Sophocles, *Hedda Gabler* by Ibsen, and *The Seagull* by Chekhov. These
plays became part of the permanent repertoire as they were presented, and were repeated alternately from time to time. Thus the
actors did not have the boring task of playing the same part every
night, but had a variety of parts, and occasionally no part, which
ensured one or two free evenings during the week.

The debut of the new theatre received an appreciative response
from public and press, and although the audiences fell off a little
after the opening, the production of Chekhov's *The Seagull* ensured the ultimate success of the company.

CHEKHOV AND THE MOSCOW ART THEATRE

Chekhov was a doctor who had taken to writing short stories of typical Russian life which brought fame and literary distinction in the award of an Academy prize. He then wrote two one-act farces, vaudeville pieces as he called them—*The Bear* and *The Proposal*—which were successful everywhere. These were followed by *Ivanov*, which achieved only moderate success at a performance in a private theatre.

The Seagull was his first great play. It had been produced at one of the Imperial theatres at St. Petersburg two years previously and had been a complete failure. Although Chekhov attended the rehearsals in St. Petersburg, the actors could make nothing of it. Chekhov had offered the play to the Moscow Small Theatre, the most advanced of the established theatres, but Lensky, the leading actor, had returned the play, advising Chekhov to give up writing for the stage.

Chekhov represented human beings as he observed them in life, and his training as a doctor made his characterizations extremely

SETTING FOR CHEKHOV'S "THE THREE SISTERS" This realistic set was typical of the Moscow Art Theatre's early naturalistic productions.

penetrating. His characters are inseparable from their own particular surroundings, and his plays are full of atmosphere: merged with his dialogue are the sounds of neighbors arriving at the house, the samovar, the rain, and the soft playing of guitar or piano. It can be understood that the actors of the old school, with their staginess of technique and their conventional style, could not hope to portray the author's conception of character and mood.

After the failure of *The Seagull,* Chekhov resolved to write no more for the theatre, but two years later Danchenko persuaded him to let the Art Theatre produce the play.

Stanislavsky's rejection of the old conventional style of acting, in which the player acted set emotions, words, or situations, and his concentration on the individual character by awakening the feelings that the particular character experienced, gave Chekhov the first possibility of a competent interpretation. Only by naturalistic acting can Chekhov's plays seem convincing; with stagey acting the dialogue seems ridiculous.

In his intricate building up of detail to create atmosphere, Stanislavsky sometimes went to extremes. Thus in *Uncle Vanya,* which was produced a year later, mosquito nets appeared on the heads of some of the characters, and the sound of a cricket chirping was heard from behind the stove.

Stanislavsky's production was always theatrical, but not stagey, in that it was real life he reproduced on the stage, but reality enlarged. In historical plays, for instance, if high hats had been worn in the period presented, the characters' hats were made even higher; if long sleeves were worn they would be so long that they had to be tucked in; if a door was to be small it was made so small that the actors had to bend double to pass through.

Stanislavsky had not Chekhov's knowledge of the provincial Russian intelligentsia of the time, with its loves, it tears, its envies, and its quarrels, but he successfully reproduced it on the stage. The greatness of Chekhov is in the lyrical qualities of his plays, which always emerge through the everyday realities of his provincial households.

Although the first season showed a loss, the enthusiastic Morozov made good the loss, and the other shareholders followed suit, so the theatre was safe for the next season. The following season other plays by Hauptmann, Tolstoy, and Shakespeare, together with Chekhov's *Uncle Vanya*, were added to the repertoire. The Art Theatre now gained a considerable reputation and began to make its influence felt in the other theatres.

In 1901 Chekhov's *The Three Sisters*, which had been especially written for the actors at the Art Theatre, was produced there. This is considered their finest production. *The Cherry Orchard* was produced in the spring of 1904. In the summer of that year Chekhov died while on a holiday in Germany.

We can sense Chekhov's awareness of the decay and futility of life among the Russian upper classes in his plays, and it is fascinating to speculate what effects the tremendous events of 1917 might have had on his writing for the theatre.

GORKY AND MAETERLINCK

Another great writer whose work was produced at the Art Theatre was Maxim Gorky. His plays, such as *The Lower Depths* (1902),

COSTUME FOR THE CHARACTER OF "BREAD" This costume was used in the Moscow Art Theatre's production of "The Blue Bird" by Maeterlinck.

dealt in a starkly realistic manner with low life in the vast interior of Russia, and could only have been produced at the Art Theatre. However, the Moscow Art Theatre was not confined entirely to naturalistic productions, and in the production of Maeterlinck's *The Blue Bird* the naturalistic element was entirely subordinated to a spirit of pure fantasy.

GORDON CRAIG

In 1911 Gordon Craig produced *Hamlet* for the Art Theatre, but in his own unique style. Gordon Craig, the son of Ellen Terry, had begun his career acting in Irving's company. After two or three years, deciding that he could no longer continue as part of a system for which he had no sympathy, he resigned from a well-paid position in order to formulate his own conception of the production of plays and the way the theatre should be organized. He evolved ideas which were so revolutionary at that time that he could find no outlet for his work, and he was compelled, in order to make a living, to write and publish his ideas and to make designs for settings, chiefly through the medium of woodcuts.

His chief objection to contemporary staging lay in the fact that on the stage the actors were three-dimensional flesh-and-blood characters who reproduced the story of the play, while the scenery merely served as a background and was largely two-dimensional. Craig conceived a bigger function for the setting; as with the actors, it should be three-dimensional, and it should play an integral part in the telling of the story or the portraying of the mood of the play. In other words, the scenery should be made to act in coordination with the players.

Craig designed settings which were composed chiefly of simple abstract forms, stairways, rostrums, blocks, and cubes, the whole effect presenting a great variety of planes. By throwing various kinds of colored lighting on the surfaces of these planes and arranging the lighting to come from different angles, he was able to achieve an appearance of change and movement, although the actual setting remained static. The actors' positions on the stage were worked out as a part of the complete setting, so that actors and scenery, both three-dimensional, formed an integral whole.

The scene painter, with years of development in representing a three-dimensional effect in two dimensions, was rejected by Craig as an anachronism. Craig's settings were usually painted in a neutral color, and lighting was the sole means of producing colored effects. Craig was the first man to understand the tremendous value of shadows in producing dramatic effect.

His method meant, of course, the complete subordination of the actor to the will of the director, for the latter would conceive the dramatic idea of the play, design the setting, arrange the lighting, and dictate the movement and speech of the actors. In those days in England, when the actor-manager was supreme, Craig found no enthusiasm for his ideas, and he has never been able to run a theatre in England.

He went to Italy to live, where he had an opportunity to study the theatre of the past and to develop his ideas further. He published a periodical called *The Mask* for many years in order to propagate his ideas and, incidentally, to earn a living. He started a dramatic school which unfortunately came to an end during the First World War. His writing and woodcut designs, however, found their way all over Europe, and his influence has been great, particularly in Germany, although he has had little influence in England, being regarded primarily as a scenic designer and secondly as a graphic artist. In Germany Adolphe Appia developed along similar lines to Craig, and was particularly noted for his staging of Wagner's operas.

In his formal production of *Hamlet* at Moscow, Craig used a series of screens which could be placed in a variety of positions, thus creating a complete change in the shape of the scene with very little actual movement. His work there, however, was considered to be little more than a novelty, and the Art Theatre remained a stronghold of naturalistic representation. What Craig's system and Stanislavsky's had in common was the unity among the various elements of production imposed by the director with strict discipline over actors and technicians of the theatre.

ACTORS AT THE ART THEATRE

By this time the Art Theatre was firmly established, and it had produced some fine actors apart from Stanislavsky, including Katchalov, Luzhsky, Gribunin, and Moskvin. The actresses never reached the heights of achievement of the men, but those who stood out were Knipper, who married Chekhov, Stanislavsky's wife, Marie Lilina, Germanova, Zhdanova, and Butova.

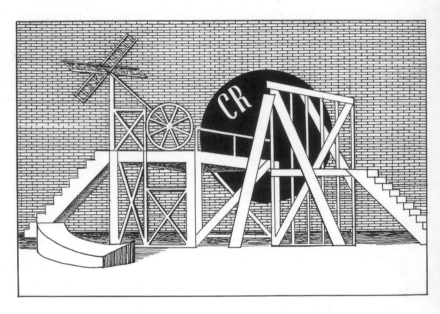

EARLY CONSTRUCTIVIST SET FOR A MEYERHOLD PRODUCTION

MEYERHOLD AND THE REVOLT AGAINST NATURALISM

Other theatres began to revolutionize their productions, sometimes in an entirely new direction. Meyerhold was probably the first and most important director to break away from the Art Theatre's naturalism. He was originally one of Danchenko's most promising students at his dramatic academy, the Philharmonic, and when the Art Theatre was founded he played in the early productions, notably as Treplef in *The Seagull* and the Baron in *The Three Sisters*.

Although an accomplished actor, Meyerhold's ambition was to direct, and after a few years with the Art Theatre he left to direct productions at the theatre of Vera Komisarjevskaya, a noted actress of the time. (Her brother, who was also developing his powers as a director there, was later to have his own theatre after the Revolution, and subsequently came to England and America to work as a director.) After a short period at this theatre, Meyerhold became director at the two Imperial theatres in St. Petersburg, the Alexandrinsky and the Marinsky.

Meyerhold was never satisfied with the intimate atmosphere of the Art Theatre, nor with the policy of naturalistic representation. In a way his ideals were more in keeping with the Elizabethan stage. He rejected the conventional stage picture seen by the audience through the "picture frame" of the proscenium arch, and he wanted the audience to be much closer to the actors and to play more than the passive part of merely watching the performance. Meyerhold regarded the audience as an integral part of the performance. At first he swept away the footlights and curtain in the large Imperial theatres and brought back the apron stage. Scenery was largely dispensed with, the bare wall at the back of the stage becoming visible to the audience, and ramps were constructed to lead from the stage to the auditorium.

The plays presented were chiefly the classics, but the scripts were completely re-edited by Meyerhold, who adopted a kind of film technique in cutting them up into a series of short episodes. Later, after the Revolution, when there were more contemporary plays

COSTUME FOR A MEYERHOLD CONSTRUCTVIST PRODUCTION

dealing with the recent upheaval of social forces, Meyerhold introduced crowd scenes, with the actors in ordinary day clothes and without makeup, thus making them indistinguishable from the audience.

ABSTRACT SETTINGS

Meyerhold also developed the use of abstract settings and was influenced by the recent development in pictorial art known as *cubism*. Cubism was a method of representing natural shapes and forms in a geometrical manner; thus a portrait head or a landscape was simplified into an arrangement of cubes or boxlike shapes, together with spheres and other regular forms. It really arose from the period of experiment in the development of painting when the problem of representing the third dimension, depth, was being explored in a new direction.

As with Craig's ideas, Meyerhold's abstract scenery was an attempt to break away from the conventional painted scenery which presented a flat background to the solid figures of the actors. Like

284

Craig, he designed his settings in three dimensions, with the actors as an integral part.

CONSTRUCTIVIST SCENERY

Immediately after the Revolution, a further development in abstract scenery was what has come to be known as *constructivism*. This was, as Komisarjevsky points out, partly thrust upon the theatres of the Revolution by the shortage of canvas in the early days of the young Soviet State. A constructivist setting was non-naturalistic, and consisted of an arrangement of wooden platforms, ladders, steps, and gangways, built as a unit, and giving the actors a great variety of levels, angles, and positions from which they could perform.

In one play, Meyerhold had only the wooden framework of a house, while in others considerable ingenuity was displayed in arranging the various platforms, ladders, and gangways into a pleasing geometrical design, which had the workmanlike effect of some

COSTUME FOR "LA PRINCESSE BRAMBILLE" AT THE KAMERNY THEATRE

piece of constructional engineering. Other theatres at this time also used constructivist settings, necessity becoming the mother of a new and exciting method of staging.

AN ABSTRACT PAINTING The abstract painter forsook the naturalistic rendering of an object and sought, rather, an interesting arrangement of shape, pattern, color, and texture.

EFFECTS OF STAGING INNOVATIONS

It is obvious that the style of acting had to be adapted to these new surroundings. Naturalistic acting would have made the settings appear ridiculous, so acting became more acrobatic and staccato in style.

The theatres in Russia eventually returned to more normal methods of staging as conditions became easier, and although naturalistic presentation is more customary at present, the abstract and constructivist period was useful in clearing away many outmoded and conventional ideas in the theatre. It made possible a new and more balanced conception of the values of the various elements in the theatre, and emphasized the need for a universal and more elastic use of the stage.

SETTING DESIGNED BY FERNAND LEGER FOR A BALLET This set shows the influence of abstract painting.

TAIROV AND THE KAMERNY THEATRE

Another experimental theatre was the Kamerny Theatre which, under its director, Tairov, produced drama, comedy, pantomime, and light opera. The presentation was frankly artificial compared with the Art Theatre's realism, and while no particular stage form was used, each production had a setting particularly suited to it, and it generally moved in the direction of abstract staging.

The impact of the Revolution naturally affected all the theatres, which had either to find new plays by revolutionary writers or to produce the classics in a style accepted by the new spirit of the times. Tairov produced several of Eugene O'Neill's plays, using a formal style, no longer abstract, with settings designed in a naturalistic but simple fashion. The shapes and forms were severe and usually monochromatic. While returning somewhat to the ideas of the Art Theatre, Tairov did not go so far as detailed naturalistic representation, and the actors were types rather than individuals, with their acting generalized rather than detailed in character.

One of the best productions at the Kamerny Theatre was *The Optimistic Tragedy,* by Vishnevsky, which concerned a detachment of sailors fighting in the Revolution. It deals with the War of the Revolution in the manner of an epic poem, and ends with the detachment's being killed off one by one, not in despair but on a note of faith and confirmation of the ideas of the Revolution. The production was presented with clarity and strength, the actors played with sincerity and restraint, and the settings were expressive of the whole struggle. Such an idea, however, to be presented on the stage, needed new forms to express it, new forms which were discovered by experimenting and by assessing new values in the setting, lighting, acting, music, and the various technical equipment of the theatre.

VAKHTANGOV

Vakhtangov, who died in 1922 at an early age, was a director who, although influenced by the Moscow Art Theatre, developed acting technique in a different direction. He saw the dangers in the exaggeration of characterization based on an inner personality, which might easily develop into a series of emotional experiences too psychological to be "good theatre." The actors of the Art Theatre built their characterizations on their conception of the mind of the particular character. Vakhtangov's actors based their interpretations on their conception of the actions of the character.

Vakhtangov's best-known production was *Princess Turandot*, a formal production that employed an abstract setting. His production methods, like Meyerhold's, made necessary the drastic editing or rewriting of the plays.

After his death the Vakhtangov Theatre produced *Hamlet*, completely ignoring the philosophical side of the play and interpreting it as a struggle for the throne between heir and usurper.

THE MOSCOW ART THEATRE AND THE REVOLUTION

What is so remarkable about the Russian theatres is that they withstood the impact of the First World War and the Revolution. Between 1914 and 1917 only three new plays were produced at the Art Theatre owing to its difficulty in getting suitable works, as it refused to produce examples of reactionary drama. It continued giving performances of its repertoire of Chekhov, Gorky, and the classics. The young Soviet Government saw the educational value of the theatres, and gave them all the material help possible when necessary. Stanislavsky and Danchenko remained the directors of the Art Theatre, which by now had a second theatre and two music studios for producing opera and musical drama.

The Art Theatre changed its name to the Moscow Gorky Theatre, but took some time to adjust itself to the needs of the Soviet. Several of its best actors had been touring in the country and were cut off by the fighting, so it was not until about 1924 that the theatre recovered its old unity. By this time, in addition to the older actors, there were the youngsters who had grown up with the Revolution. The repertoire of classics was still retained, and new plays were gradually introduced.

The policy of the supreme importance of the individual, which had been the Art Theatre's guiding star to fame in the past, had to be subjugated to political needs, to the portrayal of social justice and purpose. The production of *The Armoured Train*, by Ivanov, marked the final adjustment to the needs of the Soviet regime.

In 1930 Tolstoy's *Resurrection* was an outstanding production of the Art Theatre. The play was about life in Tsarist Russia, and the most interesting feature of the production was the commentator, played by the great actor Katchalov, who stood in the orchestra and interpreted the author's and the theatre's views on the past.

The productions of the Art Theatre were still realistic, but of a painted rather than a photographic realism. In the past the Art Theatre had kept out of politics; now it devoted certain productions to the political problems of the day.

The actor remained the most important element in the productions, and his purpose was to disclose the philosophical ideas underlying the plays through the creation of great characters. During the revolutionary period of the theatre, acting had to be simple and sincere, all subtlety was lost, and any false declamatory style would have been quite out of place.

THE SOVIET THEATRE

Now that the period of revolution in the theatre—which manifested itself by the searching for new forms, the development of new techniques, and the acquirement of new values—has passed, certain common principles have been established in all Soviet theatres. Neither time nor expense is spared in the preparation of new plays or in the fresh presentation of the classics. In every production the Soviet has accepted the Art Theatre's principle of complete unity of all the elements of the theatre—acting, scenery, lighting, and technical equipment—and of the form that the production will take. This unity must express the idea of the play, whether it be of a philosophical or of a social nature. Cubism, constructivism, or abstraction in any form has been rejected, whether it is present for a purely experimental or aesthetic reason or for its own sake.

During the thirties, the Russian Government exerted a more posi-

A CUBIST PAINTING   This oil indicates how the cubist painter broke down a natural form into geometric patterns.

A SURREALIST PAINTING   The surrealist artist attempted to create a dreamlike atmosphere by distorting naturalistic objects. A weird landscape was commonly employed for background.

SETTING FOR "ROMEO AND JULIET"   Presented at the Kamerny Theatre and designed by Alexander Exter, this set shows cubist influence.

tive political influence on the theatre. The policy of socialist realism was rigidly enforced, and some of the individuals who felt that their work could only thrive in an atmosphere of freedom, like Meyerhold, disappeared from the scene, never to return.

The theatres continued to operate during the Second World War, although the propaganda plays presented are unlikely to survive.

After the long years of Stalin's domination, when the Party line had to be strictly adhered to, a certain relaxation has come, and there is currently a greater freedom in the theatre. Okhlopov, who was a leading pupil of Meyerhold's, is now Director of the Mayakovsky Theatre, where he has staged Pogodin's *Aristocrats* in the arena style of his original production at the Realistic Theatre. The comedies of Mayakovsky, which were previously proscribed for their satirical comments on Party bureaucrats and bourgeois mentality (*The Bath House, The Bed-Bug,* and *Mystery-Bouffe*) are now popular offerings at Moscow's Satiric Theatre. The Moscow Gorky Theatre has even staged Arthur Miller's *Death of a Salesman.*

It is too early as yet to foresee what will happen in the future, but theatrical people are much the same the world over, and it is likely that they will seize the opportunity to develop further the theories and ideas of staging which so distinguished the experiments of their predecessors in the early years of the Revolution. The need for freedom of expression, in both the writing of plays and in methods of staging them, is essential to an experimental theatre from which any advance is to be made.

COSTUME FOR "ROMEO AND JULIET" A character on the stage of the Kamerny Theatre.

English Theatre
of the 20th Century

DISSATISFACTION WITH THE STATE OF THE THEATRE

Toward the end of the nineteenth century, a feeling of dissatisfaction with the state of things in the theatre arose in Europe among some theatregoers. This manifested itself in the formation, in most countries, of small groups of individuals who joined together with the common purpose of encouraging writers and directors of serious contemporary plays that would be unlikely to receive production in the established theatres. In spite of technical advances in the theatre during the century and the inevitable development of realism in presentation, the staginess of the acting and the commercial manager system, with its emphasis on starring roles, were a disappointment to many people. The new plays produced, although excellent vehicles for the star players, were usually without any great literary merit and did not arouse much serious thought in their audiences, being primarily intended to entertain or amuse.

GHOSTS

In London, a group was formed by J. T. Grein with the object of producing, at a series of semiprivate performances, Continental and British plays which would hardly see production on the popular stage. Ibsen's *Ghosts* was produced by Grein's Independent Theatre Group (later to become the Stage Society) in 1891, its first production in England.

It is impossible to estimate the great importance Ibsen has had on dramatists of the present century. He is the first great playwright to delve below the surface of polite behavior seeking out fundamental urges and to express them in cleverly constructed plays set in the matter-of-fact surroundings of provincial towns and delivered in simple everyday language.

Ghosts was censored by the Lord Chamberlain, who to this day can prevent a work from receiving public performance in Britain should it not conform to certain requirements. His powers of veto, however, are not extended to plays produced for members of a club or association, so *Ghosts* received its first performance by the Independent Theatre Group.

This play, when first produced in Ibsen's native Norway, received much adverse criticism, and although it was not without advocates of stature, much abuse was showered on its production in London. With its story of the shams and hypocrisy of an arranged marriage and the implication of venereal disease, insanity, and euthanasia it was at the time perhaps too powerful and daring in dealing with subjects which could hardly be mentioned in polite society. The years since then have brought greater understanding.

Ghosts is an immensely actable play, particularly the central character of Mrs. Alving, who remains faithful to her dissolute husband, to find in later life that her son is doomed to insanity through congenital venereal disease. The husband, who is dead before the play begins, pervades the entire action of the drama by his influence on the interplay between all the characters—in the stupidity of Manders, the hypocritical pastor; in Regina, the maid of the household; in Engstrand the carpenter, her supposed father; in Oswald, the son, who becomes fatalistic in his acceptance of an early death; and in the suffering of Mrs. Alving, powerless to prevent the evil consequences of that influence.

IBSEN'S INFLUENCE

Ibsen's method of implying certain truths by raising questions to which he provides no answer is one which has been carried further and in various directions by many later playwrights, notably Strindberg, Shaw, Galsworthy, and Chekhov. *Ghosts* was written in 1881 after Ibsen had spent many years in the theatre. His early plays were in the main poetical and historical works such as *The Warriors at Helgeland* and *The Pretenders*. He went to live in Rome in 1864 and produced *Brand*, his first major poetical drama of contemporary Norwegian life, dealing with the grim tragedy of a poor minister who refuses to compromise in his struggles against the forces of a materialistic society. *Peer Gynt*, which followed in 1867, is perhaps the greatest of his early verse plays. With its fascinating, highly irresponsible and selfish character of Peer and its long passages of lyrical beauty it is in some ways complementary to *Brand* in expressing national characteristics. Ibsen's first prose work, a satire on the politics of the time, *The League of Youth*, followed in 1869. He then went back to the days of early Christianity under the Emperor Julian for his theme in *Emperor and Galilean*, which was completed in 1873.

It is, however, Ibsen's next plays, written between 1875 and 1882 —realistic dramas of small-town life in which he exposes the hypocrisy, lies, and meanness of parochial society—which have had the greatest influence on the drama of our time. *The Pillars of Society, A Doll's House, Ghosts,* and *An Enemy of the People* are plays which, although set in his own country, have a universal validity.

In *The Wild Duck* (1884) he introduced an element of symbolism which was to pervade his later plays, but it remains perhaps his most appealing and beautiful work. *Rosmersholm* and *The Lady from the Sea* followed, in which Ibsen delved further into the psychology of personality, which is expressed even more powerfully in

Hedda Gabler, a study of an emotional woman whose bitter envy and obsession for what she does not possess leads to tragedy. *Hedda Gabler* has naturally attracted some of the greatest actresses of the times. In England Mrs. Patrick Campbell, Laura Cowie, Jean Forbes-Robertson, and Peggy Ashcroft have played the part with great distinction; while in America Mrs. Fiske, Nazimova, and Eva Le Gallienne have also been highly successful.

In *The Master Builder* (1892) Ibsen pursues the element of symbolism still further in this drama of youth and age and the artist in society, a theme which he continues to some extent in all his last plays —*Little Eyolf, John Gabriel Borkman,* and *When We Dead Awaken* —written between 1894 and 1899. He died in 1906.

As a craftsman in the theatre Ibsen was a great reformer. Observing as he does the unities of time and place, he drops the artificial methods of the soliloquy for revealing the thoughts of his characters; yet in his dialogue of everyday language it is what he implies in the wealth of meaning *behind* the words and actions of his characters that gives his work its stature. Through his plays he is somewhat an observer of life, exposing the evils, the follies, and stupidities; recognizing the importance of sexual attraction; revealing both the weakness and the strength of individuals in their reactions to the implied rules of a materialistic society. Yet he offers no solution to the problems inherent in his exposition. He was no social reformer; he offers us no way out, only a plea for understanding.

THE COMEDY OF MANNERS

Although the way was now open for dramatists to express a more profound and serious view of life in writing for the stage, and generally this occurred in work such as that of John Galsworthy, there was a reaction to the domestic drama of the late Victorian period in other directions. A revival of the comedy of manners in the witty, satirical plays of Oscar Wilde, the fantasy and imagination displayed in the works of James Barrie, among others, somewhat offset the seriousness of the themes revealed in such problem plays as those of Galsworthy.

OSCAR WILDE

The first important success of Oscar Wilde, *Lady Windermere's Fan*, was staged in 1892 at St. James's Theatre by Sir George Alexander, a leading actor-manager. It contains the strong part of Mrs. Erlynne, originally played by Marion Terry, and some very witty lines for the men. Wilde's epigrams and the brilliance of his dialogue, with its sharpness of satire and wit, brought him great popularity in the 1890's.

A Woman of No Importance was produced by Tree at the Haymarket in 1893. It was a success, although it is the weakest of his plays. In 1895, he wrote his two best plays, *An Ideal Husband*, a play involving political intrigue (perhaps to give more substance to his work), and the lighthearted gallop, *The Importance of Being Earnest*, with its hilarious picture of a grand lady of Victorian society vetting the suitability of marriage partners for her daughter and nephew. Wilde, like Sheridan, wrote these plays at breakneck speed, but when played by expert actors they retain their appeal.

He wrote one other play, *Salome,* in French for Sarah Bernhardt, although she never undertook the part when it was produced in Paris. A poetic fantasy on the biblical theme, it was censored in England, although it was later made into an opera with music by Richard Strauss.

JAMES M. BARRIE

James M. Barrie had already made a reputation as a novelist before turning to the theatre with a dramatization of his *The Little Minister,* which proved to be as popular on the stage as in the book. *Quality Street* in 1902 was also a great success, giving a well-considered picture of a bygone age. *The Admirable Crichton,* written the same year, is a delightful comedy of a shipwrecked upper-class family, helpless and pathetic on a desert island, whose butler and maid find a new status when their natural leadership is asserted, a leadership which is swiftly relinquished when the family is rescued and returns to its old home. Underlying the topsyturvey-dom of the escapade is a delicious satire of social distinction.

Peter Pan, perhaps the best known and most continually successful of Barrie's fantasies, the story of the boy who never grew up, was written for children and its royalties were donated to a famous London children's hospital. It is performed every year at Christmastime in London, has been seen as a musical in New York, and remains a delight to both children and adults.

What Every Woman Knows (1908) is a well-constructed comedy of the unseen power of woman over her man. The fantasy of the real and an imagined world is delightfully blended in his later plays, *Dear Brutus* and *Mary Rose,* written in 1917 and 1920. His last work, *The Boy David,* was a serious attempt to present the well-known Bible story in contemporary terms. It was not seen on the stage until 1936, when the part was played by Elisabeth Bergner for whom it had originally been written, but it was considered too lighthearted a piece for the subject and was not a success.

Barrie wrote many other plays, some of which were short pieces, and in all of them he displayed a mastery of stage effect. Although his impish delight in underlining the fact that things are never what they seem leads him at times to sentimentality, he revealed much in life of great beauty, giving his works a timelessness which enables them to be constantly revived.

JOHN GALSWORTHY

John Galsworthy also made a reputation as a novelist before writing for the theatre. His great novel of late Victorian society, *The Forsyte Saga,* in which he aptly describes the changing social patterns of his time through the characters he creates with consummate skill and understanding, remains a masterpiece of English literature.

The Silver Box was his first play, written for Granville-Barker and produced by him at the Court Theatre in 1906. In this, as in many of his plays, Galsworthy was concerned with the social injustice of one law for the rich and another for the poor. The action of the play hinges on the drunken son of a well-to-do family who takes into his home Jones, the husband of the family charwoman, for a final drink. Jones takes a silver cigarette case from the house and a purse which the young man himself had taken from an earlier party. Mrs. Jones is charged with stealing, but although she is eventually discharged, Jones is convicted, while the young man goes scot free.

Galsworthy's characters are never stock types, but are drawn from his own acute observation of life. There are no heroes and no true villains. His plays are realistically written in simple language, with no false heroics or artificial devices. What makes them so distinguished is that his sympathy for the underdog and his great belief in humanity in conflict with the conventions of society are made so convincing through the ordinary everyday dialogue.

In *Strife* (1906) he deals with labor relations in a tinplate works and the effects of a strike on the members of both sides of the conflict, which in the end leads to purposeless tragedy. In *Justice*, Galsworthy draws on the experiences of his early life as a barrister for the action, which takes place in a solicitor's office, a court of justice, and a prison, and in which the plight of two young lovers ends in tragedy. The first production of this play at the Duke of York's Theatre in 1910 was distinguished by many fine actors, including Dion Boucicault, Edmund Gwenn, Charles Maude, and Lewis Casson.

Among Galsworthy's other works, the most important are perhaps *The Pigeon, The Eldest Son, Escape, The Fugitive, The Mob, The Skin Game,* and *Loyalties,* although he wrote many others which were consistently successful. His enduring qualities lie in the serious questioning of the cruelty, ugliness, poverty, and the elements of chance that in real life so often create the circumstances in which the individual finds himself imprisoned. He was, however, unable to present in his plays the more rounded view of life evident in his novels, and there is no humor or optimism to be found in them.

GEORGE BERNARD SHAW

Standing apart in his own prolific writings for the theatre is George Bernard Shaw, who learned much from Ibsen in the underlying seriousness of his themes, yet in his fifty plays expressed his ideas with a sense of aptness, logic, and whimsical speculation that has made him one of the greatest dramatists of our time. He approaches Wilde in wit, excels Barrie in fantasy, and his themes are deeper in implication than those of Galsworthy. He was, above all, eloquent. His plays were published with extremely detailed stage directions and prefaces intended to be read in which he postulates his ideas of social and political reform.

In contrast with Ibsen, Shaw seeks an answer to the problems inherent in the world in which he lives. The evils of slum landlords, prostitution, the cant of the medical profession, the hypocrisy of certain aspects of religious belief, the needless tragedy of war, and the economic power of the great industrialists—in fact the whole question of life itself—provided a basis for his questioning, rational outlook. Yet he did not use the stage merely as a platform to air his theories of reform. He was a great dramatist by his extraordinary power of stimulating thought through the dialogue between his very individual characters, created in a fresh dramatic mold.

Little happens in a Shaw play except talk—but what talk! what eloquence!—a continuous rain of paradox, satire, a shattering of established beliefs, an exposing of false ideals, a questioning of almost every social convention, leavened with a riotous humor and a sparkling wit which hold his audience spellbound. His power of language, the breadth and depth of his knowledge and intellect, the clearness of his vision, bring to the theatre a distinction of thought unequaled in this century. He can fairly be called the father of the theatre of ideas.

Shaw started late as a dramatist, after years as a novelist and a critic of books, music, and art, as well as drama. He was persuaded by J. T. Grein to write something for the Independent Theatre Group after the production of *Ghosts* already mentioned. *Widowers' Houses,* already begun some years earlier during a period of collaboration with William Archer, was completed and received its first production in 1892. It was received with very mixed feelings by the audience of the day. The younger, more liberal elements applauded its obvious attack on vested interests, while the more conservative minded regarded him as subversive and as introducing political matters which they considered outside the sphere of the theatre.

The encouragement that Shaw gained from seeing his work on the stage set him to writing plays in earnest. The following year saw *The Philanderer*, a lighthearted comedy on a subject he rarely touched—sexual attraction—and *Mrs. Warren's Profession*, a serious play dealing with prostitution. The latter was not produced until 1902 by the Stage Society, and did not see a public performance until the Lord Chamberlain's veto was relaxed in 1920. When the play was first produced by Arnold Daly in New York during a two-month season of Shaw's plays, the police arrested Daly, Mary Shaw his leading actress, and other members of the cast as a result of complaints by the more shocked members of the audience. The judge, who had the advantage of knowing neither the author nor the play, after suspending proceedings while he took a week to read the play, returned to acquit the company as he pronounced nothing wrong with it.

The American theatre has always made Shaw welcome on its stages, and no less than nine of his plays were first produced there, chiefly by the Theatre Guild. Indeed, *The Devil's Disciple*, with Richard Mansfield as Dick Dudgeon, was played in America two years before the first London production.

These three plays were published together with another three—*Arms and the Man, Candida,* and *The Man of Destiny*—in 1898 as *Plays Pleasant and Unpleasant*, with prefaces and very detailed descriptions of the characters and stage directions intended to be read as literature. *Arms and the Man*, an antiromantic view of Balkan cloak-and-dagger warfare, was remarkably forward thinking in its view of the successful conduct of military operations as businesslike and efficient as the Swiss hotel that its hero, Captain Bluntschli, inherits. *Candida* is a domestic play with a strong title role, a woman who has to make a choice between an adoring youthful poet and her middle-aged husband, an idealistic and philanthropic cler-gyman. *The Man of Destiny* is a short play that gives an unconven-tional picture of Napoleon.

Before the 1890's dramatists in England were wary of publishing their plays because of the laxity of the copyright laws in America, but an agreement in 1891 gave them the opportunity of publishing with full protection. Thus the works of the important writers for the theatre rapidly enjoyed wide interest and in many cases brought them not only literary fame but royalties from worldwide produc-tion by both amateur groups and repertory theatres.

Although it was some considerable time before Shaw gained com-plete popularity as a dramatist, he poured out plays in the following years. *You Never Can Tell* (1896) was an amusing light comedy, as "commercial" as any seen in the theatre at that time. A melo-drama set in the time of the American Revolutionary War, *The Devil's Disciple*, followed, also in 1896. *Caesar and Cleopatra* was written in 1897 (perhaps as a challenge to Shakespeare) for Shaw's favorite actor, Forbes-Robertson, and *Captain Brassbound's Conver-sion*, a tilt at imperialism, was especially written for Ellen Terry. In 1900 he wrote *The Admirable Bashville*, based on his earlier un-successful novel.

The next year saw one of his greatest plays, *Man and Superman*, in which, perhaps, his pen ran away with him. This play, which may be briefly described as a parable of love and life, romantic and realistic, has a play within a play, the third act, which is a scene of Don Juan in Hell, in which the main characters of the play appear. Jack Tanner, the liberal free thinker, appears as Don Juan, Anne Whitefield as Donna Anna, Roebuck Ramsden as the statue of the Commander, and Mendoza, the bandit chief, as the Devil. They engage in a long and amusing discussion on the advantages of being in either heaven or hell. This third act makes the complete play too long for practical purposes in the theatre (although it has been per-formed in its entirety, notably by Esmé Percy), but the play is often given successfully without it.

Shaw's Irish origin and his friendship with W. B. Yeats encouraged him to write *John Bull's Other Island* for the Abbey Theatre in Dublin in 1904, but the play failed, although the dramatization of English and Irish characters and attitudes was wonderfully apt and is still basically valid. At the request of Arnold Daly he wrote *How He Lied to Her Husband*, another short play to complete the bill with *The Man of Destiny*.

Major Barbara (1905) was an attack on the power of the great munitions manufacturers, with a glimpse of the work of the Salvation Army in its fight against the evils of poverty and drink. The following year came *The Doctor's Dilemma*, a tragicomedy in which the medical profession, almost the bitterest of Shaw's detestations, is mercilessly exposed. In 1908 *Getting Married*, a discussion of divorce and marriage, was followed by *The Showing-up of Blanco Posnet* (1909); *Misalliance* (1910), in which religion and eugenics are considered; and *Fanny's First Play* (1911), an attack on suburbia and drama critics. In this play, Shaw drew on his own experiences by introducing real critics into his cast, thinly disguised under other names. Trotter, for instance, was a recognizable portrait of the *Times* critic of the day, A. B. Walkley.

Shaw chose the Roman period of early Christianity for *Androcles and the Lion* in 1912, and the same year produced one of his best plays, *Pygmalion*, for Mrs. Patrick Campbell, whom he much admired and who made a brilliant success of the role of Eliza. This play has become more widely known through the film of the same name and, further, from the musical version, *My Fair Lady*, one of the greatest successes of our time.

Some lesser works were written during the next few years, which also cover the period of the First World War, when the time was not ripe for the performance of serious works. But during this period Shaw began writing *Heartbreak House* (which saw completion in 1919), a comedy with a Chekhovian flavor which must be ranked with his best plays. His next great work, *Back to Methuselah*, a collection of five plays, was about life itself and the conse-

quences of an enormous increase in longevity, in which the last
part is set 30,000 years in the future. This was first produced in
America by the Theatre Guild.

Shaw's next great work was his interpretation of medieval history
in *Saint Joan* (1923), in which Sybil Thorndike was a great success
in the London production. Then, in 1930, *The Apple Cart* was produced, in which that fine actor, Cedric Hardwicke, gave an excellent performance as the wily and intelligent King Magnus, manip-
ulating the weaknesses of his ministers. *Too True to be Good,* a
fantasy completed in 1931, introduced many interesting characters,
including Private Meek, based on Shaw's own friend (Aircraftsman
Shaw), T. E. Lawrence. In the next two years he wrote *Village
Wooing, On the Rocks, The Simpleton of the Unexpected Isles,*
and *The Six of Calais,* which are perhaps not as dramatically strong
as his previous works, although they are, as usual, full of exciting
dialogue. *The Millionairess* followed in 1936, another play with a
dynamic bossy woman as the main character, which has given many
fine actresses a wonderful opportunity, including Ellen Pollock
and Katharine Hepburn.

With the rise of fascism in Europe *Geneva,* written in 1938,
reflected Shaw's awareness of the coming struggle for power, although his caricatures of Mussolini and Hitler (in Bombardone and
Battler) seem perhaps too lighthearted in the event. *Buoyant Bil-
lions,* a play put together from earlier fragments, was produced in
1939. His last play, *In Good King Charles's Golden Days,* was written when he was eighty-three, and gives us a picture of a sympathetic and intelligent monarch in the days of the Restoration.
Shaw lived, still writing on a wide range of topics, until his ninety-
fifth year.

Shaw was never completely popular with London audiences until J. E. Vedreune and Harley Granville-Barker introduced a repertory season at the Court Theatre in Sloane Square between 1904
and 1907 during which no less than eleven of his plays were performed, together with other fine productions of Euripides, Maeter-

SYBIL THORNDIKE As St. Joan, the actress appears in the original production of Shaw's play at the New Theatre, London, 1924. It had a successful run of 244 performances.

linck, Hauptmann, Yeats, Masefield, Galsworthy, and Granville-Barker's own dramas.

Shaw took an active interest in the productions of his plays, taking many rehearsals and going over the plays in every detail, explaining and demonstrating how each character should speak. Most of his life he retained this practical interest in the stage, and should any producer decide to present a Shaw play at a time when he was conveniently nearby he would descend on the theatre during rehearsals to give the actors first-hand knowledge of his intentions in writing the piece. The writer remembers a fascinating time when the Open Air Theatre at Regent's Park was rehearsing *Androcles and the Lion* and Shaw demonstrated with great ability the most effective way of drawing the lion's cage onto the greensward which serves as a stage in those sylvan surroundings.

HARLEY GRANVILLE-BARKER

Granville Barker was a fine combination of scholar and theatrical craftsman of artistic sensibility. Apart from his plays, the chief of which are *The Voysey Inheritance* and *The Madras House,* he wrote prefaces to Shakespeare, the fruit of his own notable productions of Shakespeare at the Savoy Theatre in 1912 and his own researches and studies. He was responsible for a new attitude toward stage presentation, using simplified settings (in contrast with the elaborated stage pictures of the customary West End production), which he was to develop further in his season at Wallack's Theatre in New York in 1915. He was an indefatigable worker for the institution of a National Theatre in England, of which Shaw was also an ardent and active supporter. Neither saw its eventual birth and extraordinary success at the Old Vic in 1962.

SHAW AT THE MALVERN FESTIVAL

In his later years Shaw had the advantage of seeing his plays at the Malvern Festival which, from 1929, Sir Barry Jackson, the founder of the famous Birmingham Repertory Theatre, ran for a month each summer. Although other plays were presented by such drama-

tists as Sheridan, Fielding, Ben Jonson, Nicolas Udall, Dion Boucicault, Rudolph Besier, James Bridie, J. B. Priestley, C. K.
Munro, and Lord Dunsany, Shaw was always strongly represented, and the
first season the repertory was confined to his works: *The Apple
Cart, Back to Methuselah, Caesar and Cleopatra,* and *Heartbreak
House.* Seven of Shaw's plays received their first performance at the
Festival and these were generally transferred later to London. Lec-
tures and discussions on the theatre were given during the Festival,
which attracted large numbers of interested parties—critics from
London, writers, producers, actors, and good enthusiastic audiences.

REVIVAL OF INTEREST IN SHAW

Although interest in Shaw's plays had slackened in England in the
last decade or so, there has been a sudden revival, and in the current season very successful productions have been staged in London
of *Fanny's First Play, Too True to be Good, Man and Superman,*
and *You Never Can Tell.* After a period of somber new plays with
rather sordid themes and commonplace dialogue, audiences are welcoming the wit, humor, and fantasy of Shaw as sparkling cham-
pagne after a diet of small beer.

THE ABBEY THEATRE

During the early years of the century, the rising Nationalist movement in Ireland found expression in Dublin's Abbey Theatre, where
the poet W. B. Yeats and Lady Gregory began a theatre in 1904 devoted to Irish themes and works by native dramatists. Within a few
years the Abbey gained a worldwide reputation as a repertory theatre based on a policy of presenting, in a simple but lively manner,
plays dealing with every aspect of Irish life. Both the founders were
dramatists of distinction, and others were attracted to it, including
J. M. Synge, A. E. (George William Russell), Lennox Robinson,
Padraic Colum, and St. John Ervine.

Lady Gregory and J. M. Synge wrote plays in the idiom of the
country people of Western Ireland by making a close study of dialect and their means of expression. This practice of a living "lan-

guage of the folk" has been maintained by other Irish dramatists, so the rich poetic fantasy of Irish speech found expression in the fine acting of the Abbey players and in the works of their own dramatists.

The Abbey continues to the present time, and of the later writers associated with it he most important are Denis Johnston, Paul Vincent Carroll, and Sean O'Casey, although these playwrights have been more widely produced in England and America.

SEAN O'CASEY

Sean O'Casey wrote some extremely powerful dramas of Dublin slum life in *Juno and the Paycock* and *Shadow of a Gunman,* in which the bitter strife of the years between 1915 and 1922 in Ireland is the background to laughter and tears. *The Plough and the Stars* was an even stronger tragic play about the Easter Uprising of 1916 and proved too powerful for the audience of the Abbey at its opening. His antiwar play, *The Silver Tassie,* with its skillful blending of naturalism and symbolism, remains to many critics the greatest expression of his deeply spiritual, if somewhat bitter, view of life.

THE GATE

A special branch of Irish drama was devoted to works in the Gaelic language. The first play was produced by the Abbey in 1901, the work of Douglas Hyde, who was the pioneer in this field. But others have followed, including the fine actor Micheal MacLiammior, who was one of the founders of the second Dublin theatre of note, The Gate. This was started in 1928 with aims, complementary to the Abbey, of presenting plays from all periods and of international importance such as works by Aeschylus, Shakespeare, Ibsen, Strindberg, Chekhov, Shaw, Eugene O'Neill, and Elmer Rice, as well as by Irish writers whose work was different in style and subject from that produced at the Abbey.

IRISH ACTORS

The Irish theatre not only has had great significance in both England and America, it has produced some notable actors who have frequently been seen in those two countries, such as Sara Allgood and her sister Maire O'Neill, Dudley Digges, Barry Fitzgerald, Siobhan McKenna, and the already-mentioned Micheal MacLiammior.

W. SOMERSET MAUGHAM

Among the large number of writers for the English theatre who established themselves in the period between the two wars, some of them still active at the present, is a group whose plays can be broadly described as the social comedy of manners. Established by Oscar Wilde in the 1890's, the success of these plays depends on the brilliance of their wit, excellent characterization, and the dexterity of their stage craftsmanship.

Without doubt, the greatest of these dramatists is Somerset Maugham, who wrote over thirty plays between 1896 and 1933. He was a superb storyteller who could create characters and situations with implications more profound than is at first apparent in his dialogue. The performance of his plays by such stylish actors as Marie Lohr, Irene Vanbrugh, Constance Collier, C. Aubrey Smith, Reginald Owen, and A. E. Matthews contributed much to their great success.

Presenting a somewhat sardonic view of humanity, Maugham does not preach, but presents us with a picture of people as they are in life, neither good nor bad, and the clash of personalities in unforeseen situations. In many ways he is the embodiment of the Restoration playwrights, and like them represents a stage of transistion.

Not all his plays run to a pattern, however, and some are in a more sentimental mood, as *Smith* and *The Tenth Man*. Others may seem melodramatic, as *The Letter*. But his most typical examples are *The Constant Wife* and *Our Betters,* plays about idle members of society whose main preoccupation is with illicit love affairs. The clinical analysis of character in these plays is in much greater depth than the general picture of the somewhat frivolous society of the 1920's which he presents so accurately. His last play, *Sheppey,* written in 1933, is entirely different in character and is a kind of Everyman morality play set in a working-class milieu. In the London production, Ralph Richardson played the role with great distinction.

FREDERICK LONSDALE

Lighter in caliber, but equally expressive of the age, with a sharp wit and an underlying satire, is Frederick Lonsdale, whose not unworthy aim appears to be limited to amusing and entertaining. *The Last of Mrs. Cheyney, On Approval,* and *Canaries Sometimes Sing,* successes of the 1920's, have been constantly performed by repertory companies since then by virtue of their amusing situations, witty dialogue, and the scope they present for sophisticated, stylish acting.

NOEL COWARD

Wider in scope and ability as a man of the theatre—actor, director, playwright, and composer—is Noel Coward. His early plays, written and produced in the 1920's, are witty and accurate reflections of society of that epoch, with its optimism, disillusionment, and greater freedom of thought and behavior.

The Vortex was his first notable achievement, in which he appeared with Lilian Braithwaite in 1924 with considerable success. The following year, *Hay Fever* and *Fallen Angels* added to his rise to fame. He wrote most of the sketches and composed the music and lyrics for *Charlot's Revue* (1924), *On with the Dance* (1925), and *This Year of Grace* (1927). He was not without his failures, as was evidenced by *Sirocco* in 1927, but he returned in triumph in 1929 with the brilliant musical play *Bittersweet,* set in the Victorian age, in which he accurately expressed the public's desire for sentiment and romance after some years of brittle and matter-of-fact pieces. This was followed by his spectacular patriotic evocation of the Edwardian age in *Cavalcade,* presented at Drury Lane with considerable success. Between the two musicals he wrote *Private Lives,* a witty and amusing battle of the sexes involving two ill-assorted couples, which merits its periodic revivals.

Coward not only wrote the plays and composed the music, he directed them as well. He returned to straight comedies in 1932 with *Design for Living*, written for Alfred Lunt and Lynn Fontanne, with whom he appeared as the third member of the *ménage à trois*. *Tonight at 8:30* was a program of nine one-act plays. Another musical, *Conversation Piece*, was again an excursion into the past, although not with the success of *Bittersweet*.

Outside the theatrical, bohemian, or society background considered typical of Coward, was the suburban setting and sympathetically created everyday family of *This Happy Breed*. During the war, he wrote *Blithe Spirit*, a gay and amusing fantasy on the subject of spiritualism, since made into a musical, and in *Present Laughter* returned to the crazy comedy of theatrical life which he had expressed so well in his earlier *Hay Fever*.

His more recent works, *Quadrille*, which saw production in 1952, and *Nude with Violin*, in 1956, were not great successes, although the latter had John Gielgud in the principal role of the supposed artist's valet. His latest work, a musical, *Sail Away*, was a failure in London in 1963, although successful in New York.

Coward's plays, with their laconic but witty dialogue, rely for their success on expert playing of great speed and technique, attributes well evidenced in his own distinguished performances, which lately have been largely confined to films. He is due to present a bill of new plays in London in which he will appear.

TERENCE RATTIGAN

The next important writer in the group is Terence Rattigan, whose first success was the long-running farce *French Without Tears* in 1939. His wartime *Flare Path*, a play about air pilots and their wives, gave a hint of greater depths. The continuing success of the farce *While the Sun Shines* in 1943 was matched with an amusing comedy, *Love in Idleness* (*O Mistress Mine* in New York), in which the Lunts appeared the following year.

At the end of the war he displayed a deeper quality and a stronger theme in his play *The Winslow Boy*, based on a *cause célèbre* of Edwardian days, the Archer-Shee case, in which the family of a young naval cadet fought for his vindication when he was wrongly accused of theft. *The Winslow Boy* indicated that Rattigan was not only a purveyor of commercially successful comedies.

Adventure Story, in the same year, was an attempt at an historical drama in which Alexander of Macedon was presented as a brash though vital young man with the ruthless actions of a fascist dictator. Although it had touching moments, the dialogue hardly matched its theme, and it must be regarded as a good try, but a failure.

In *The Browning Version,* a short piece given with a light comedy of theatrical life, *Harlequinade,* he created a memorable character in the sensitive, aging schoolmaster, Crocker-Harris, married to a rapacious, vulgar woman. *The Deep Blue Sea* (1952) provided a wonderful full-length role for an actress, magnificently played by Peggy Ashcroft in the London production, of a woman whose deep, unsatisfied love for a ne'er-do-well drives her to an unsuccessful attempt at suicide, but whose dilemma remains unresolved at the close of the play. *The Sleeping Prince* was a return to the light-hearted comedy of manners set in the Edwardian age dealing with the affairs of European aristocracy.

In 1954 came *Separate Tables,* which had the unusual form of being two separate plays, the action of which takes place in the same setting, a genteel residential hotel. Each play had two main characters, a man and a woman suffering variously through a perpetual torment of introspection and loneliness, but who are finally attracted to each other, at first by sympathy for their respective weaknesses and then by deep love. In London the finely contrasted double parts were played with great feeling and distinction by Margaret Leighton and Eric Portman.

Rattigan is a dramatist who provides the West End theatre with successes (except rarely, as in *Variations on a Theme*) and, like Coward, has a respect for the intelligence of his middle-class audience to whom he frankly directs his plays. He has a depth of feeling and thought which may yet produce a masterpiece within the limits he sets himself.

OTHER WRITERS OF COMEDIES OF MANNERS

Other notable dramatists of social comedy were Dodie Smith, whose *Autumn Crocus, Dear Octopus,* and *Call it a Day* were among her many successes of the 1930's; John Van Druten, who wrote *Young Woodley, There's Always Juliet, After All,* and *The Voice of the Turtle;* and W. Chetham Strode, whose *The Guinea Pig* is a comedy of class distinction set in a famous public school and whose *The Gleam* dealt with the affairs of doctors in the National Health Service.

More recent successes are Hugh Williams, in collaboration with his wife Margaret, with such current light comedies as *The Grass is Greener, The Plaintiff in a Pretty Hat, The Happy Man,* and *Past Imperfect;* and William Douglas Home, who is quite at home with politics and reluctant peers, as befits one whose brother relinquished his peerage to become Prime Minister. *The Chiltern Hundreds, The Reluctant Debutante,* and *The Reluctant Peer* are some of his successes.

SOCIAL PLAYS

In an age when the pressure of world events and international and internal political tensions have had such an incursive effect on social activities, as might be expected there have been many dramatists who have taken a much more serious view of life and in their work have reflected various aspects of the troublous times through which we have lived in the present century. Others have attempted historical plays, choosing themes which could often be paralleled in our own time. There has been an awareness that the theatre, as in the great epoch of the classic plays or in the equally troubled Shakespearean age, should present a deeper and more purposeful view of life and humanity. This aspect of the drama, which must stem from the inherent questioning of Ibsen, is reflected in the work of the next group of playwrights under consideration.

JOHN DRINKWATER

John Drinkwater was primarily a poet and is mainly known for his historical plays, although he also worked in the theatre as an actor, director, and manager. Although he chooses his subjects from the past, his themes are eternal ones: the impact of circumstances on a strong moral purpose; the clash of personalities. His early plays were in verse, with clear and simple dialogue, and include *Rebellion,* written in 1914, set in Victorian times, and *X = O: A Night of the Trojan War,* an antiwar play with a hint of Euripides.

It is, however, his later prose plays that made his name as a dramatist of power and integrity; the most important is *Abraham Lincoln.* It had a successful run in 1919 of over a year outside the West End of London at the Lyric Theatre, Hammersmith, under the enterprising management of Nigel Playfair, and has been revived several times. It has a number of dramatic scenes, realistically portrayed, linked by two chroniclers who explain and comment in verse. *Oliver Cromwell* was written in 1920 but was not produced until two years later. Although it is a rare incursion into a strangely neglected period of English history, it was not a success. He returned to the American scene with *Robert E. Lee* in 1923. His last historical play was *Mary Stuart,* which was not successful, although it presented a fine dramatic picture of that unfortunate woman.

In complete contrast, he wrote a delightful modern comedy set in a country inn, *Bird in Hand,* which opened the season in 1927 at the Birmingham Repertory Theatre, where most of his works were first produced, and was later seen in London, where it had a successful run. It is also revived frequently in repertory.

RUDOLPH BESIER

Rudolph Besier, in his early days, also wrote a poetic play, *The Virgin Goddess,* in which there was an obvious appreciation of the power of Greek tragedy. After some run-of-the-mill comedies, he produced *The Barretts of Wimpole Street,* for which he is chiefly known. This penetrating study of a tyrannical Victorian father, cruelly dominating his family, and the merciful escape of his daughter Elizabeth through the love of Robert Browning is a beautifully told and powerfully realized story which was a great success in

London, where Cedric Hardwicke and Gwen Francon-Davies played the main parts with great distinction. It was later made into a successful film with Charles Laughton, and turned into the musical *Robert and Elizabeth*, playing in London at present to a long run.

JAMES BRIDIE

The Scottish dramatist James Bridie (O. H. Mavor) originally trained and practiced as a doctor, serving as an Army surgeon in both World Wars. Yet he found time to write no less than thirty plays. He found his themes in the Bible, as in *Tobias and the Angel, Jonah and the Whale*, and *Susannah and the Elders;* in medical history, as in *The Anatomist;* or in Scottish Calvinism, as in *The Devil and Mr. Bolfry.* He also wrote many imaginative plays based on affairs of the day, such as *The King of Nowhere*, and satirical comedies such as *It Depends What You Mean* (a comedy of a local brain trust), *What Say They, The Black Eye, Dr. Angelus*, and *A Sleeping Clergyman.*

His plays are written with a facility for witty dialogue which sometimes makes us remember Shaw, although Bridie does not always possess the force to resolve the predicaments in which his characters find themselves.

He played a leading part in establishing the Glasgow Citizens Theatre, the most important of the few repertory theatres in Scotland.

R. C. SHERRIFF

R. C. Sherriff is known chiefly for his first play, *Journey's End*, which had a memorable impact on the London audience in 1929. This was the first play dealing with the horrors of trench warfare in France during the First World War to be produced in the West End. A moving and dramatic story, it tells of a small group of officers waiting to carry out one of the futile orders to attack the enemy in the face of greater odds so characteristic of that holocaust. This tragic play, with its small cast of men, has since been played all

over the world, and remains the most powerful plea for the abolition of war the modern theatre has produced. The long success of
the London production was partly due to the fine playing of Colin
Clive, Maurice Evans, and Robert Speaight.

Sherriff went on to write many plays, none of which possesses the
underlying seriousness of his first play, but many of them have been
successful. *Badger's Green,* a comedy about a village cricket match,
written in 1930, was followed by *St. Helena* in 1935, in which he
collaborated with Jeanne de Casalis, and which was about Napoleon's last years, splendidly played in the Old Vic production by
Kenneth Kent and Ian Swinley. *Miss Mabel* was a popular success
of 1948. *Home at Seven,* a study of a victim of amnesia, provided
an excellent part for Ralph Richardson, which was repeated,
although with less success, the following year in *The White
Carnation.*

Sherriff's recent work has a more imaginative quality, as evidenced
by *The Long Sunset,* a drama about the closing years of the Roman
occupation of Britain, which has many moments of beauty and
pathos.

J. B. PRIESTLEY

One of the most far-ranging dramatists of the plays of ideas has
been J. B. Priestley, who was first known as the author of a very
successful novel, *The Good Companions.* With the aid of Edward
Knoblock, this was adapted for the stage and produced in 1931 with
John Gielgud in the leading role. Its success led Priestley to write
more for the theatre, and since that time he has produced well over
twenty plays. These differ widely in scope and purpose, but most
of them are serious enough in their implications, although he is
able to produce, from time to time, lighthearted comedies such as
When We Are Married, Ever Since Paradise, and *Are They the
Same at Home,* when the apparent intention is limited to entertainment and amusement.

Dangerous Corner, his first original play, produced at the Lyric
Theatre in 1932, has an ingenious plot showing how a group of

people are affected by a chance remark. It goes on to reveal a serious underlying involvement between each of them. When their problems reach an unsatisfactory climax, the play begins again and we then understand that what we have witnessed is only what might have been. The chance remark is not made this time, and the play ends with the characters in full control of their thoughts and emotions.

Priestley's interest in the theories of time of J. W. Dunne enabled him to experiment with ideas which led to dramatic expression in *Time and the Conways* and *I Have Been Here Before,* both produced in 1937. Priestley is often very topical in his themes and his war play, *Desert Highway,* reflects the soldier's thoughts in a questioning mood. In *Are They the Same at Home* life in evacuated Britain is presented as a comedy of muddling through. With *They Came to a City,* a vision of a new life and existence set in the future, he reflected many of the thoughts, idealistic perhaps, which were current in the minds of a people at war.

The Linden Tree was written after the war in 1947, in a difficult period of adjustment to spiritual needs and material shortcomings. The same year, in *An Inspector Calls,* Priestley sets the scene in 1912, and he thoroughly works out the theme of inhumanity and its tragic consequences. The inspector at first appears to be from the police, investigating the death of a poor girl, but at the end of the play it is apparent that he is a fiction of the mind, a mysterious figure who questions all the characters in the play who have in some way been responsible for the tragedy. The greatness of this work lies in its theme, the interplay of characters, and the creation of atmosphere, while the fantasy of the inspector—the symbol of conscience—is skillfully integrated with the characters drawn from real life.

Priestley's later plays, some of which have been in collaboration with Jaquetta Hawkes, have been unsuccessful on the whole, until an amusing comedy of love life, *The Severed Head,* which was written in collaboration with the novelist Iris Murdoch. This is a

long way from the serious basis of his prewar plays, but it has settled down in London for a long run.

EMLYN WILLIAMS

Emlyn Williams, equally known as an actor and dramatist, created
an early success with his playing of the main character, a psycho-
pathic killer, in his thriller *Night Must Fall*. Drawing on his own
upbringing in a Welsh mining village, he wrote *The Corn is Green*,
a study of a woman teacher in the early years of the twentieth century with the absorbing desire to give one of her pupils, a young
miner, the chance to compete for an Oxford scholarship. Emlyn
Williams played the part of the young student to a magnificent
performance by Sybil Thorndike as the teacher. *The Wind of
Heaven*, produced in 1945, the action of which again takes place in
a Welsh village in Victorian times, is an ambitious play based on
the theme of the Second Coming. Although it may be claimed that
he gets very near to sentimentality at times, Williams' work is extremely effective on the stage.

W. C. HUNTER

W. C. Hunter has written several plays somewhat in the mood of
Chekhov. *Waters of the Moon, A Day by the Sea*, and *The Tulip
Tree* have been successful in London, partly due to the fine opportunities they gave for the sensitive playing of some of England's
greatest actors, including Sybil Thorndike, Edith Evans, John Gielgud, and Ralph Richardson.

ENID BAGNOLD

Enid Bagnold has written two plays, *The Chalk Garden* and *The
Chinese Prime Minister*, in which Edith Evans made a rather rare
appearance in plays on contemporary subjects. Her novel *National
Velvet* was adapted for the stage, and she wrote *The Last Joke* in
1960.

PETER USTINOV

Peter Ustinov is probably more widely known as an actor, author, and director of broadly comic creations in films, radio, and television; but in the theatre his work as a playwright has more serious qualities. Graduating as an actor from the Drama School of Michel St. Denis in 1939, he began writing plays almost as soon as he made his debut as a performer. During the war he served almost five years in the Army. He performed occasionally in satirical revues, and wrote his first successful play, *House of Regrets,* which was produced in 1942. It is a sensitive study of aged emigrés from Eastern Europe in a seedy London boarding house, reliving their earlier lives through their memories and failing to adjust themselves to their new situation. Although there is a preoccupation with the problems of age in many of his plays, there is a richly comic vein running through them all which often has an underlying satire on behavior governed by national characteristics.

His next play, in 1943, *Blow Your Own Trumpet,* although presented by the Old Vic Company, was not a success. The following year, *The Banbury Nose* enjoyed a long run. In this play, members of a military family are seen to have been in conflict with the Army traditions of the past generation and attempt to resolve their problems by their own influence on the next. By moving from the present backward in time, he skillfully presents the inability of a conventional people to understand the changing values of their children. In *The Love of Four Colonels* Ustinov had another great success in 1951. It is a delightful satire of the well-contrasted national characteristics of the four colonels — American, English, French, and Russian — in occupied Austria just after the war, written with great wit and understanding. *Photo Finish* was again an experiment with time, as the principal character, an eighty-year-old author confined to his bed, watches and converses with himself personified first as a young man, then middle-aged, and finally elderly, re-enacting his past life. In the London production of 1962 Ustinov played the main part with great distinction.

His most impressive play to date is *The Moment of Truth,* produced in 1951. It concerns a European country in the recent past, defeated in war, in which a very old and ailing Marshal is made the nominal head of the unoccupied part of the country, as he is the only one to retain the respect of the people. Although he is manipulated by the wily Prime Minister and is unaware of the puppet nature of his position, he fulfills his duty to the country. After some years the victors are finally defeated by the Allies, together with the Army of Resistance, whose General triumphantly returns to take over. The Marshal and his daughter, who has looked after him throughout the war, are imprisoned as collaborators. As he is now very senile, his daughter is eventually returned to him, but she dies in his arms as the result of her suffering in prison, and he has a momentary vision of clarity in which he becomes aware of the tragic train of events in which he has been involved. While at the beginning of this play one is reminded of Pétain and Laval, it develops into a powerful argument against war, in which there are no victors or vanquished.

In *Romanoff and Juliet,* a lighthearted comedy, Ustinov sets the scene in a mythical European country of minute size which is nevertheless strategically important to both East and West, and the American and Russian Embassies face each other across the town square. The Prime Minister plays one against the other, and the fun begins with the son of the Russian Ambassador falling in love with the American's daughter. The Prime Minister becomes a go-between in the reactions of the two families to the implications of such a match, and provides a rich field for Ustinov's sense of humor and satire.

While Ustinov makes admirable attempts at serious drama from time to time, he is naturally suited to the creation of pure satirical comedy, and he gives much pleasure to large audiences when he provides just that. He has written many other plays which see worldwide production, and no doubt will continue to write many more for the theatre, of which he is an undoubted master craftsman.

CHARLES MORGAN

Other plays which have contributed to the drama of ideas have been the occasional plays by two writers whose chief work has been in the novel. Charles Morgan's *The Flashing Stream* (1938) concerns a man and woman engaged in important and secret mathematical calculations who decide that although they are much in love, their respective duties, which require their full and complete attention, are more imperative in view of the coming war than their own personal relationships. While the theme is well conceived, the characterization is never completely realized. His *River Line* and *The Burning Glass* are other attempts at a serious theme, but he never quite manages to create real-life characters, and sometimes the action of the play is forced to the point of melodrama.

GRAHAM GREENE

The other distinguished novelist, Graham Greene, has written four plays: *The Living Room, Potting Shed, The Complaisant Lover,* and *Carving a Statue.* They have all seen production, with varying degrees of success, in London during the last decade. His novels, *The Power and the Glory* and *The End of the Affair,* have also been successfully dramatized.

Graham Greene has a rather pessimistic view of life, and his plays all have a cry of despair from his characters, who rarely come to terms with their world. It is true that this is an almost universal quality among contemporary dramatists, a sensible compromise with life by which most of us survive seeming to offer little scope for drama. This compromise never happens in Greene's plays, infidelity, suicide, or emotional breakdown being the means of giving force to his drama. Yet, depressing though it may be, Greene's work in the theatre postulates the battle between material and spiritual values and a searching by man for the redemption of his soul which is inherent in all great drama.

POETIC DRAMA

For a time in England it seemed that the way was clear for a development of poetic drama. Attempts had been made earlier in the century with the plays of W. B. Yeats, John Masefield, and John

Drinkwater to establish a poetic form in contemporary language, which worked well with historical subjects but which was less convincing in plays of contemporary life. The plays of W. H. Auden and Christopher Isherwood were attempts to resolve this problem. *The Ascent of F.6* and *The Dog Beneath the Skin* were serious contemporary themes written in a form of satirical verse.

T. S. ELIOT

A further development was seen in the plays of T. S. Eliot who, although of American birth, spent most of his life in England and achieved a reputation as its leading poet of the younger generation in the period after the First World War with *The Waste Land* and *Four Quartets.* His first attempts at writing for the theatre were in a short experimental piece based on an ancient Greek drama, *Sweeney Agonistes,* and *The Rock,* a pageant play in which he used a chorus of voices to explain the action.

This was followed in 1935 by the production of *Murder in the Cathedral,* first performed at Canterbury Cathedral, which recounts the events relating to and the murder of Thomas à Becket in that very place eight hundred years ago. This play, although written at the instigation of the Dean of Canterbury for a Canterbury festival, was later produced in London with great success. As might be expected, Eliot, who was a practicing member of the Church of England, was aware of the importance of ritual, and skillfully interweaves it with his dramatic narrative. He also has a chorus of the women of Canterbury, who comment and explain the action and by their chanting emphasize the sense of ritual.

Eliot's next play, *The Family Reunion,* in 1939, was set in modern times, but the underlying theme was taken from classical drama, that of Orestes pursued by the Furies. At the country home of a dowager, her son arrives after an absence of eight years, during which time he has made an unfortunate marriage. He now has a guilt complex, as he believes he is responsible for his wife's death. The reunion of the various members of the family is dominated by the necessity to explain or excuse his mistaken guilt feelings. When he is finally convinced that it is only in his imagination that he killed his wife he decides to leave, now no longer pursued, and this brings about the death of his mother. The play has many deep and hidden meanings and its language of blank verse is an attempt to arrive at a poetic form of everyday speech. The form of blank verse used does not, however, approach it, and the uncles and aunts chanting as a chorus in a kind of ritual break away from any sense of surface reality, although when played with sincerity the son's dilemma comes across.

In *The Cocktail Party,* written in 1949, the theme is again the redemption of the soul and the revaluation of spiritual needs in a rather futile and materialistic postwar world in which the psychiatrist has become a universal father confessor. The language is less poetic, although still in the form of blank verse.

Eliot's last two plays, *The Confidential Clerk* and *The Elder Statesman,* continue this trend, although with an attempt at greater characterization and a simplicity of meaning. Although Eliot may not have reached a solution to his dramatic problems, he underlines the need for a greater sense of spiritual values in the contemporary theatre and provides it with a language of heightened style.

CHRISTOPHER FRY

The style of language is also a fundamental attribute in the plays of Christopher Fry. His plays have been extremely successful, with their fecundity of imagery, witty phraseology, and his almost Elizabethan ability to play with words. While his meaning is obscure at times, the facility of his poetic fancy and his ornamentation of language provide a delight after the laconic matter-of-fact ordinariness of much contemporary dialogue.

His first play was of one act, *A Phoenix Too Frequent,* produced in London in 1946. *Venus Observed* (1950) gave opportunities to Laurence Olivier. In the same year Fry wrote *Ring Round the Moon,* adapted from the French of Anouilh. He also wrote some religious dramas in verse and an historical play, *Curtmantle.* Of recent years he has been chiefly occupied with writing for the films, although he has written *The Dark Is Light Enough*, *The Lark* (also adapted from Anouilh), and two adaptations from Giraudoux, *Tiger at the Gates* and *Duel of Angels*.

Fry's happiest creation to date, *The Lady's Not for Burning*, is set in the early fifteenth century. A young woman is being held as a suspected witch and is expecting to be burned at the stake, as was the custom. A young man insists that he should be hanged for the murder of the rascally tinker whose body has disappeared and whom the young woman is supposed to have turned into a dog. The young woman is confined in the mayor's house with the young man, they fall in love, and she talks him into giving up the idea of confessing. Finally, the tinker turns up after waking from his long drunken sleep in a ditch, and the lovers are free to face life together.

Fry can create a mood with felicity, and although his plays are naturalistic, there is in them a perpetual wonder at life which arouses the sensibilities through his heightened use of words.

THE NEW YOUNG PLAYWRIGHTS: SOCIAL REALISM

During the last decade, England has seen a number of new plays by younger men which have, with great vitality, broken away from almost all accepted conventions of the West End theatre. They have been chiefly associated with two theatres in London, both outside the West End: the Royal Court Theatre (of the early Granville-Barker regime), home of the English Stage Company directed by George Devine; and the Theatre Royal, Stratford, in East London, occupied during the crucial time by Joan Littlewood's Theatre Workshop. Many of the productions of both theatres were eventually transferred to the West End and became very successful.

JOHN OSBORNE

Generally acknowledged as the spark which ignited this explosion in the English theatre is the work of John Osborne, *Look Back in Anger*, first produced at the Court in 1956. In a return to realistic language, often of a blunt and savage character, it gives voice to the despairs and frustrations of contemporary life among a younger generation eager to rebel but without any clear conviction of its cause. The chief character is an egotistic antihero who reviles the conventions of the society in which he lives—class, the Church, the Press—and behaves with cruelty to his wife, who leaves him, and to her friend who replaces her. Although he has had a university background, he ekes out an existence by running a stall in a street market with another young man, who also shares his flat. The play has little action and a sordid setting, but with the vociferous, challenging Jimmy Porter, Osborne holds his audience in suspense at the prospect of his fulfillment. But little happens. His wife returns after her friend has duly left him and we are at the beginning again. Osborne created a character which was theatrically convincing, although not likeable, and the dialogue was powerfully effective in a fresh evocation of so-called realistic language. That polite sensibilities were not shocked by the bad manners, the crudities, and the sordid nature of this play is evidenced by its long run.

Osborne followed this play with another success in *The Entertainer*. This gives a picture of a seedy vaudeville comic and his family in the world of the old variety houses, a third-rate performer in a dying profession. Again the milieu is that of a sordid provincial household. The chief character, an utter failure in his profession and his life, remains unconvinced of his ability to rise above either his audience or the problems of his home life. During the action of the play, Archie Rice, the comic, performs his act before us, with his patter of vulgarities, jokes, and songs, and this is contrasted with scenes of his home life with his drunken wife; his old father, a variety performer in the Edwardian heyday, still living in the past; and his grownup children. The production of *The Entertainer* at the Court in 1957 was made memorable by the performance of Laurence Olivier as Archie Rice, a performance which evoked great feeling for the tragedy behind the mask.

Osborne has since written two other successful plays. *Luther*, written for the Royal Shakespeare Company, was an attempt to see the implications of the Reformation through the individual character of its chief protagonist. The title role provided a magnificent part for Albert Finney, one of the rising stars of a new generation of actors. *Inadmissible Evidence* was another study in the despair and dissolution of its main character, a solicitor, a difficult part played with distinction by Nicol Williamson in London and New York.

ARNOLD WESKER

The next playwright of importance among the younger writers, whose work has been almost universally praised, is Arnold Wesker. His *Chicken Soup with Barley,* the first play of his triology of a Jewish family, the Kahns of the East End of London, and their friends, set in 1936 during the time of the Mosley marches, displays an unerring ear for the nuances of working-class language, and its overtones of a socialist striving for a better life.

In the second play of his triology, *Roots,* the setting is changed to the deep country of Norfolk and none of the earlier characters appear. Beatie, a young girl, has, however, come into contact with the idealistic Ronnie Kahn, to whom she becomes engaged and who exerts a considerable influence over her relationships with her family. He awakens in her a desire to break away from the working-class life of her parents; and although she has little learning, at the end of the play she becomes articulate, although what she is going to do with her life, since she receives a letter from Ronnie breaking off the engagement, we are left to guess. Joan Plowright's touching performance as Beatie brought the Court production to life.

With the third play, *I'm Talking About Jerusalem,* we return to the Kahn family, with their daughter now married to Dave Simmonds, the socialist hero of the Spanish Civil War from the earlier play. This play begins in 1946 and tells the story of the young couple's attempts to build a better life in the country. Dave's efforts to emulate the teachings of William Morris in a happy life, making fine furniture by hand, are doomed to failure, and the close of the play sees the family (it is now 1959) packing to return to the city.

The first two plays were first performed at the Belgrade Theatre in Coventry in 1958; the complete triology was performed at the

Court Theatre in 1960. Wesker's characterization is excellent and well founded in life, and his dialogue is completely convincing. Yet, one is aware of a certain missing ingredient. Is it hope or faith?

Of Wesker's other plays—*The Kitchen, The Four Seasons,* and *Chips with Everything*—only the last was well received and transferred to the West End in 1962 for a long run. An all-male cast tells the story of a group of National Service men in their various reactions to the ardors and discipline of service training with humor and understanding, which in many ways is an advance over the plays of his triology in that the characters are complete in themselves and not symbols for Wesker's ideas of socialist revolution.

THE LONG AND THE SHORT AND THE TALL

Another remarkable play of wartime service life by Willis Hall, also with an all-male cast, *The Long and the Short and the Tall,* was produced at the Court in 1959. A small infantry patrol is cut off in the Malayan jungle and established in a small hut when a Japanese soldier stumbles in and is captured. The development of the play is concerned with their treatment of their prisoner and his eventual killing and ends in the decimation of the patrol by the enemy. It is, in its own terms, an antiwar play as potent as *Journey's End*.

THE THEATRE OF THE ABSURD

Social realism is one direction to which the younger writers are turning, but the other main trend is chiefly in the realm of fantasy, currently known as the Theatre of the Absurd. Here the main inspiration is perhaps the work of Pirandello, Ionesco, and Samuel Beckett. Other Continental writers such as Adamov, Genet, Arrau, and Arrabal have been published in England and their plays occasionally performed.

Ionesco's *Rhinoceros* was produced in London and New York with considerable success. It is a play in which each of the characters changes into a rhinoceros. The development of the play lies in the varied degrees of opposition and eventual acceptance of this metamorphosis. Other plays by Ionesco which have been produced in England include *The Chairs, The Lesson, The Bald Prima-donna,* and *Amédée.*

Beckett's *Waiting for Godot* is perhaps the greatest triumph of this particular school. It is a play in which the acting, although keeping correctly to the script, appears to run away with the whole meaning. It is considered by some people as a parable of life, an eternal question with no answer (as it was played in London), while others regard it as a fantastic comedy (as it was played in New York). His other plays, *Endgame* and *Krapp's Last Tape,* present great production difficulties, but offer excellent acting opportunities. It seems that the actor has overtaken the dramatist. Beckett is an Irishman, although he lives in Paris, and his plays were first produced there and written in French.

The work of N. F. Simpson comes into this group with his *A Resounding Tinkle* and *One-Way Pendulum,* fantastic displays of nonsense in ordinary domestic surroundings.

Harold Pinter is an English playwright whose work seems to fall between both schools. His plays are set in dingy working-class households and the behavior of his characters toward each other is quite unaccountable, although in themselves they seem to have some conviction. He has a gift for dialogue which is at times remarkable, although much is crude and violent. *The Caretaker* has only three characters, two brothers and an elderly tramp who has been invited to stay in the house, presumably to look after it in their absence. The two brothers are opposite in nature and react differently toward the tramp, who rambles on about himself. Although he wants to retain the chance for shelter, he is unwilling to be involved in the affairs of others. As in *Waiting for Godot* the meaning, if any, is obscure, but it could be taken as an expression of the complete inability of people to communicate once the social conventions are dispensed with.

There is something of a parallel between the state of affairs in the theatre and the development of fine art in the early years of the century. First the break away from established conventions, with a revolutionary fervor and vitality which brought with it violence and crudity, as in the paintings of the fauvists, followed by the greater formality and discipline of the cubists and, on another tack, the revolt against this discipline with the Dada group, who seemed content to destroy all the conceptions of art. The surrealists retired from the dilemma with their obsessions with meaningless dreams, in turn to be awakened and their work concluded by the even greater nightmare of war. Yet, in the pursuit of their aims, the artists broke much new ground and found some fascination in their means of expression, which otherwise would not have been discovered. The creation of their own set of conventions and the fact that some work is painted with a heightened sensibility have meant that the viewer has to be prepared to meet the artist halfway. Full communication is only possible with the already converted.

PLAYWRIGHTS' WORK IN THE THEATRE

Many of the younger dramatists in England have been closely connected with the theatre, perhaps as actors or directors, and the literary qualities of the earlier playwrights have been replaced with a working knowledge of theatre, which accounts for much of the success of the acting opportunities in their plays. Shelagh Delaney, whose *A Taste of Honey* brought her fame, worked closely with Joan Littlewood's Theatre Workshop and has acknowledged her debt to this experience. Pinter has acted and directed. Most of the new plays are successful primarily for their acting opportunities.

THE OLD VIC

With the passing of the old actor-managers' stock companies early in the century, the production of the classics fell into decline. The West End theatres of London were generally concerned with modern plays and these were usually well produced with players of expert though somewhat limited skill. The West End, like Broadway, is composed of many theatres owned by people who never have a hand in the production of plays, who are merely landlords, letting their buildings to producing companies. In some cases they are sublet by those companies to others who wish to present a particular play. The finance involved in putting on a play is very considerable, and this may very well be a gamble in the case of new and untried plays. Actors are engaged simply for the particular play, and when performances come to an end, as the bookings cease, the play comes off and the cast is dispersed.

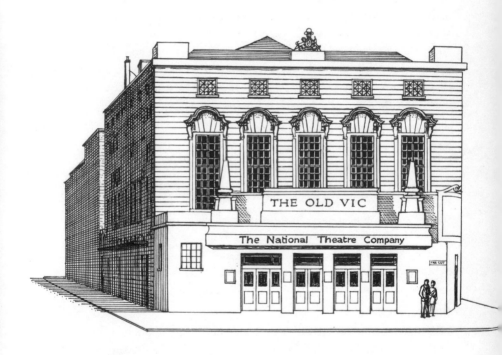

THE OLD VIC   The famous Old Vic Theatre building is currently the home of the National Theatre Company. Permanent quarters for the Old Vic are being completed on the south bank of the Thames.

The idea of a repertory theatre in London in which the classics could be performed and actors could be employed for a whole season seemed a desirable aim for both sides of the footlights. This was established early in the century at an old playhouse just south of the Thames known as the Old Vic. At the time it was built in 1818 there were other theatres nearby (Astley's and the Surrey), although it was largely a rural area. The outer walls and the horseshoe plan of the interior and much of the original structure remain today. In its day it had seen some great figures. Its first manager was William Barrymore, an ancestor of the famous Broadway family. Junius Brutus Booth, Samuel Phelps, Macready, Edmund Kean, Grimaldi, Charles Mathews, and Madame Vestris had all performed there.

But as the years of the century passed, the neighborhood deteriorated to a slum and the theatre, first known as the Royal Coburg and then as the Royal Victoria, suffered accordingly, providing a program of crude melodrama and variety which was acceptable to the noisy, disreputable audience, although eventually even this fare became unprofitable.

In 1879 the management passed to Miss Emma Cons, an alderman and a well-to-do lady of middle age, much interested in social welfare, who had an idea that the theatre might be used as a means of education. Universal primary education had only just become a fact with the passing of legislation, but there was little chance of any further education among the masses of the working people. During this period the mechanics and polytechnic institutes began their work, and Miss Cons's intentions with the old theatre must have been regarded as part of this liberalizing effort in her wish to enlarge the leisure life of the poor.

She opened with a mixed program of lectures, recitals, and music hall turns, abolished the sale of liquor, and began to attract a different kind of audience, many of them quite young and anxious to benefit from the opportunities of more serious fare.

Miss Cons employed various managers to attend to the day-to-day running of the theatre, one of whom was young William Poel, who was there from 1886 to 1888. During this time he experimented with his own ideas of staging plays, although not yet those of Shakespeare. He was later to become well known for his theories of a return to the actual text of Shakespeare, the much greater speed of delivery in speaking, and the simplified method of staging analogous to that of the Elizabethan stage.

Many of the audience who attended the lectures asked for more information and soon evening classes on a variety of topics were being held in the various rooms behind the auditorium. Indeed, at one time the classes became more popular than the stage productions and part of the auditorium was curtained off for this purpose. Eventually, this side of the theatre's activities was moved to its own building nearby, where it has flourished ever since as Morley College.

LILLIAN BAYLISS' MANAGEMENT AT THE OLD VIC

In 1898, Miss Cons introduced her niece, Lillian Bayliss, to the theatre and she became an assistant manager. Miss Bayliss had been a music teacher and had danced in South Africa. Like her aunt, she was deeply religious, but she developed a burning enthusiasm for the theatre, and when her aunt died in 1912 she took over the management.

By now the presentations were including recitals of operas, and a small permanent theatre orchestra was built up under Charles Corri. Eventually a license was obtained by Miss Bayliss and a fund was started to stage the operas in full, when the First World War brought these activities to an end. Early films were shown and occasional single performances of Shakespeare were given. These must have decided Miss Bayliss on her next course of action, and in 1914 she began the productions of Shakespeare's plays which were to become the Old Vic's lasting glory in the next forty years. She had the help of some experienced actor-managers—Matheson Lang, who also played in *The Merchant of Venice*, *The Taming of the Shrew*, and *Hamlet*; Ben Greet; and Andrew Leigh.

Many well-known actors played at the Old Vic during these early years, often for a nominal fee, pleased to be able to help in establishing the theatre. Lilian Braithwaite, Angela Baddeley, Florence Saunders, Estelle Stead, Nancy Price, Hermione Gingold, Sybil Thorndike, her sister Eileen, her brother Russell, Robert Atkins, Basil Sydney, Ernest Milton, and Malcolm Keen were a few of the players who appeared in those early years.

Miss Bayliss was emphatic in her policy of low admission prices. The gallery was twopence and a stall seat was two shillings. This was the only income for the work of the theatre, out of which the expenses of production and salaries of actors had to be paid, although various appeals were made to the public from time to time for development funds.

The old theatre equipment was still in use, the scenery was mainly composed of painted flats in grooves, and the principal stage lighting was still by gas. In spite of all the material difficulties (which in some ways were a blessing, economy of means often leading to ingenuity in staging), the enthusiasm of the players and the invincible character of Miss Bayliss succeeded in establishing the Old Vic as the London home of Shakespeare and opera.

A permanent and faithful audience was gradually built up, strengthened occasionally by parties of school children. This became a permanent feature when the educational authorities, the London County Council, took over the whole theatre for special matinees. An Old Vic magazine was instituted, and two theatre clubs were formed to foster interest in the theatre, the players, and the productions; occasional lectures were given to members.

A special annual event was Shakespeare's Birthday celebration. This evening's program was made up of short excerpts from the plays in which well-known players, many of them currently appearing in the West End theatres, would appear with members of the resident company. Even such stars as Ellen Terry and Lady Forbes-Robertson were seen in these revels.

By 1923 the Old Vic became the first theatre to have presented the complete cycle of Shakespeare's plays. Other plays were also

DAME EDITH EVANS   As Lady Bracknell in Oscar Wilde's "The Importance of Being Earnest," the actress appeared at the Globe Theatre, London, in 1939.

produced—Sheridan's and Goldsmith's comedies; Marlowe's *Dr. Faustus; Everyman,* the medieval morality play; Ibsen's *Peer Gynt;* and occasionally the work of contemporary writers, such as Barrie's *Pantaloon,* Lawrence Binyon's *King Arthur,* and Gordon Bottomley's *Britain's Daughter.* Except for a month or so in the summer, the Old Vic was open throughout the year and the plays were given in alternate weeks with opera.

During the 1920's greater attention was given to standards of production, and the pioneer work of Robert Atkins as director of the plays made a lasting contribution to the Old Vic's success. Influenced by William Poel in his theory of a return to the more fluid movement possible on the Elizabethan stage, which resulted in a much quicker development of the action, Atkins created a kind of apron stage by the erection of a false proscenium behind the existing one but in front of the stage curtain. An entrance door in either side enabled actors to play in front of the curtain, behind which another scene could be erected during the action. The old system of stage grooves was discarded and the scenery was now especially designed for each production. The stage lighting was modernized with electricity.

Another innovation was the establishment of a permanent wardrobe for the theatre; hitherto costumes had been hired.

Atkins, a fine actor, played in most of the productions with such players as George Hayes, Hilton Edwards, John Laurie, Francis L. Sullivan, Austin Trevor, Russell Thorndike, Marie Ney, Florence Buckton, Dorice Fordred, Jane Bacon, and Florence Saunders.

Robert Atkins left the Old Vic in 1925 to take his own company on tour, eventually becoming a producer at the Stratford-on-Avon Memorial Theatre and, during the summer, at the Open Air Theatre created in London's Regent's Park. His place as director of the Old Vic was taken by Andrew Leigh.

The company had the advantage of two brilliant new players, Baliol Holloway and Edith Evans, and for a season saw the return of Sybil Thorndike with her husband Lewis Casson. Edith Evans in comedy and Sybil Thorndike in tragedy became the particular favorites of the Old Vic audiences, and both of them have returned there from time to time throughout their long and successful careers. In the 1920's, Harcourt Williams, Henry Cass, and Tyrone Guthrie were the directors, and the cast lists included almost all the present distinguished leading actors of the English stage.

JOHN GIELGUD

John Gielgud played his first *Hamlet* there in 1929, and soon established himself as a rising favorite, playing Romeo, Richard II, Macbeth, and many other parts. His fine stage presence and magnificent voice, his sensitive poetic reading of Shakespeare, were to be developed even further when he left the Old Vic at the end of the season. *Richard of Bordeaux,* a play by Gordon Daviot at the New Theatre in 1933, was a modern treatment of the story of Richard II, and in this production, beautifully mounted with designs by three young women who called themselves Motley, Gielgud made a great success. Then followed his *Hamlet,* which achieved a long run in both London and New York.

Although he is probably at his best in Shakespeare, Gielgud has given excellent performances in *Love for Love, The Importance of Being Earnest, Noah, The Lady's Not for Burning, Ivanov,* and many contemporary plays. He has also done much directing of plays, besides those in which he has appeared, at seasons of repertory at the Haymarket toward the end of the war and notably at Stratford-on-Avon in the 1949–1950 season.

RALPH RICHARDSON

Another of England's present leading actors, Ralph Richardson, made his reputation at the Old Vic, chiefly in the 1930's seasons, with John Gielgud. Richardson had been a member of the Birmingham Repertory Company and was playing a small part in *Othello* at the Savoy Theatre—the production with Paul Robeson and Peggy Ashcroft—when he was offered the opportunity of a season at the Old Vic under Harcourt Williams' direction. He played

SIR JOHN GIELGUD He appears in his own production of "Hamlet" at the New Theatre, London, in 1934.

Bolingbroke, Sir Toby Belch, Prince Hal, Henry V, Iago, Caliban, and Bluntschli in Shaw's *Arms and the Man* with much success. Later he was to be seen in modern plays, appearing several times at the Malvern Festival.

He returned to the Old Vic after the last war, with Laurence Olivier, in their seasons at the New Theatre. He appeared with great distinction as Falstaff, Uncle Vanya, Bluntschli, and Peer Gynt. He has superb gifts as a character actor, and in his rendering of the main roles in J. B. Priestley's *Johnson over Jordan* and in Somerset Maugham's *Sheppey*, he vividly created the universal man struggling against his destiny with humility and resignation.

THE BEGINNINGS OF THE ROYAL BALLET

The Old Vic was firmly established in the 1930's and Miss Bayliss had enlarged her sphere by engaging Ninette de Valois to form a small ballet company to perform short ballets in the operas. Further expansion came with the chance to take over the old Sadler's Wells Theatre at Islington, then being rebuilt with publicly raised funds. For some two or three years, the Old Vic Company would repeat their performances at Sadler's Wells, alternating with the opera, but eventually it was decided to concentrate the plays at the Old Vic, and Sadler's Wells became the home of the opera and ballet. The ballet then developed into a separate entity, and eventually some evenings were devoted entirely to ballet performances. After the war, the ballet moved to Covent Garden, still under Ninette de Valois, and became the famous Royal Ballet of today.

CHARLES LAUGHTON AT THE OLD VIC

During the 1930's, the artistic standards of the Old Vic rose considerably. By bringing in established stars, the company could attract audiences from all parts of London. This was largely the work of Tyrone Guthrie, who began directing in 1933. His first introduction of the stars was of Charles Laughton and his wife, Elsa Lanchester. Laughton had already made a reputation in the West End in modern plays in such parts as the gangster Perelli in *On the Spot*

RALPH RICHARDSON   He appears as Falstaff in the Old Vic production of "Henry IV, Part I," presented in 1945 at the New Theatre, London, the war-time home of the Old Vic Company.

and the respectable suburban murderer of *Payment Deferred*, and he had become universally known for his performance in the film *The Private Life of Henry VIII*. He stayed the entire season of 1933–1934 at the Old Vic and played a wide range of parts, including Prospero and Macbeth·(not his best roles). He was memorable as Lopakhin in *The Cherry Orchard*, the first time the Old Vic had played Chekhov.

He appeared in *Henry VIII* with Flora Robson as Katherine, but although it was beautifully played and the production designed by Charles Ricketts, a noted stage designer, it was something of an anticlimax after the film. Perhaps his happiest creation in this season was Tattle in *Love for Love*, with Athene Seyler as Mrs. Frail. Elsa Lanchester presented an unusual characterization of the sprite Ariel in *The Tempest*, but although Laughton was a dignified Prospero, he failed to bring out the lyrical qualities of the fantasy.

MAURICE EVANS AT THE OLD VIC

Another young director, Henry Cass, directed the next two seasons, 1934–1936, during which Maurice Evans made a new reputation in Shakespeare, to be furthered later in America. His magnificent voice and lively, intelligent interpretation were much admired in *Richard II* and in *Hamlet*, played in its entirety, but he was perhaps more at home in comedy, as in his Benedick to Mary Newcombe's Beatrice in *Much Ado About Nothing*. Other newcomers were Marius Goring, Kenneth Kent, William Devlin; Ian Swinley returned for occasional roles.

THE 1936 SEASON AT THE OLD VIC

Tyrone Guthrie returned as director in 1936 and remained for the next twelve years. His most brilliant production of 1936 was without doubt Wycherley's *The Country Wife*. This was presented in the original unexpurgated version, and the brilliant cast played it with all the wit and sparkle that one imagines was produced in the Restoration theatre. The title role was played by Ruth Gordon, the American actress, and the cast included Edith Evans, Ursula Jeans,

LAURENCE OLIVIER   He is costumed for the role of Richard III in the Old Vic Company's production, shown at the New Theatre in 1944.

Kate Cutler, Iris Hoey, Eileen Peel, Freda Jackson, Patrick Barr, Richard Goolden, Alec Clunes, Ernest Thesiger, James Dale, and Michael Redgrave. The costumes and settings were designed by Oliver Messel, England's leading designer who, without slavishly reproducing the period, aptly caught its spirit.

This season also saw the Old Vic debut of Laurence Olivier, who had by then made a great reputation in the West End and in films. He made an agile, quicksilver Hamlet, a riotous Sir Toby Belch to the Aguecheek of Alec Guinness, and a noble Henry V, in which Jessica Tandy played the French princess. He won his audiences completely and joined the happy band of their special favorites.

Edith Evans played a memorable Rosalind in a production of *As You Like It* set in Watteauesque costumes and decor in which the Orlando was Michael Redgrave. A scintillating season of talent.

LILLIAN BAYLISS' CONTRIBUTIONS TO THE OLD VIC

The theatre sustained a great loss the following year with the death of Miss Bayliss, who had been ailing for some time. This remarkable woman had tremendous character, a deeply religious background which was her great strength, and an ability to bring unexpected talent to the surface. She was eccentric in some ways, but these eccentricities endeared her to her players and staff, who returned her love and affection. She had steered the Old Vic from its beginnings through a period of some forty years, years of great change and development, and she was responsible for the auspicious beginnings of opera and ballet at Sadler's Wells.

ACTORS AND PRODUCTIONS AT THE OLD VIC

By now, Old Vic audiences were widely drawn from all classes of the community, and particularly from among the young. Among the players of the next few seasons were Laurence Olivier, Ralph Richardson (who returned again), Roger Livesey, Alec Guinness, John Mills, George Benson, Stephen Murray, Robert Morley, Anthony Quayle, Robert Helpmann (who had hitherto been seen in ballet), Lewis Casson, Harry Andrews, Frederick Bennett, Andrew

Cruickshank, Malcolm Keen, Esmé Percy, Morland Graham, Angela Baddeley, Pamela Brown, Jean Cadell, Freda Jackson, Ursula Jeans, Agnes Laughlan, Vivien Leigh, Marie Ney, Veronica Turleigh, and Sybil Thorndike.

Some notable productions were *Coriolanus,* in which Laurence Olivier extended his range in tragedy, with Sybil Thorndike; *Hamlet* in modern dress with Alec Guinness; a lively revival of *Trelawney of the Wells;* Ibsen's *An Enemy of the People; A Midsummer Night's Dream,* charmingly reminiscent of the early Victorian prints, with the music of Mendelssohn; and *The Taming of the Shrew,* produced in the manner of the *commedia dell'arte.*

THE OLD VIC DURING THE WAR

During the years of the war, the Old Vic Company went on tour, performing sometimes in remote parts of England and Wales, and established a headquarters at the Victoria Theatre in Burnley in the north of England.

Early in 1940 the Old Vic Theatre opened tentatively with a fine *Lear* by John Gielgud, to which Jack Hawkins, Robert Harris, Nicolas Hannen, Stephen Haggard, Andrew Cruickshank, Fay Compton, Jessica Tandy, and Cathleen Nesbitt contributed much distinction. Lewis Casson and Harley Granville-Barker directed. This was followed by a remarkable production by George Devine and Marius Goring of *The Tempest,* with Gielgud as Prospero and settings and costumes beautifully designed by Oliver Messel. This was the last production at the Old Vic Theatre until it reopened long after the war.

During 1943, the Playhouse Theatre in London was taken over as a temporary home for the Old Vic, but it failed to attract the changing wartime public. Three plays were produced: Drinkwater's *Abraham Lincoln,* in which Herbert Lomas gave a fine interpretation of the title role; *The Russians,* an English version of a topical play by Konstantin Simonov about life among the Russian partisans, with Freda Jackson; and Peter Ustinov's *Blow Your Own Trumpet.*

REPERTORY AT THE OLD VIC

Then, in the autumn of 1944, the Old Vic was renewed by the formation of a new company at the New Theatre to present plays in repertory. This was headed by Tyrone Guthrie, Laurence Olivier, Ralph Richardson, and John Burrell. The intention was to rehearse three plays for a beginning, which would be given alternately, and gradually to add further plays. Hitherto each play at the Old Vic had run for three weeks, or occasionally for four, and was then abandoned for the next production. The new form of repertory, as it exists on the Continent, implied a permanent company, and the actors would have a variety of parts during the week.

The opening plays were *Peer Gynt, Arms and the Man,* and *Richard III. Uncle Vanya* was added later in the year. Laurence Olivier and Ralph Richardson played the leading roles, and the excellent casts which had been assembled included Sybil Thorndike, Margaret Leighton, Joyce Redman, Nicolas Hannen, George Relph, Michael Warre, and Harcourt Williams.

Peer Gynt was the opening piece, in which Ralph Richardson was magnificent as the willful, erratic, and hapless Peer, portraying the change from youth to old age with remarkable skill. Sybil Thorndike was extremely moving as Ase, Olivier took the small part of the buttonmoulder, and the whole cast played together with an ease and ability that promised well for the future of the company. Tyrone Guthrie directed, and the decor was the work of a young designer, Reece Pemberton, who made interesting use of semitransparent settings on which various cutout shadows were projected, enabling a rapid change of scene. A regular Old Vic audience received the production and Richardson's performance with rapturous applause.

There was no doubt that the Shaw play was going to be a success as it was tried out in Manchester beforehand. The two leading parts of Sergius and Bluntschli were taken by Olivier and Richardson, and Nicolas Hannen played Petkoff. Joyce Redman, Margaret Leighton, and Sybil Thorndike made it a gay romp. John Burrell directed *Arms and the Man* and the following plays of the season with great attention to movement, action, and ensemble playing, which the company so successfully achieved.

Richard III was a triumph for Olivier, a Richard without the passion of historical interpretations but with the logic of satanic evil. *Uncle Vanya* was the time for Richardson to shine as the tragic failure, but wholly human, Vanya.

At the end of the season, in the summer of 1945, the company toured the Continent, appearing with great success wherever they played in Antwerp, Brussels, Hamburg, and finally at the Comédie Française in Paris.

This first season of brilliant playing and production of standard plays and the alternating repertory was wholly successful, both financially and artistically, despite the fact that at the time of opening London was being bombarded with flying bombs and rockets. The leading players added further distinction to their already considerable reputations, and the repertory system of playing was firmly established. The Old Vic Company continued operations at the New Theatre for the next four years, during which time more distinguished players joined the company, including Alec Guinness, Bernard Miles, Harry Andrews, George Relph, Baliol Holloway, Miles Malleson, John Clements, Trevor Howard, Edith Evans, Pamela Brown, Celia Johnson, and Rosalind Atkinson.

The Old Vic Company had some notable tours abroad in 1946, in America (playing at the Century Theatre in New York), and in Paris. In 1948 they went to Australia. Later, further tours were made with special productions. America and Canada were visited three times, Australia again, South Africa, and many tours were made to various countries on the Continent, including Russia.

THE BRISTOL OLD VIC

A branch of the Old Vic was established at Bristol in the beautiful Georgian Theatre Royal, and became known as the Bristol Old Vic which, however, was autonomous, with its own productions and players, although they were presented from time to time in London.

THE POSTWAR OLD VIC

In 1950, the Old Vic Theatre in the Waterloo Road reopened, its war damage repaired and refurbished, and settled down to some years of steady progress with a new generation of players and directors. Olivier, Richardson, and Guthrie departed from the company to their own individual activities in the West End theatres and elsewhere. The new system of repertory was retained and the new directors, Hugh Hunt and Michael Benthall, worked steadily through the Shakespeare cycle of plays, completing it in 1958.

THE NATIONAL THEATRE

In 1962 the Old Vic became the National Theatre under the directorship of Laurence Olivier, with the backing of Government finance. It continues at the old theatre at present until an entirely new building, already designed, is constructed on the South Bank. The National Theatre's policy is to provide a home for Shakespeare and the classics, but also to produce new plays, and in this it has been very resourceful. The plays are performed in repertory, and in the current season no less than eight plays are being given alternately, four of which are new plays.

THE ENGLISH STAGE COMPANY

The English Stage Company at the Court Theatre (now the Royal Court), which was established under the direction of George Devine in 1950, has also been a major influence, particularly in its encouragement of plays by new writers. These have generally been plays of serious purpose, and often iconoclastic (as John Osborne's *Look Back in Anger*), but there are never enough new plays for a continuous program, and Devine falls back on established works, mostly Continental or American. Even Shakespeare sees occasional production. Some fine players have been associated with the Royal Court, including Robert Shaw, Ronald Fraser, Alfred Lynch, and Peter O'Toole.

With the recent death of George Devine it is perhaps difficult to visualize the future policy of the English Stage Company, but it may well add to its discoveries of talented young writers, directors, and players.

THE ROYAL SHAKESPEARE COMPANY

Another important influence in the English theatre is the Royal Shakespeare Company, whose home is the Memorial Theatre at Stratford-on-Avon. Although this theatre was built in 1930, for some years it housed only a summer festival of Shakespeare's plays, for which many distinguished players and directors made the journey from London for the short season.

W. Bridges Adams, Iden Payne, Robert Atkins, and Theodore Komisarjevsky made many interesting productions. The company was not fully developed, however, until after the war when first Anthony Quayle, as director, lengthened the season from early spring to late autumn, and later Peter Hall extended the activities by taking over the Aldwych Theatre as a London showplace.

Quayle concentrated chiefly on presenting Shakespeare in a fresh, vital manner, a policy continued by Peter Hall, who has also introduced contemporary plays into the repertory at the company's London home. Some present-day dramatists have been commissioned to write plays for the company. As at the Old Vic and the present National Theatre, these are presented in alternating repertory, so that in one week audiences at Stratford and London can see three or four varied productions.

The Royal Shakespeare Theatre and the National Theatre have recruited large permanent companies of players, many of whom are proving themselves brilliant actors, equally at home in period and modern productions. It is among these players that the stars of the future will undoubtedly be found.

VISITING FOREIGN COMPANIES

During the summer months, when the emphasis is on Shakespeare at Stratford, the company relinquishes the Aldwych Theatre to a season of productions from Continental theatres. Companies from France, Poland, Greece, Italy, and elsewhere on the Continent have given weeks of their repertory, played in their own languages, with modern electronic devices providing a simultaneous translation should the individual member of the audience require it. Lee Strasberg's Actors' Studio Theatre from New York has also performed during this season. A good deal of contemporary experience in the theatre has thus been available in London, and much has been learned of methods of staging and production. The Moscow Art Theatre Company has made two visits to London with their great productions of Chekhov and other Russian works.

THE BERLINER ENSEMBLE COMPANY IN ENGLAND

The Berliner Ensemble Company of Bertold Brecht has also had two London seasons, in 1956 at the Palace Theatre and in 1965 at the Old Vic. The interest they created in their unique methods of presentation has been widespread, although the content of their propaganda for a Marxist view of history has been accepted with much reservation. The meticulous production of their work in all its detail—sometimes in an expressionist manner, often in a formal symbolic mood, and at other times quite realistically—is blended in a rapid and continuous flow of the unfolding of the main theme. Actors play short scenes, the lights fade, and the minimal scenery changes are made to the next part of the action. During such short pauses, a screen is lowered on which is projected a commentary on the action or on the political background. This is useful when they are playing abroad, as the players act in German. The acting is often brilliant in the broad, but to English eyes rather old-fashioned, Continental manner.

Brecht's essential aim was to create audience participation in the production, and to this end no curtain is used, the stage is open at the beginning and the end, and the climax is obtained by an extremely skillful building up of theatrical effects, using all the technical resources of the modern theatre in lighting and electronically produced sounds and music. Actors sometimes address the audience directly, and occasionally appear in the audience.

To some, the transition of the stage as an illusory picture to a

platform on which a thesis is propounded may be considered outside
the realm of the theatre, but others consider that much can be
learned in the methods used and the powerful vitality of the performances. Certainly Joan Littlewood, in her Theatre Workshop
production of *The Hostage* by Brendan Behan, found that the actors can bring the audience closer to a play by the direct approach,
by the rapid movement of the drama using the absolute minimum
of scenery, and by the interpolation of songs and dances.

THE MERMAID THEATRE

Another new center of theatrical activity was created with the opening of the Mermaid Theatre on the banks of the Thames in the
City of London in 1959, the first theatre to be opened in that center
of trade and commerce for some four hundred years. It arose on the
bomb-blasted but solid walls of a Victorian warehouse, and its in-
ception was largely the work of its director, the fine character actor
Bernard Miles.

It is a simple theatre, with a rectangular racked auditorium sloping directly into a wide-open stage without a proscenium. A large
revolve is built into the stage and is used in much of the action.

The opening production was a musical play based on a comedy
of London in 1730 by Henry Fielding, retitled *Lock up Your
Daughters*. This production had all the vitality of a new company
anxious to show their paces and, without any great stars, it became
a smash hit. Although intended to last only six weeks, it ran for
several months and firmly established the new theatre. Since then,
the policy has been to present a varied program of classical plays
other than Shakespeare's, and new plays of interest — English,
American, and Continental. Among these have been the *Galileo* of
Bertold Brecht, Pirandello's *Right You Are (If You Think So)*,
Maxwell Anderson's adaptation of Alan Paton's novel *Cry the
Beloved Country*, Dekker's *The Shoemaker's Holiday*, Gogol's *The
Marriage Brokers*, the *Oedipus* plays of Sophocles, Beaumont and
Fletcher's *The Maid's Tragedy*, and *The Wakefield Mystery Plays*.

Links with the off-Broadway theatre in New York were forged

with a visit of the Living Theatre company in their production of *The Brig* by Kenneth H. Brown during the early summer of 1965.

THE THEATRES AND THE REAL ESTATE COMPANIES

The West End theatre suffered occasional onslaught by the developments of real estate companies. As in New York, the theatres are chiefly old buildings sitting on land which has increased enormously in value. Since London's authorities have removed the building-height limit, and office blocks in tower form are becoming a familiar feature of the city, the St. James's Theatre and the Stoll Theatre among others have been demolished by these incursions. There are, however, still some forty theatres which are open most of the year. Some of these, such as Drury Lane, are too large for anything but musicals and these, chiefly from America, they continue to provide very successfully. The longest-running productions (excluding the phenomenal thriller *The Mousetrap* by Agatha Christie, now in its fourteenth year at a small theatre, the Ambassadors), have been musicals and the farces such as Brian Rix has provided at the Whitehall Theatre for the last twenty years, echoing the success of the Tom Walls–Ralph Lynn gambols at the Aldwych Theatre in the 1920's.

THE CHICHESTER FESTIVAL THEATRE

Some new theatres have been established outside London; among the most notable is the Chichester Festival Theatre, a summer repertory theatre which has been under the directorship of Laurence Olivier. Many of their productions were subsequently absorbed into the National Theatre at the Old Vic, including Peter Shaffer's *The Royal Hunt of the Sun* and *Black Comedy* and Strindberg's *Miss Julie*.

PROVINCIAL THEATRES

Other new theatres of note in the provinces are the Nottingham Playhouse, the Belgrade Theatre in Coventry, the new Shakespeare Theatre in Liverpool, and the latest—a delightful theatre in the

THE CHICHESTER FESTIVAL THEATRE   Founded in 1962 by Leslie Evershed-Martin, the Chichester Theatre was inspired by the Shakespeare Theatre in Ontario, Canada. The open stage, with its two playing areas is surrounded on three sides by the audience. No seat is more than 66 feet from the stage. A gallery encircling the top of the auditorium can be used as a third playing area.

country outskirts of Guildford named after Yvonne Arnaud, the well-known West End actress, which opened with a fine production of *A Month in the Country* with Michael Redgrave and Ingrid Bergman. The production was later transferred to the West End. These, in addition to the well-established repertory companies at Birmingham, Manchester, Liverpool, Glasgow, and many other cities, continue to provide the drama of today and the classics of the past.

TELEVISION AND THE THEATRE

Generally, the theatre in England has made considerable progress since the last war. The cinema, which closed many theatres in the period between the wars, has itself been overcome by television. But drama has become one of the most popular offerings on television in England. Television has given new opportunities to dramatists, directors, and players, particularly in spreading their fame to millions. Television has also offered excerpts directly transmitted from an actual theatre with a live audience, which have proved to be greatly beneficial to the future run of the production.

ACTING ADVANCES

Acting has perhaps seen the greatest advance, no doubt due to the establishment of the repertory system and the wide range of contemporary and classical drama being constantly produced. The actor of today must be prepared to speak the verses of Shakespeare and of his contemporaries, to move in the affected manner of the Restoration beau, or to speak in the Cockney accent of Wesker's characters. He must be something of an acrobat and dancer, as in Theatre Workshop productions, and have to endure playing his part completely immobile, as in *Endgame*.

Without doubt, the English actor has gained tremendously in his grounding in Shakespeare, in the infinite range of characters, and in the fine shades of meaning which he can interpret. Generally, with his experience in the classics of the past he acquires a sure sense of period acting, and perhaps this is his forte. But many younger actors, without this grounding, have also been highly successful in the contemporary plays of social realism. They may be more limited in their range, but they have developed a naturalistic style well suited to the demands of the play.

STAGING

As yet, there have been few advances in the actual staging of plays, apart from some minor Brechtian influences. It is possible that the old theatres do not lend themselves to advances in this field, and it is salutary that the new theatres in America have either an arena stage or a thrust stage, which brings audiences in much closer contact with the players. A possible return to the elements of the Elizabethan theatre, with all its make-believe, would require a wealth and richness of language which has not been evident among the new dramatists. So far, the greatest impact they have made has been in a naturalistic setting in the traditional stage picture. It remains to be seen whether the play of ideas can also become the play of the heart and the emotions.

American Theatre —20th Century

NEW TRENDS IN THE AMERICAN THEATRE

While the theatre prospered materially in the early years of the twentieth century, with its large new theatres, growing audiences, and its productions of great technical skill, from the standpoint of both acting and staging, the plays presented were chosen mainly for their entertainment and commercial value. The theatre was indeed Big Business now. The great dramas in which the leading actors could extend the range of their interpretation were still largely those of the past or by foreign dramatists.

It is the development of the work of the newer writers of the century that has lifted the American theatre to international acclaim. It is a development, on one side, into the field of serious drama, an attempt to relate the fundamental truths beneath the surface of contemporary American society in terms of a questioning of the motives and problems of life itself. On the other side there have been many excellent comedies which have an underlying seriousness. A further advancement in the theatre, on the lighter side, has been the universally acknowledged rise of the American musical.

In an age of great material advancement, there has naturally been great disruption and reassessment of personal and spiritual values, and the theatre has reflected this turmoil of thought and ideas in the work of its younger dramatists. There was a natural reaction to what had gone before—the well-worked-out plot, the spectacular climax, and the submission of truth-to-life to theatrical effect. General trends in the new plays have been away from these attributes, with a more serious and vital theme, a less contrived story, and essential truthfulness of character.

New American writers had to learn the business of stagecraft and its importance to dramatic form, and in the early years of the century there were several small groups of individuals, interested in serious writing for the theatre, who put on semiprivate performances which enabled them to see their work in practice. The actors were interested amateurs, as were the directors and designers, and what was lacking in technical skill was partly replaced by an infectious group enthusiasm which enabled the group to press on with their activities, gradually improving their skills and ultimately the standard of the drama. Eventually, they made the difficult crossing into the professional theatre and became, in the 1920's, the potent force in the American theatre. As they had to learn their craft from scratch, they were fortunate in avoiding the influence of traditional theatricality in acting, presentation, and scenic design. The result was something fresh and vital, expressive of the new generation.

GEORGE PIERCE BAKER

Perhaps more than anyone, a professor of English Literature at Harvard, George Pierce Baker, was the important influence in this upsurge of the American theatre. Although he was never able to persuade the Governing Board to ratify his drama course into full academic acceptance, he was able to instigate his "47 Workshop," in which his students actually produced their own plays and, in the process, learned much of acting, directing, costume and scenic design, lighting, and the innumerable practical problems of staging. He was able to continue this work for nearly twenty years at Harvard. In 1925, he moved to Yale, where he became professor of a newly created Department of Drama, with a new University theatre and the work raised to graduate status. He remained there, directing his department, until shortly before his death in 1936.

Many of his students became major figures in the American theatre of this century. Among the playwrights were Edward Sheldon, Eugene O'Neill, S. N. Behrman, Sidney Howard, Philip Barry, Percy MacKaye, Edward Knoblock, George Abbott, Hubert Osborne, and Thomas Wolfe. Others became producers and directors: Winthrop Ames, Alexander Dean, Sam Hume, Irving Pichel, Theresa Helburn. Some became critics: John Mason Brown, Robert Benchley, Heywood Broun, Walter Prichard Eaton, and Kenneth Macgowan. Three of his students became leading designers in the American theatre: Robert Edmond Jones, who also directed; Lee Simonson; and Donald Oenslager. Others became well-known actors: Mary Morris and Osgood Perkins.

Professor Baker must have had an extraordinary enthusiasm and faith in the theatre, with great ability as a teacher, to inspire so many of his students to go on to great things. They brought to the American theatre an integrity in human and artistic values which has been vital in its rise to international status.

COLLEGE THEATRES

Since those early days, colleges and universities throughout the country have offered degrees in drama and partake actively in public performances. Indeed, many of the best new theatres built since the last war have been college theatres, some of them becoming firmly established, with professional schedules for eight months of the year, playing not only to students and friends, but serving the whole community and occasionally undertaking road tours of the locality. Others have summer seasons of drama with professional casts and visiting stars in addition to the normal work of the academic year.

EUGENE O'NEILL

The most outstanding of the new dramatists, without doubt, was

Eugene O'Neill. Born in 1888, the son of a well-known actor, James O'Neill, who for many years toured the country playing the leading role in *The Count of Monte Cristo,* Eugene spent much of his early life accompanying his father. He must have acquired a taste for and a knowledge of the theatre at a very early age.

After a varied education leading to Princeton University, where he spent a year in 1906, he drifted into many occupations—prospected for gold, worked in business, and served in the Merchant Navy on many voyages to the various ports of the Atlantic. He began writing as a newspaper reporter, but he was discovered to be suffering from tuberculosis and spent six months in a sanitarium in 1913. It was during this time that he first began to write for the theatre.

THE PROVINCETOWN PLAYERS

O'Neill became known to a group of amateur and professional actors, the Provincetown Players, who at first were summer visitors to Provincetown, performing at the house of one of their number, Hutchins Hapgood, but later converting an old fish warehouse into the Wharf Theatre. In the summer of 1916 an association began which was to lead to the production of many of O'Neill's works. The Provincetown Players produced two of his short plays, *Bound East for Cardiff* and *Thirst.* The following winter, an ambitious move was made by establishing a small playhouse in Greenwich Village. Here the company prospered until the Depression of 1929 finally closed it. Among the original members were Susan Glaspell, John Reed, and Robert Edmond Jones. Many other talented people were attracted to the company as writers, directors, designers, and actors, including Floyd Dell, Lawrence Langner, Mary Morris, Henry O'Neill, Walter Huston, Otto Kruger, Donald Oenslager, and Kenneth Macgowan.

O'Neill wrote some other plays, drawing on his experience at sea — *In the Zone, The Long Voyage Home,* and *The Moon of the Caribbees*—in 1917–1918. They expressed his views of humanity with a realism hitherto unknown in the theatre. He soon began to be noticed by the critics as a coming dramatist, and within the next few years he developed broader themes and a more ambitious means of expression.

Although he rejected his early religious background as a Roman Catholic, his concern was for the void left by the failure of the old religious beliefs to be appropriate in a world of scientific and materialist thought. That the advancement of this new world failed to supply any intrinsic values was his constant concern. Although he went to the German philosophers for guidance, his later plays are suffused with a failure to find a positive attitude to the problem. In the end, he became a pessimist and heavily despondent.

His early work shows his wonderful grasp of essentials, the creation of real character, and a deeply sympathetic understanding of a humanity caught in the toils of circumstance. There is an intensity in his feeling for the sweep of the drama, and the inexorable gloom of his tragic situations is occasionally lit by flashes of real humor.

He was fortunate in having many of his plays produced by the Provincetown Players, who were seeking by various experimental means a way of presenting the new plays. O'Neill, who was closely associated with Robert Edmond Jones and Kenneth Macgowan, clearly learned much of value in his search for a means of expressing his ideas in an atmosphere of untrammeled freedom.

O'NEILL'S FIRST BROADWAY PRODUCTIONS

He had his first Broadway production in 1920 with *Beyond the Horizon,* a success endorsed by his gaining the Pulitzer Prize, an award established in 1917 by the will of the publisher, Joseph Pulitzer, for the best play of the year. This bitter tragedy of a man tied to a farm life in which he is unsuccessful while longing for the sea established O'Neill in the professional theatre. In the following years he became a prolific and ever-questing writer who was rapidly accepted as the leading American dramatist.

The Emperor Jones was also produced in 1920. This has remained one of his best-known and most-often-produced plays. Its study of primeval fear, effectively suggested by the constant background of tom-toms, presented a wonderful opportunity for a Negro actor, perhaps the best known in the part being Paul Robeson.

The following year came *Anna Christie,* a second version of an earlier work, *Chris Christopherson,* a story of romantic and venal love played against a background of the sea. This earned O'Neill his second Pulitzer Prize.

In 1921 *The Straw* and *The First Man* were written. Although minor works, they present very actable parts. The following year saw *The Hairy Ape,* a study in a style of expressionism in which the main character is seen not wholly as a person but as a symbol for a whole aspect of life. O'Neill returned to his sea background in this story of a rough ship's stoker and his desire to be someone. Although the profanity of the crew in the stokehole shocked some of the audience, the realism and novelty of the setting and its characters were effectively and successfully achieved.

The next important work was *Desire Under the Elms,* produced in 1924, which created much discussion with its tragedy of an elderly New England farmer of the 1850's whose young wife becomes passionately in love with her stepson, bears his child, then in desperation kills it and is led away to be tried for murder. Walter Huston was memorable in the part of the old puritanical farmer, Ephraim Cabot, and Mary Morris played the tragic young wife, Abbie, with an extraordinary sense of warmth and humanity. This was also a triumph for Robert Edmond Jones for his sensitive direction and his unique farmhouse setting in which the various rooms and the action taking place in them were seen simultaneously by the audience.

O'Neill experimented further with symbolism in 1926 with *The Great God Brown.* The characters appear masked to denote their appearance to others and remove the masks to reveal their true selves. This play excited much interest at the time as an experiment in modern drama, although it is not now considered one of his most important works. The following year came *Lazarus Laughed,* in which O'Neill postulated the idea of a return from the grave with no longer a fear of death, to him perhaps the most potent evil in life.

Marco Millions, the presentation of Marco Polo as a brash young business go-getter, and *Strange Interlude,* were both produced in 1928, the latter play earning him his third Pulitzer Prize. *Strange Interlude* is an extremely long play of nine acts in which the characters voice their innermost thoughts in soliloquies to the audience, effectively contrasting their speech to each other. It tells the tragic story of a neurotic woman, extremely possessive by nature, and the men in her life who are alternately attracted and repelled by her. In the Theatre Guild production in New York, O'Neill reached the high point of his success with a run of no less than 432 performances, followed by a long road tour. The Theatre Guild produced *Marco Millions* at their own theatre, taking over the John Golden Theatre for *Strange Interlude.* The cast of this production, which was directed by Philip Moeller with sets by the young Jo Mielziner, now America's leading stage designer, included Lynn Fontanne, Tom Powers, Earle Larrimore, and Helen Westley. Alfred Lunt led in *Marco Millions,* with Morris Carnovsky, Ernest Cossart, Dudley Digges, Baliol Holloway, and Mary Blair.

Dynamo, in 1929, did not achieve the success of the previous year for O'Neill, although it contained some interesting ideas and its main theme of the failure of modern science to provide a valid foundation for spiritual values is a pertinent one today. The first production, which the Guild presented at the Martin Beck Theatre, was directed by Philip Moeller, with striking constructivist settings by Lee Simonson. The cast included Claudette Colbert, George Gaul, Helen Westley, Glenn Anders, Ross Forrester, Edgar Kent, and Dudley Digges.

THE MOURNING BECOMES ELECTRA TRILOGY

For the next two years, O'Neill was busy on his trilogy, *Mourning Becomes Electra,* which became his most widely acclaimed work throughout world theatre. First produced by the Guild in 1931 at the Martin Beck Theatre with Philip Moeller directing and the magnificent settings of Robert Edmond Jones, it was an immediate success. In a long evening of six hours, O'Neill unfolds his version of the Orestean tragedy set in a New England mansion at the time of the Civil War. He does not keep closely to Aeschylus' framework, but his departures from it are merely incidental.

The first play, *The Homecoming*, sees the return from the war of Ezra Mannon (Agamemnon) and his son Orin (Orestes), the murder of Ezra by his wife Christine (Clytemnestra) for the love of Captain Brant (Aegisthus). *The Hunted* continues the impelling story with Lavinia (Electra), moved by the deep love she had for her father and her hatred of her mother, persuading Orin to avenge the crime. He confronts Brant and shoots him before Christine, who then commits suicide. In the final play, *The Haunted*, Orin, overcome by remorse at the death of his mother, whom he loved, and beset by fears of madness and his father's influence over him, takes his own life. Lavinia, in punishment, is left to live out her own life alone in the gaunt Mannon house, haunted by the consequences of hate and passion and her own part in the tragic story.

There are great psychological depths in the play, subtle in their implications and carefully woven into the dialogue. In spite of its length the story is gripping, with a considerable building up of suspense. It was an attempt by O'Neill to parallel, in terms of modern psychological drama, the old Greek sense of fate, and one can accept the play for the art and great skill with which it is written. To many critics, however, it lacks the essential feeling for human qualities, the characters seeming too subservient to the theme, although in most of O'Neill's other plays the reverse is more often true.

OTHER O'NEILL PLAYS

Like the old Greek tragic plays, *Mourning Becomes Electra* was followed in 1933 by a comedy, *Ah, Wilderness!*, in which small-town life in the early years of the century is aptly caught. George M. Cohan played the father with all the whimsical geniality for which he was so well loved, and Will Rogers took it on the road. *Days*

Without End (1934), with its study of the faith of a split personality, in which O'Neill employed two actors to interpret the same
character, had a mixed reception in New York, although it was well
received when produced at the Abbey Theatre in Dublin.

For the next twelve years, O'Neill retired from the theatre and
settled down to writing a long cycle of plays which were to represent American life in the present century. Nine of them were to be
interrelated, and three or four to be independent of the cycle. His
intention was that none of them should be produced until they
were all completed. He was awarded the Nobel Prize for literature
in 1936, but he remained in retirement. He completed many of his
plays, some of which were inordinately long; but with some he
achieved only the first drafts, which he destroyed, being unable,
through illness, to complete their revision.

THE ICEMAN COMETH

New York saw the production in 1946 of *The Iceman Cometh*. It
had a long run but a very mixed critical reception. It was the beginning of that gloomy despair of life with which the later plays
of O'Neill are permeated. The scene is a cheap saloon in 1912, and
the characters are drunks who spend their days living in the past
or in pipe dreams. Although attempts are made by one of the characters to arouse them from the depths of their despair, he eventually
confesses to the murder of his deeply loved wife through his own
inability to control his cravings, and the gloom descends still deeper.
In this long play, O'Neill returned to the naturalism of his early
works, and conveys the atmosphere of his sleazy bar with consummate skill and dramatic effectiveness. It seems that his intention in
this play was to find a means of expressing the eternal searching
of the soul by man to find an understanding of life, which he finally
rejects as beyond him.

O'NEILL'S LAST PLAYS

His later plays—*Long Day's Journey into Night, A Moon for the
Misbegotten,* and *A Touch of the Poet*—were not produced in New

York until some years after his death in 1953, partly because of the wishes expressed in his will. While they were received with a deference due his position as the leading dramatist in America, they did not have the impact on his audiences that might have been expected. O'Neill, throughout his career in the theatre, had experimented with various methods of expressing his views on the inner meaning of life, and in these later plays, although still with dramatic effectiveness, he returned to the realism of his early work. But underlying it was a heavy despondent philosophy, without hope.

O'Neill's life in the theatre spanned a period of great development. During this time many other dramatists produced work which, although never reaching the heights or the depths of his achievement, nevertheless added considerably to the stature of American drama. Generally speaking, they reacted more closely to the affairs of the day, or to periods of history wherein the main theme had a parallel validity.

MAXWELL ANDERSON

Maxwell Anderson, who was born in the same year as O'Neill, wrote plays on many varied subjects and in many different styles, and his poetic imagination colors most of them. His earliest success was with the popular hit *What Price Glory?* (1924), a realistic presentation of the American soldier in World War I which was written in collaboration with Laurence Stallings. This was followed by *Saturday's Children* (1927), the first popular success by his own hand. A realistic comedy of young love and marriage, with serious implications, it was an outstanding success. *Gypsy*, another realistic play, is a tragedy of city life, with its story of the young girl passing from one man to another without finding that special someone with whom she could remain, her disappointment leading to suicide.

Anderson experimented with verse drama, and in *Elizabeth, the Queen* (1930) he produced a moving dramatic play, perhaps idealistic in conception, but with considerable beauty of language. He continued this trend in 1933 with *Mary of Scotland* in which he took artistic license with history by making Mary and Elizabeth meet. Other historical plays were *Valley Forge,* an attempt to dramatize the life of Washington and his struggles with Congress; *The Masque of Kings,* the tragedy of Crown Prince Rudolf and Maria Vetsera; *Night Over Taos; Joan of Lorraine,* in which Ingrid Bergman was memorable as Joan of Arc; *Anne of the Thousand Days;* and *Knickerbocker Holiday,* with music by Kurt Weill, in which Walter Huston splendidly characterized old Peter Stuyvesant.

Anderson turned to political satire in *Both Your Houses,* which earned him a Pulitzer Prize in 1933. His best play was *Winterset,* a verse tragedy of injustice which received a memorable production in New York with Burgess Meredith as the young man who sacrifices his life to vindicate the father unjustly executed for murder, Margo as the girl who befriends him, and Richard Bennett as the judge whose mind is unhinged by his conduct of the case. The setting by Jo Mielziner of the vast background of Brooklyn Bridge was admirably expressive of the inexorable march of fate.

Other Anderson plays, in different styles, have been *Key Largo; The Star Wagon; Truckline Café; The Wingless Victory; High Tor; The Bad Seed;* and *Journey to Jerusalem,* an attempt to present the early life of Jesus. Anderson's plays display a practical understanding of the theatre, and as a fine craftsman he never loses sight of the basic need to entertain, however tragic his theme may be.

ELMER RICE

Elmer Rice, who was trained as a lawyer and practiced for a time, became equally well-known as a director and a dramatist. His first play, *On Trial* (1914), was an outstanding success with its use of the flashback, a technique much employed by later dramatists. In *The Adding Machine* in 1923, he employed with great skill the expressionist technique then being used by German dramatists, in a satire of the machine-age man. *Mr. Zero* was well staged by the Theatre Guild, with Dudley Digges, Helen Westley, and Margaret Wycherley.

Many consider *Street Scene* his best play. Produced in 1929, it is a realistic treatment of life in a New York tenement. It was awarded the Pulitzer Prize. *Counsellor-at-Law* gave Paul Muni an excellent role as a Jewish attorney, and drew on Rice's own expert knowledge of the law. In *Judgment Day* (1934), Rice made a powerful dramatization of the Reichstag Fire trial, the first of those travesties of justice staged for political ends which have become so familiar in our day.

During the 1930's, Rice's obvious allegiance to the underdog was evidenced in his work for the Federal Theatre Project. His ideas of providing employment for the numbers of unemployed actors crystallized in the "Living Newspaper," a dramatization of current events using many short scenes with different actors and rapid changes. His interest in social problems was also expressed in *We, the People* (1933), in which the theatre becomes a political meeting.

Between Two Worlds was a failure, although it was a serious attempt to dramatize the differences between the American and the Russian way of life. *Two on an Island* is a romantic and charming comedy of Manhattan. In *Flight to the West* (1940), Rice deals with Nazi madness and introduces an element of melodrama. *A New Life,* two years later, is a slight work of youthful idealism and its conflict with conventionality. *Dream Girl* (1945) gave Betty Field a good role as a very imaginative girl discovering romance in the least expected place.

GEORGE S. KAUFMAN

George S. Kaufman, known as "The Great Collaborator," and also as one of the best directors of farce and comedy, had a keen sense of satire. He wrote many plays with Edna Ferber, including *The Royal Family,* inspired by the Drews and the Barrymores of Broadway; *Dinner at Eight;* and *Stage Door.* His other chief collaboration was with Moss Hart, which produced *Once in a Lifetime,* a 1930 satire on Hollywood; *Merrily We Roll Along;* and *You Can't Take It With You,* which won a Pulitzer Prize in 1936. With Moss Hart, he also painted a hilarious portrait of Alexander Woollcott in *The Man Who Came to Dinner* in 1939. (He had previously collaborated with Woollcott on *The Channel Road* [1929] and *The Dark Tower* [1933].) These were all extremely successful farcical comedies, witty, and with an underlying feeling for humanity. He also collaborated with Marc Connelly in several plays, including *Beggar on Horseback*. His most important solo effort was *The Butter and Egg Man*, a farce of theatrical life.

ROBERT E. SHERWOOD

Robert E. Sherwood began as a critic, and after serving in World War I in which he was gassed and wounded, became a distinguished dramatist between the wars, with both comedy and the serious play of ideas. His first success, in 1927, was a satirical farce about Hannibal, *The Road to Rome*, in which he debunked the glory of the ancient Carthaginian general's march, giving fine parts to Philip Merivale, Barry Jones, and Jane Cowl. The following year *The Queen's Husband* gave Roland Young an amusing opportunity as the henpecked king of a Central European country.

London found *Waterloo Bridge* (1930), a melodrama of World War I, more acceptable than did New York. Its story of the streetwalker and the American soldier in London, however, showed Sherwood's ability to write plays impregnated with a deeply human sympathy. A very successful excursion into high romantic comedy followed in 1931 with *Reunion in Vienna*, in which the Lunts appeared brilliantly in both New York and London.

In 1935 came *The Petrified Forest*, a melodramatic play of the disillusion of a young writer and his choice of death at the hand of the escaping gangster rather than the negative, empty life in which he was drifting. The play was made memorable by the performances of Leslie Howard and Humphrey Bogart, repeated for universal enjoyment in the film.

Tovarich (1936) was an adaptation from the French·of Jacques Deval's amusing comedy of Russian *émigré* life in America. Sherwood's awareness of the coming storm in Europe was evidenced by *Idiot's Delight*, in which his earlier pacifism developed to a positive protest against fascism. It earned him the Pulitzer Prize in 1936. In

1939, Sherwood wrote *There Shall Be No Night,* the drama of a pacifist scientist turning to war during the Russian invasion of Finland (later changed, in the London version, to Germany's invasion of Greece). *Abe Lincoln in Illinois* was directed by Elmer Rice in 1938, and Raymond Massey brought distinction to this story of the great man's formative years.

No more plays were written until 1945, when *The Rugged Path,* a philosophical account of the motives of soldiers and journalists during World War II, was successfully produced with Spencer Tracy.

PHILIP BARRY

Philip Barry was a student of Professor Baker's 47 Workshop at Harvard, where he won the Prize Play contest in 1922 with *You and I,* an inherently serious play which has a surface polish of witty comedy. This was to be a quality of most of his plays. *The Youngest* (1924), a satire of social pretensions, was followed by *In a Garden,* an obscure play which was remembered largely for Laurette Taylor's performance. *White Wings* (1926) proved a failure with the public, although it was well received by the critics for its satire and symbolism. Other comedies of manners followed, including *Paris Bound, Holiday,* and *The Animal Kingdom.* Perhaps the best of his comedies is *The Philadelphia Story,* of 1939, brilliantly witty, and remembered for Katharine Hepburn's sparkling performance.

In *Tomorrow and Tomorrow* (1931), Barry turned to a more serious theme of married happiness and sexual passion. *Hotel Universe* (1930) was another serious play in which an attempt was made to dramatize the revelation to a group of individuals of the naked truth within them in a symbolic expiation for their sins. This is probably his most ambitious work, but it failed with the public. In *The Joyous Season,* Barry attempted to deal with the underlying importance of religious faith which colors the impulses and actions of individuals. Although a sincere and moving play, it failed with the public, as did *Bright Star* in 1935. *Here Come the Clowns* was produced in 1938, with Eddie Dowling giving a fine performance.

Barry later contributed *Liberty Jones* (1941), *Without Love* (1942), and *Foolish Notion* (1945).

MARC CONNELLY

Marc Connelly often collaborated with other writers, particularly with George S. Kaufman. Their partnership proved to be most successful, and included *Dulcy,* in which Lynn Fontanne established her reputation as a star in 1921; *To the Ladies,* a comedy of the astute young wife behind her not-so-ambitious husband; *The 49-ers; Merton of the Movies,* a hilarious satire of Hollywood from the original novel of Harry Leon Wilson; *Beggar on Horseback;* and *Be Yourself.*

Connelly then parted company with Kaufman and wrote *The Wisdom Tooth* (1926), following this with his masterpiece, *The Green Pastures.* This retelling of the Bible stories in terms of the Negro spiritual greatly impressed the public with its reverence, its humor, and its deep and sympathetic understanding. Connelly himself directed the New York production in 1930, with Robert Edmond Jones designing the settings and Richard B. Harrison as "De Lawd." It had a successful run of nearly two years, won the Pulitzer Prize, and continued for three years on the road.

In 1934, Connelly began a collaboration with Frank B. Elser that resulted in a moderate success with *The Farmer Takes a Wife,* a comedy of canal life in New York State in which Henry Fonda and June Walker gave fine performances. Other plays on which he has collaborated with various authors have been *Having Wonderful Time, The Two Bouquets, Everywhere I Roam, The Flowers of Virtue,* and *A Story for Strangers.*

THORNTON WILDER

Thornton Wilder is known chiefly for his two plays, *Our Town* (1938) and *The Skin of Our Teeth* (1945), both of them experimental in form and unusual in the way in which they were produced. *Our Town* was an attempt at a close-up view of some of the inhabitants of a small New England town. The town itself, and the various settings in which the action takes place, are left to the imagination of the audience, as the whole play takes place on a bare stage, except for a few chairs and rostrums, and there is no scenery. A member of the town acts as a stage manager and sets each short scene by his description and introduction of the characters. In spite of this apparent lack of realism, the action of the characters in their daily lives, in falling in love, and in dying is played out in a natu- ralistic style, with an imaginative use of lighting, and is extremely effective and moving.

The Skin of Our Teeth is a rather rambling play, lacking the unity of the earlier *Our Town,* but it does set out to embrace the whole of mankind in his struggles to make a comfortable and mean- ingful life against the various national disasters he has been faced with since the Ice Age. This is not done historically, but in terms of contemporary American life, and it uses many devices of the expres- sionistic technique, later developed further by Brecht. Wilder, how- ever, has no ax to grind, and the play conveys its story as a kind of modern morality play, although with many lighthearted moments of humor.

Wilder has written other plays, more conventional in form, of which *The Matchmaker,* a later reworking of his *The Merchant of Yonkers,* is perhaps the best known. This farcical comedy about a designing widow, set in the early years of the century, provided an excellent part for Ruth Gordon, who was magnificent. This was later made into the successful musical *Hello Dolly.*

S. N. BEHRMAN

Among other important dramatists of this generation who have used the conventional form is Samuel Nathan Behrman, noted for his social comedies, which appeared regularly throughout the twenties and thirties, providing entertaining vehicles for such stylish players as the Lunts, Ruth Gordon, Constance Collier, and Henry Daniell. Among these were, notably, *The Second Man, Serena Blandish, Brief Moment, No Time for Comedy,* and *Amphitryon 38,* the last adapted from the French comedy by Jean Giraudoux.

LILLIAN HELLMAN

Also in this group is Lillian Hellman, who has displayed in her plays great dramatic force and an impressive command of the stage. Her first play, *The Children's Hour,* first produced in 1934, was about a private children's school and the slander of two women teachers which, set in motion, relentlessly pursued its evil path to a final tragedy. The subject was dealt with both delicately and powerfully, and with a sure dramatic touch. It had a successful run for two years. *Days to Come* and *The Little Foxes* were also strong dramas of character in which evil and avarice were given full rein. Other notable works have been *Watch on the Rhine, Another Part of the Forest,* and *Toys in the Attic.*

REGIONAL WRITERS

Some dramatists have written plays with a definite regional character, and among these are Lynn Riggs, DuBose Heyward, and Paul Green. Lynn Riggs has written both tragedies and comedies devoted to life in the South and Southwest. His best-known play is the comedy, *Green Grow the Lilacs,* in which Franchot Tone made his name in 1930. This became much more widely known during the last war, when it was adapted as a musical by Oscar Hammerstein II and Richard Rodgers, to become the record-running *Oklahoma!* Other Riggs plays have been *Russet Mantle, Roadside,* and *The Cream in the Well,* a fine tragedy of farm life which was unfortunate in its presentation on Broadway because of the imminence of threatening clouds of war.

DuBose Heyward, a native of Charleston, with his wife as collaborator, is chiefly known for his sympathetic treatment of the Southern Negro, first displayed in *Porgy,* produced in 1927. This, perhaps for the first time in the theatre, provided a serious view of the Negro which was advanced for its time. Previously on the stage the Negro had been treated largely as a figure of fun. The play also provided fine acting opportunities for the Negro cast. Some years later, Heyward reworked this play for George Gershwin, and it became the folk opera *Porgy and Bess,* produced with great success in 1935. *Mamba's Daughters* (1938), also written with Mrs. Heyward, provided a fine character part in which Ethel Waters, of revue fame, came to be regarded for the first time as a serious actress on Broadway.

PAUL GREEN

Paul Green had been a student of Frederick H. Koch who, like Professor Baker with whom he took his M.A. degree at Harvard, had a great influence on American drama through his college work. Koch ran playwriting courses, first at the University of North Dakota and then at North Carolina. There he established the Caroline Playmakers, a group of his students who wrote and produced their own plays and, as well as giving college performances, took them on tour. Koch's main interest was not to provide dramatists for Broadway but the establishment of folk drama, and it is in that field ·hat Green made his reputation. He wrote many one-act plays dealing with tenant farmers, outlaws, and Negro life in the South. His first full-length play, *In Abraham's Bosom,* was produced by the Provincetown Players in 1926 and earned him the Pulitzer Prize. It is a tragic story of a young Negro of mixed parentage trying to establish a school for Negro children who comes into conflict with the forces of hatred and obstruction, culminating in his death at the hands of a lynch mob.

Green's next play, *The Field God,* produced the following year, dealt with the farmers of the eastern part of North Carolina in their religious prejudice, and its influence on their daily lives.

His next important work was *The House of Connelly,* a drama of conflict between a decadent planter family of the old South and a virile new generation of tenant farmers. This was important in another way, as it was the first production of the Group Theatre. It opened in New York at the Martin Beck Theatre in 1931.

Green returned to the subject of Negro life with *Roll Sweet Chariot* in 1934, a reworking of his earlier play, *Potter's Field.* In 1936, he broke away from folk drama to a play with a universal theme, *Johnny Johnson,* which he subtitled *The Biography of a*

Common Man. It is a play about war, the powerful evil of war fever, and the attempts of a cheery, simple soul to bring an end to the holocaust of the battles in France in 1918. His efforts resulted in his being certified insane, and the last act is his return to America to a "house of balm." This play is partly in blank verse, full of humor and satire, but with many sad and touching moments. The music of Kurt Weill, which was interwoven throughout the action with many songs, has a biting quality which recalls that of his earlier collaboration with Brecht. Although the critics were generally favorable to the production, it was not a success, partly because the only theatre available on Broadway at the time was the very large Forty-fourth Street Theatre, and the impact of satire is greatly weakened by distance.

Green also wrote two pageant plays—*The Lost Colony,* which is performed annually as a summer attraction at an open-air theatre on Roanoke Island, and *The Highland Call,* for Fayetteville. He wrote many other one-act plays dealing with Negro life and the South, including the powerful drama of the chain gang, *Hymn* to *the Rising Sun,* and dramatized the novel *Native Son* by the Negro writer Richard Wright.

THE GROUP THEATRE

The Group Theatre was a new group of actors led by Harold Clurman, Cheryl Crawford, and Lee Strasberg, who had been associated in various ways with the Theatre Guild. It was to become a powerful influence during the 1930's, not only because of the extraordinary quality of the ensemble acting in a company with no stars (although several of the players later became stars of the films and theatre), but through the new plays by dramatists who worked within the group. The main trend of the plays was presenting, from a leftish point of view, the social, political, and economic problems of the times, dramatizing the conflicts of the individual in his struggle for a better life.

The Group Theatre established itself with *The House of Connelly,* but had some failures with its next productions: *1931,* an attempt to dramatize the great depression by Claire and Paul Sifton, and *Night Over Taos,* a poetic drama of the Mexican War by Maxwell Anderson. *Success Story* by John Howard Lawson had a run of 121 performances toward the end of 1932, but this was followed by another failure, *Big Night,* from Dawn Powell's *The Party.* These were all plays dealing in some measure with social conscience.

The next production was a melodrama about hospital interns by Sidney Kingsley, *Men in White.* This included a scene in the operating theatre played completely in pantomime. In this play, the actors of the Group Theatre found a level of quality they had not previously reached, and the production was a great success. The fruit of two years of hard work, with a mixed bag of failures and part successes, now culminated in the most finished and unified presentation. Lee Strasberg directed, and the quiet, simple settings of Mordecai Gorelik, who created so many of the Group's designs, served admirably to enhance the mood and atmosphere. The play won the Pulitzer Prize of the season and had a long run of nearly a year, which put the company's finances, for the first time, on a firm basis.

The actors of the Group Theatre, although paid a small salary during actual performances, had to keep themselves between rehearsals and productions, but they generally managed to remain together as a group. They included Stella Adler, Luther Adler, Clifford Odets, Franchot Tone, Morris Carnovsky, Elia Kazan, Frances Farmer, J. Edward Bromberg, Mary Morris, Jules (John) Garfield, Russell Collins, and Lee J. Cobb.

Lee Strasberg developed a new system of rehearsal inspired by Stanislavsky's direction at the Moscow Art Theatre, in which training of the individual actor had a vital part. There was a good deal of discussion of the meaning behind the play and the actor's expression of that meaning beyond his particular role. To encourage and develop the actor's powers of imagination scenes were improvised outside the action of the play, but having an emotional relation to it. Also, the scenes of the play were run through without the actual dialogue, with actors improvising their own speeches. They were also called upon to do exercises in emotional memory, dramatizing incidents or events in their own lives.

All this was intended to further the Group's principle of a theatre based on life itself and the creation of really spontaneous acting working from the inside outward. This implies a naturalism in style, and is most successful in realistic productions. In poetic drama, however, the need is for a lyricism which must come from the language itself, whether in prose or verse, and a different approach is necessary.

CLIFFORD ODETS

From the success of *Men in White,* the Group went on to produce the plays of one of its own actors, Clifford Odets. Odets had his first work produced early in 1935, a Sunday night performance of *Waiting for Lefty,* a violent one-act play about the taxi drivers' strike of the previous year. The audience responded both to the effective performances of the Group and to the sentiments expressed in the play, and Odets became accepted as the voice of "revolutionary drama." The success of this short piece led to further work from Odets, and soon full-length plays were being written which were to see production on Broadway. Another one-act play, *Till the Day I Die,* an anti-Nazi piece, and *Waiting for Lefty* were quickly taken up by many new theatre societies being formed all over the country.

Odets' first full-length play, *Awake and Sing,* in a quieter mood, expressed the hopes and disappointments of a Bronx family during the Depression of 1932. Although not a great financial success, it established Odets in wider theatrical circles outside the radical elements associated with the Group's activities, and he was offered lucrative employment as a Hollywood writer. This was accepted, and for some years he alternated this work with writing plays for the Group.

Odets' next play, *Paradise Lost,* was produced by the Group Theatre in 1935. It was a study of the effect of bankruptcy on a middle-class family, and it had a rather mixed reception, running for only two months. This was followed by the great success of *Golden Boy* at the Belasco Theatre in 1937. This tragedy of a young violinist who is tempted to become a prizefighter and, with the financial rewards, help his family, but who in doing so ruins his hands and his ability to play, was written with great sympathy and conviction in its characterization. It did not deal with any particular political issue of the times, and perhaps because of this it attracted a wide audience. Luther Adler played the title role magnificently, and the rest of the company (which included Jules Garfield, later to be a movie star as John Garfield, Frances Farmer, Lee J. Cobb, Morris Carnovsky, Elia Kazan, Howard Da Silva, and Karl Malden) supported him with the accustomed Group ability. It ran in New York for 248 performances, then new companies were formed to take it to London and on tour in America.

Odets' subsequent plays were *Rocket to the Moon* (1938), a psychological study of an elderly dentist, his wife, and his inane young mistress; *Night Music* (1940), a lyrical fantasy of a boy searching for a home in the big city; *Clash by Night,* produced in 1941 (when the Group Theatre was disintegrating), a drama of despair on Staten Island. None of these plays had the clarity and power of his earlier works, and they failed to achieve the success of *Golden Boy*.

OTHER GROUP THEATRE PRODUCTIONS

During the ten years of its existence, the Group Theatre produced plays by many other authors. Irwin Shaw, whose grim antiwar play *Bury the Dead* was a notable production of the short-lived American Repertory Theatre, wrote *The Gentle People* for the Group, a comedy of honest and practical souls who do away with a racketeer. He later wrote *Sons and Soldiers* and *The Assassin,* which were not successful on Broadway.

Robert Ardrey's *Thunder Rock* was produced by the Group Theatre in 1939. It was a moving fantasy of a writer's futile attempt at isolation from the affairs of the day, in which the characters he creates people the stage and finally persuade him to return to the darkening world. This play was also very successful in London in

1940, with an English cast led by Michael Redgrave, where it was received as a note of optimism amid the perils of the first year of war. Ardrey later wrote *Jeb*, a notable play of Negro life.

WILLIAM SAROYAN

The Group also produced *My Heart's in the Highlands* by William Saroyan, a tender and lyrical study, possessing great charm, of a poet's attempts to maintain his integrity against an encroaching materialism. This was well received, and encouraged Saroyan to develop his style in *The Time of Your Life* which, although rejected by the Group, was produced by the Theatre Guild the following season. This play, set in a San Francisco saloon, is full of philosophy and humor, a fantasy of anarchism and benevolence among the motley characters, each seeking happiness in his own way, but sustained by the comradeship of the others and the efforts of an outsider to give them the time of their lives. Eddie Dowling, as the dispenser of encouragement and money, gave a fine performance and helped the play to great success. It won both the Pulitzer Prize and the Critics Prize of 1939. Saroyan wrote many other plays, some of which were not professionally produced, but among his produced plays were *Love's Old Street Song*, *The Beautiful People*, and *Get Away Old Man*.

VISITS BY FOREIGN COMPANIES

A potent force in the development of theatre technique in America during the twenties and thirties was the appearance on Broadway of a large number of European plays, sometimes with foreign companies for short seasons, but more frequently in translations. There were many enterprising managements who brought in works which had long been known in literary circles but had never received production in America.

This trend had already begun with such visits as those of Jacques Copeau and his Vieux-Columbier Company between 1917 and 1919 at the Garrick Theatre. In 1921, the Chauve-Souris Company from Moscow gave a season of their unique blend of musical revue, and the following year the Moscow Art Theatre had a season of repertory. This included Chekhov's *The Cherry Orchard* and *The Three Sisters,* Turgenev's *The Lady from the Provinces,* and Gorky's *The Lower Depths.*

With Stanislavsky came the great players Katchalov, Moskvin, Knipper-Chekhova, and Maria Ouspenskaya. With Ouspenskaya, two of the Moscow company decided to remain in America, Leo Bulgakov and Richard Boleslavski. Ouspenskaya and Boleslavski set up as teachers of the Stanislavsky system of acting, and it was with them that Lee Strasberg studied between 1923 and 1926, going on later to his great work with the Group Theatre. (He now dominates the Actors' Studio of New York, where he has further developed his technique of training actors and where established actors turn for inspiration.) Also from Moscow came the Habimah players in 1926, with a repertory of Hebrew plays, including their renowned production of *The Dybbuk.*

Max Reinhardt staged his production of *The Miracle* in 1923, and four years later brought his Berlin company for a season, including such works as Büchner's *Danton's Death,* Von Hofmannsthal's version of *Everyman,* and Shakespeare's *A Midsummer Night's Dream.* From Freiburg came the *Passion Play,* with its German company.

Such Continental stars as Eleanora Duse and Sacha Guitry appeared with their companies, and the Spanish Art Theatre came with a repertory of modern Spanish plays. There were, of course, a large number of productions transferred from London with English players, and periodic seasons by the Abbey Theatre of Dublin.

THE THEATRE GUILD

In the production of foreign plays with American actors, the most important organization was the Theatre Guild. This was primarily an organization of actors and directors which stemmed from the Washington Square Players, who from 1914 to their disbanding in 1918 gave performances of musical and noncommercial plays at the little Band Box Theatre, and later at the Comedy Theatre, in New

York. Their primary interest was in acting and staging plays which would not normally be seen on Broadway but which should be of artistic merit. They encouraged their members to write plays, usually of one act, which they staged with other short pieces. At first the actors were unpaid, and only two performances a week were given, but as they became established they lengthened the number to seven, and paid both actors and staff a small wage. In 1917, they moved to the Comedy, having outgrown the tiny Band Box, and put on full-length plays, including Ibsen's *Ghosts,* Andreyev's *The Life of Man,* Shaw's *Mrs. Warren's Profession,* and O'Neill's *In the Zone.*

The leaders of the company were Edward Goodman and Lawrence Langner, both of whom wrote plays and directed. Among the talented members of the casts were Katharine Cornell, Roland Young, Rollo Peters, Jose Ruben, Frank Conroy, Margaret Mower, Glen Hunter, and Marjory Vonnegut. Lee Simonson began his career as a designer with them, and others who designed and directed were Rollo Peters, Robert Edmond Jones, and Philip Moeller.

In 1919, the Theatre Guild was established by Lawrence Langner and some other members of the Washington Square Players with the intention of acting as producers of plays of merit, staged to the highest artistic standards. They took over the small Garrick Theatre, which had once been conducted by Richard Mansfield, and began a subscription scheme of selling tickets for the entire season. This proved to be an extremely successful way of financing their activities, and to this day it is used by the more important repertory companies in the country.

The Theatre Guild did not build up a permanent company, however, and engaged actors for each production, although some, of course, were constantly employed, including Dudley Digges, Helen Westley, Henry Travers, and Erskine Sanford. Perhaps the most notable and consistent players in leading roles have been Alfred Lunt and Lynn Fontanne.

By 1925, the Theatre Guild was flourishing sufficiently to build

ALFRED LUNT AND LYNN FONTANNE   America's foremost acting team
is shown as Jupiter and Alkmena in the 1937 Theatre Guild production
of Jean Giraudoux' "Amphityron 38," a play which enjoyed a moderate
success.

RUTH GORDON   She apepared in her London debut as Margery Pinch-
wife in "The Country Wife," presented at the Old Vic in October, 1936.
She repeated the role on Broadway two months later.

its own theatre, with a thousand seats. Their audiences numbered no less than 15,000 regular subscribers, and eventually this figure was doubled in New York alone.

The majority of the plays were by European authors, although the American offerings included O'Neill's *Marco Millions, Strange Interlude, Dynamo,* and *Mourning Becomes Electra;* Elmer Rice's *The Adding Machine;* Dorothy and DuBose Heyward's *Porgy;* and Sidney Howard's *The Silver Cord* and *They Knew What They Wanted.*

Of the British dramatists, Shaw was the chief contributor, and the Guild Theatre became his main platform in America. They produced *Heartbreak House, The Devil's Disciple, Saint Joan, Caesar and Cleopatra, Arms and the Man, Pygmalion, Androcles and the Lion, The Doctor's Dilemma, Major Barbara, The Millionairess,* and *Back to Methusaleh,* which was presented in three parts, each played in successive weeks.

German dramatists produced included Georg Kaiser, Stefan Zweig, Ernst Toller, and Franz Werfel. Plays from France have included those by Claudel, Courteline, Giraudoux, Anouilh, and many others. From further East have come works by Capek, Molnar, Vajda, Andreyev, and Evreinoff. From Scandinavia came Ibsen and Strindberg.

The Theatre Guild's activities have extended to other cities, and as far as the Pacific Coast, where season subscribers make touring productions less of a gamble. As time went on, the Theatre Guild became rather more of a backing organization for other plays which they had not originated, and the early standards of artistic merit required in·their plays somewhat faltered.

THE CIVIC REPERTORY THEATRE

Another venture in New York which operated through the difficult time and was finally closed by the Depression of 1932 was the Civic Repertory Theatre started by Eva Le Gallienne in 1926 at a theatre off Broadway in Fourteenth Street. Until recent years and the establishment of the Lincoln Center Repertory Theatre, this was the only repertory theatre New York has had.

Miss Le Gallienne had played leading roles in some of the Guild Theatre's productions, notably Julie in Molnar's *Liliom*. She became the leading interpreter of Ibsen in America, and is remembered particularly for her Hilda Wangel in *The Master Builder*, Ella Renthein in *John Gabriel Borkman*, and Mrs. Alving in *Ghosts*.

With keen young players, she established a company which performed a large number of European plays to an audience who were attracted by intelligent drama at very low prices of admission, the best seats being under two dollars. The choice of plays was of an exceptional standard and included works by Molière, Goldoni, Ibsen, Chekhov, Schnitzler, Dumas, Benavente, the Quinteros, and occasionally Shakespeare. Miss Le Gallienne not only directed but acted in most of her productions. Had times been more favorable, Miss Le Gallienne's company might easily have developed into something like London's Old Vic, with an analogous importance to the American theatre as a whole.

THE FEDERAL THEATRE PROJECT

During the difficult times for the theatre in the mid-thirties, much good work was done by Hallie Flanagan, previously teacher of drama at Vassar, who directed the Federal Theatre Project aid to the theatre in many enterprises throughout the country. She organized countless productions—often in towns where there was no theatre, in converted movie houses and lecture halls—which kept many actors alive by employment at low but regular salaries. In many instances, new and permanent audiences were built by means of low-priced seats, which uncovered an enormous potential for the establishment of repertory theatres producing serious and intelligent drama. Much of this ground was lost in the following years of the war when, although the theatres experienced a period of boom, the accent was naturally on entertainment and comedy.

A.N.T.A.

Out of the Federal Theatre Project grew A.N.T.A., which a group of theatre lovers established by having introduced and passed in Congress a charter incorporating the American National Theatre and Academy as a nonprofit corporation (without drawing on Government finance) to present theatrical productions of the highest type, to advance public interest in the drama as an art belonging both to the theatre and to literature.

Although nothing much came of this until after the war, in 1946, with a new board of officers including Vinton Freedley, Robert E. Sherwood, Gilbert Miller, and Rosamund Gilder, A.N.T.A. began a vigorous campaign to acquire a nationwide membership. Through subscription and benefit performances it built up funds for a long-range program to encourage the theatre throughout the nation. Much of its work has been in the educational field, but it served in an advisory capacity in the theatre generally and sponsored various experimental performances.

In 1950, A.N.T.A. took over the Guild Theatre and began to sponsor a series of interesting American and foreign plays. Later it established its own theatre in Washington Square, New York, where the Lincoln Center Repertory Company held its first two seasons while awaiting the completion of the Vivian Beaumont Theatre in Lincoln Center, which is to be its permanent home.

ORSON WELLES AND THE MERCURY THEATRE

Also from the Federal Theatre Project came Orson Welles, a true directorial genius, who had produced many revivals for the Project, including Marlowe's *Dr. Faustus*. After the demise of the Federal Theatre Project, he and John Houseman formed the Mercury Theatre, where they produced many striking revivals in a new and original manner. They presented modern-dress productions of *Julius Caesar* and Dekker's *Shoemaker's Holiday* and, departing from their more usual revivals, presented a new offering in 1937, Marc Blitzstein's memorable *The Cradle Will Rock*; it was performed without scenery. The Mercury Theatre, however, is perhaps best remembered for its celebrated and frighteningly realistic radio performance of H. G. Wells's *War of the Worlds* in 1938, which caused panic in many places. Welles later went on to produce, direct, and star in the film *Citizen Kane,* which has become a modern classic.

POSTWAR PLAYWRIGHTS: WILLIAMS AND MILLER

Of the many dramatists who have had work produced since the war, the two dominant figures are Arthur Miller and Tennessee Williams. Although both are sensitive interpreters of American life, they differ widely in their means of expression, and yet are to some extent complementary. Arthur Miller, who has also written novels, uses the medium of everyday language in his powerful dramas of social purpose, and his plays are written for a naturalistic style of acting, while Tennessee Williams is a writer in whose language symbolism and poetic expression are subtly interwoven, giving greater scope for imaginative production. Both are still actively writing, and may yet display new developments.

Williams wrote several one-act plays in the 1930's and aroused the interest of the Group Theatre. His first produced play was *The Battle of Angels,* which failed to reach Broadway; it was rewritten, and in 1957 was successfully produced in New York and London as *Orpheus Descending.*

THE GLASS MENAGERIE

Williams' first great success was *The Glass Menagerie,* produced in 1945 in New York and later in London. It is a play about a mother and her two children—Laura, a crippled girl, and Tom, a quite normal young man who, although he loves his mother and sister, really wants to join the Merchant Marine. Amanda, the mother, and Laura live in a world of illusion, dwelling chiefly in the past, while Tom finds the atmosphere too constricting and seeks to break away from the home.

Laura, who is completely withdrawn from life outside the home, finds comfort in arranging a group of tiny glass animals, while her mother seeks to persuade Tom to bring home a friend, a "gentleman caller," for Laura. He finally does so, and his friend turns out to be a pupil from the same high school whom Laura has always worshiped. But the occasion is a disaster for Amanda, as the young man is apparently already engaged and has called out of friendship to Tom. He persuades Laura to dance with him, and although she demurs, she is swept into a clumsy waltz during which they bump into a table and one of the glass animals is broken. This animal is a special favorite of Laura's, a unicorn, and when it falls the horn is broken off, making it appear like the other animals. This does not seem to upset her, as one would imagine, perhaps because to her it symbolizes that she is no longer different from others and the end of her withdrawal from life. The play ends on a note of despair, with Tom going off to sea and Laura blowing out the candles which illuminate the scene.

It has many passages of sheer beauty, and has depths of emotion which Williams expresses with great feeling for his characters. It is a memory play, and is staged with a dim all-over lighting and transparent scenery. Areas of the stage are illuminated from time to time with shafts of light, not always on the chief action, but used symbolically. The Broadway production in 1945 was distinguished by the presence of Laurette Taylor as Amanda, which contributed much to its success.

SUMMER AND SMOKE

Summer and Smoke, written in 1948, is a play in which Williams explores the forces of spiritual and physical love. It is a story of a young woman whose failure to reconcile the two values in the man she loves, a young doctor, eventually turns her away from him. He does not reciprocate her love, being too conscious of his respect for her finer feelings. When she learns of her lover's approaching marriage, she abandons her attitude and goes off with the first young man she meets, a traveling salesman.

Despite the simplicity of the plot, the play is full of incident and unusual characters, and the main theme is stressed in a symbolic way by spotlighting an anatomical chart in the doctor's office. As in

The Glass Menagerie, the settings are intended to be fragmentary, with most of the mood and atmosphere achieved by lighting.

A STREETCAR NAMED DESIRE

Tennessee Williams' next play was *A Streetcar Named Desire*, which dealt with the problems of a woman trying to come to terms with a life she was never fitted to meet. Blanche Dubois and her sister Stella are the last members of an old Southern family which has fallen on hard times. Although Blanche has become a school-teacher and clings to the old respectability, an unfortunate experi-ence in an early marriage turns her toward drink and promiscuous sexuality. She leaves her teaching post and eventually drifts into prostitution.

At the beginning of the play Blanche, a once attractive woman now prematurely aging and losing her looks, visits her young sister, who is now married to an uncouth but passionate and vigorous young man, entirely without sensibility, but with whom Stella finds completeness through the bonds of sexuality. The visit gradually lengthens, and looks like being permanent, much to the opposition of Stanley, the young husband, who recognizes Blanche's dissolute character. For a time, Blanche has hopes of marriage with a friend of the husband's who is unlike him in character, being sensitive and quiet. But Stanley sets out to unearth something of Blanche's immediate past, and when he passes on his knowledge of her prosti-tution his friend's reaction is to break away from her. This final dis-appointment leads Blanche eventually to a complete mental break-down.

The conflict of personalities is very revealing in Blanche's in-ability to face the harsh reality of life and in Stanley's contempt for her show of refinement. Rarely allowing herself to be seen in day-light, she shields the lamps with Chinese shades; a naked bulb to her is like a vulgar word or action, and she seems continually about to take, or to be coming from, a bath. The husband's drunken poker parties and Stella's attempts to reconcile her love for the husband and her sister build up the tensions in the home.

THE ROSE TATTOO

In *The Rose Tattoo,* Williams again explores the realms of physical love in a drama of a Sicilian immigrant widow seeking a lover in the likeness of her former husband, in spite of her knowledge that he had been unfaithful to her. This was written for the Italian film actress Anna Magnani, who did not appear in the stage production, but made a memorable film Serafina, in spite of her lack of facility with the English language.

CAMINO REAL

Perhaps Williams' most controversial play to date has been *Camino Real,* a fantasy which takes place in a kind of limbo in which Don Quixote, Lord Byron, Casanova, Marguerite Gautier, and many other characters appear. It is set in a mythical Central American town full of decadence, violence, and cruelty. There is no clear story, but much action, some of which startlingly takes place in the auditorium. Most of the characters are waiting to pass through to somewhere else, although it is not clear where, and in the waiting they meet, talk, and part. There are crowds, and a fiesta with a mock fertility ritual. It is so full of symbolism that the author's meaning appears confused, and although conceived on a grand scale, it must be regarded as a failure.

CAT ON A HOT TIN ROOF

After this, Williams came to earth with *Cat on a Hot Tin Roof,* a drama of a wealthy Southern family whose head, "Big Daddy," is dying of cancer. His son Brick is an alcoholic who sleeps apart from his wife, Maggie, whose frustrated sexuality explains the title. Other members of the family are scheming to get control of the estate, and Maggie tries to resolve the situation by announcing that she is pregnant. The play ends with Brick coming together with his wife to make good the claim.

In the action of the play, the characters are starkly revealed in an exposing of the emotional lies of conventionality, and there is much bitterness, cruelty, and passion.

JOHN BARRYMORE Shown as he played Hamlet in the famous production of 1922 at the Broadway Theatre. Barrymore was considered the greatest Hamlet since Edwin Booth. He broke Booth's record of 100 consecutive performances.

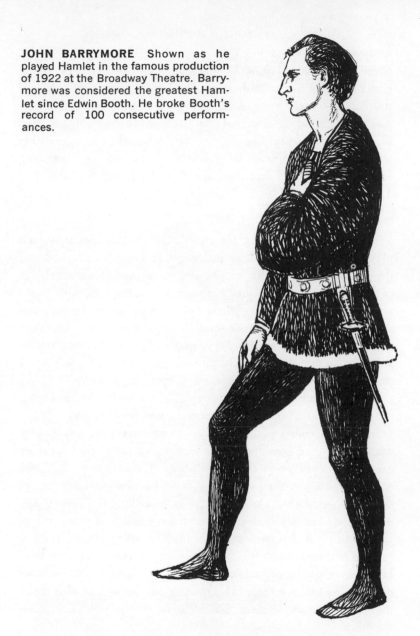

WILLIAMS' LATER PLAYS

Some of the later plays of Williams may be considered too sensational in their nightmarish stories of sex, violence, and physical
mutilation, but the view of life expressed in them is an abnormal
one in which the emotions are charged to an explosive degree, and
his dialogue is always convincing, even when the characterization
and the action appear to be contrived. They include *Something
Unspoken, Suddenly Last Summer, Baby Doll,* and *Sweet Bird of
Youth.*

NIGHT OF THE IGUANA

With *Night of the Iguana,* which Williams announced as his last
play for Broadway (although his *Slapstick Tragedy* was produced
during the 1965–1966 season), he returns to the quieter searchings
of the inner soul of *The Glass Menagerie.* The story concerns Shannon, an unfrocked minister whose fall has been due to his unortho-
dox beliefs and his passionate sexuality, which led him to conduct
irreconcilable with his calling. He now makes a living as a tourist
guide in Mexico, leading lady tourists astray on back roads for a
small commission from hotel and inn keepers. He has a more or less
permanent affair with the proprietress of the Costa Verde Hotel,
the seedy surroundings of which form the setting of the play.

Into his life comes a New England spinster, traveling the country
with an old blind grandfather who was once a minor poet and now
ekes out an existence reciting his works. They come to the hotel
and are refused by the proprietress, but Shannon persuades her to
take them in. Shannon has a violent fit, to which he is periodically
prone, and after his recovery he and the spinster, a wise, sympathetic and virginal person, reach an understanding, despite the difference in their personalities. They seem to be about to fall in love,
but their very disparity allows nothing more than a brief moment
of sympathy for each other. The spinster and her grandfather move
on to their next engagement, and Shannon returns to his sex-ridden
existence.

ALL MY SONS

Arthur Miller began his career with *The Man Who Had All the Luck,* which was produced on Broadway in 1944 but achieved only four performances. From this play, he elaborated the theme of the relationship of two sons with their father which was presented in two further plays, although they dealt with different characters.

All My Sons, which Elia Kazan staged in 1947, deals with Joe Keller, a war profiteer whose partner is in jail, unjustly taking the consequences of Keller's actions. One of Keller's sons has been killed in action during the war and the other, Chris, is possessed with a guilt complex at having survived an action during the war, when he was a company commander, in which all his men were killed. He wants to marry Ann, the former fiancée of his brother, and brings her to the Keller home. She is attracted by his honest idealism, and agrees to marry him. The mother still lives in hope that her other son was not killed, and although he has been missing for three-and-a-half years, thinks he may still be alive. She is therefore against Chris's marrying Ann.

The tension mounts when Ann's brother arrives, having visited his father in prison and now believing that Keller is in fact the guilty party in the action of disguising faulty airplane parts. Although he appears at first to be friendly to the family, he finally discovers the truth, that Keller was responsible, and passes on his knowledge to Chris. There is a dramatic scene when Chris confronts his father with the accusation, and although Keller admits his criminal responsibility, he tries to excuse his action through his love for his family. Chris is completely stunned, his love for his father shattered. Ann then produces a letter she received from his brother, written just before he took off on a mission, which indicates that he knew of his father's disgrace and was so moved that he couldn't bear to live anymore.

This finally drives Keller to seek the only way out he knows. He leaves the room quietly, and shortly after a shot is heard, which brings the play to an end. Although this appears somewhat melodramatic, it is a play with complete conviction of characterization, and the simple but effective dialogue has the authentic flavor of real life.

DEATH OF A SALESMAN

Miller's next play, *Death of a Salesman,* is perhaps his most successful work to date. It is a strong drama of a weak personality for whom Miller arouses our sympathy throughout the story. Willy Loman, a traveling salesman, is a complete failure in life, in his job, in bringing up his two sons, and in his inability to realize the great strength of his wife's love for him. He lives partly in a dream world; some of the characters in the play exist only in that world, and there is a constant shift from the present to scenes in the past. This is most skillfully done, however, so that there is a continuity and flow in the narrative. It is a play in which the emotions are given full rein, particularly in the relations between Willy and his elder son, Biff, whom he has always idealized.

Although the boy has had his moments of popularity at high school, where he had been a football star, he fails to graduate, drifts from one job to another, and has sunk to stealing, for which, unknown to his father, he has spent three months in jail. He has also surprised his father, on one of the latter's selling trips, in a hotel room with a strange woman. In spite of his own optimistic views of his own powers of salesmanship, Willy finally loses his job. He tries to make a success of his son's life, but the climax of the play arrives when Biff, who knows that he can never be anything but a failure, forces his father to accept the truth, revealing his prison sentence. This finally breaks Willy, whose love now turns to hatred. Unable to face life without his remaining dream, Willy drives off in his car to a fatal crash.

The tragedy reaches its most poignant expression in the part of Willy's wife, Linda, who has all along borne with his salesman's exaggerations, his massive dreams, his occasional cruelties and infidelity through her deep love and understanding, although by temperament she is completely unable to express that influencing stability he so badly needs.

Death of a Salesman was a great success on Broadway, where it had a run of 742 performances and gained Miller the Pulitzer Prize for 1949. It also had a long run in London, with Paul Muni and Katherine Alexander, in the same year.

THE CRUCIBLE

Miller's next play, *The Crucible,* was written in 1953, and in it he has obviously sought an historical parallel to McCarthyism. In this story of a group of wantons, discovered apparently practicing black magic by dancing naked in the moonlight, who try to absolve themselves by accusing other members of the town of witchcraft, Miller goes back in time to Salem in the seventeenth century. The terror in the town, which is created by ignorance, intolerance, and bigotry, is starkly revealed as the story unfolds.

Abigail, the leader of the supposedly bewitched, accuses the wife of her ex-lover, John Proctor, of being a witch, hoping thereby to obtain his return to her. Proctor is arraigned with his wife in court, and seeking to prove the underlying reason for Abigail's accusation, he confesses his past infidelity. His wife, however, denies the charge, mistakenly thinking it will help to set him free. But in the feverish atmosphere of the town, which requires scapegoats, her attempts to shield him ensure their condemnation.

In this play Miller creates an intensely dramatic situation and atmosphere and, as he has explained, he was not attempting to give real depth to his characters but was presenting them as personifications of his theme of injustice. The moral purpose is conveyed in writing of great force, in which Miller aptly reproduces the rhythms and cadences of the period speech. *The Crucible* was produced at the Martin Beck Theatre in 1953, but had only a modest run. It is, however, a popular addition to the current repertory of London's National Theatre Company, and a film was made from it in France.

A VIEW FROM THE BRIDGE

A View from the Bridge was originally of one act and was given with another short piece, *A Memory of Two Mondays,* in its Broadway production. For the London production in 1956, it was lengthened to two acts and given alone. Miller sets his story of a longshoreman in a slum near the docks seaward of Brooklyn Bridge. With Eddie Carbone and his wife Beatrice lives Catherine, the seventeen-year-old daughter of his wife's dead sister. Eddie has gradually and unconsciously fallen in love with Catherine, who is just leaving school to start work as a stenographer when the play opens.

The arrival of two Italian immigrants who have entered the country illegally, and the interest which Catherine shows in Rodolpho, the younger of the two brothers, causes Eddie to realize the depth of his passion, and he determines to use any means to stop the two young people from coming together. He tries to persuade Catherine that Rodolpho would be interested in marriage only because his illegal position would thus be regularized. When she refuses to accept this, he tries to humiliate Rodolpho before her by claiming that Rodolpho is a homosexual. When she will not accept this and is quite unshaken, he decides to inform on the two brothers to the immigration authorities. They are duly taken away, with two others discovered in another apartment, but are released on bail while awaiting their court hearing. Marco, the older brother, shattered by the sudden end of his chance for a new life, as he will have to return to Sicily where his wife and children are sustained by his earnings, returns to denounce Eddie to the neighbors. Although Eddie tries to bluster his way out, a fight with Marco ensues in which Eddie draws a knife, but in the struggle it is turned against him and he is killed.

As in his earlier plays, Miller sees the main character of Eddie in the round, and a brief outline of the plot cannot give more than a hint of the deeply felt and forceful sweep of the tragedy of a common man.

AFTER THE FALL

There was an interval of nine years before Miller's next play was produced. *After the Fall* became the first production of the new Lincoln Center Repertory Company in January of 1964 at their temporary home, the A.N.T.A. Washington Square Theatre. Later in the same year, another of Miller's plays, *Incident at Vichy,* was produced by the same company.

After the Fall is a memory play, at the beginning of which Quentin, a writer, addresses the audience and tells of the high moments of his life, revealing his past with an intense self-searching and a somewhat fearful contemplation of the future. In the background are the key figures, who come forward and enact with him various scenes of his life. His childhood, life with his mother, who turned against his father when their business failed; his first marriage to Louise, a woman who wanted to be a separate person; his second marriage to Maggie, a sexy, popular entertainer who was a touching, pathetic character underneath, but who drove him away with her outward violence; and the German girl he may yet marry, with her outlook permanently overshadowed by the concentration camp in which she grew up, are brought into a long narrative of three hours.

His men friends and other characters are brought in to sustain the action, which moves smoothly from scene to scene. The play was imaginatively directed by Elia Kazan on the bare thrust stage of the A.N.T.A. Theatre with the absolute minimum of setting and properties, while the changing mood and atmosphere of the story were well created by Jason Robards, Jr., and an able cast.

In this work, Miller poses the question of whether, in the eternal chaos, pain, and muddle of life, it is possible to find an order, a stable basis for the future. At the end he arrives at a quiet but affirmative answer. *After the Fall* had a mixed reception, some critics regarding it as Miller's most mature work to date, others seeing in it certain autobiographical trends which they felt weakened an objective approach.

INCIDENT AT VICHY

Incident at Vichy is a play about the Nazi barbarity in their treatment of Jews during the last war; but it has a wider moral preoccupation in uncovering the tragedy of indifference to the fate of others implicit to some degree in all men.

A group of individuals are brought in for questioning, and the widely contrasted reactions to their unknown fate, and to each other, forms the development of the drama. The characters are a temperamental painter who is unable to control his fright; a businessman; a Communist electrician; a young waiter; a flamboyant and confident actor; a proud and sensitive doctor; an aged and silent bearded man; and an Austrian prince, a homosexual, humane, sensitive, but weary of life, who is the only Gentile in the gathering.

While they are waiting to be interrogated, the doctor questions them on their likely behavior when their dreaded call comes. The actor sees himself as a hero in a dramatic climax, outwitting his enemies by sheer force of self-confidence. The electrician asserts that he will be upheld by his conviction of the ultimate triumph of Marxism. Others show a paralyzed fear as the realization that they are doomed becomes clear. A long discussion on the inexplicable evil that has entered their world follows, and as the characters are taken off one by one, the Austrian prince makes the ultimate sacrifice by exchanging his identity papers with those of the doctor.

The play has not received the critical acclaim of his earlier works, either in New York or in London (where it had a distinguished cast led by Alec Guinness and Anthony Quayle). However, Miller's future plays will be awaited with eager interest for his vision, his depth of human understanding (in spite of his obsessions and pessimism), and his ability to create characters with a language rooted in life.

EDWARD ALBEE

Most of America's younger dramatists have been influenced in some way by Arthur Miller or Tennessee Williams, although, as in Britain, there have been incursions from abroad. Edward Albee has written some short plays in the vein of Ionesco—*The Zoo Story,*

The American Dream, and *The Death of Bessie Smith*—which are popular offerings off-Broadway. He made a great success of his first full-length play, *Who's Afraid of Virginia Woolf,* in which two couples engage in an amusing ping-pong of nonsense which reveals much of their inner personalities, their hopes and despairs, with a quite savage wit.

His more recent *Tiny Alice,* described by its author as two mysteries in one—metaphysical and conventional—did not repeat his earlier success on Broadway, although it was played by a distinguished cast including Irene Worth as Miss Alice, the richest woman in the world, and John Gielgud as Brother Julian. *A Delicate Balance* was presented in the fall of 1966, and is considered by some critics to be his best play to date, exhibiting more compassion for humanity than had his earlier works.

ARCHIBALD MacLEISH:

Archibald MacLeish is a poet who has written many plays for stage and radio since the 1930's, including the sensational *The Fall of the City* of 1937. It is, however, with *J. B.,* produced in 1958, that MacLeish has made his mark in the contemporary theatre. In *J. B.* he re-creates the story of the Old Testament Job in terms of contemporary American life, not in a naturalistic manner but in the fantasy of a play within a play. There is no curtain, and the setting is suggestive of a vast circus tent, old and battered after unsuccessful years on the road. Various employees wander on, depressed at their failure to attract an audience, and in pantomime decide to perform a play for their own entertainment—the story of Job.

Using the props of the circus, an old actor (now selling balloons) and a popcorn vendor don masks as God and the Devil, and as they do so, a disembodied voice begins to introduce the play. Job is represented as J. B., successful businessman whose fear of God and love of his family is beset by the tribulations of our own time—the failure of his business, disasters happening to each member of his family, war, and the atom bomb. He does not know if he is being punished for past sins, and in a long debate on the question of justice in the world his friends and his wife fail to persuade him to "curse God and die," and finally his wife leaves him. But J. B. has withstood the test of faith and, as in the Old Testament, she returns to him and they begin life together again.

The play was directed by Elia Kazan (who has been responsible for so many of the best productions in the American theatre) with great imagination and creative skill, while the players—Raymond Massey as God, Christopher Plummer as Satan, Pat Hingle and Nan Martin as J. B. and his wife—contributed much to the success of the play, which gained MacLeish the Pulitzer Prize.

OTHER SIGNIFICANT PLAYS

Of the many other notable plays of recent times, space permits only the merest mention of a few. They include William Inge's *Come Back Little Sheba*, in which Arthur Miller's influence is strong, and *The Dark at the Top of the Stairs*, with its Freudian undertones; Arthur Laurents' psychological study of a neurotic woman, *A Clearing in the Woods*; Jack Richardson's *The Prodigal* and *Gallows Humor*; Arthur Kopit's satire, *Oh Dad, Poor Dad, Mama's Hung You in the Closet and I'm Feeling So Sad*; and Jack Gelber's remarkable documentary of drug addiction, *The Connection*.

THE OFF-BROADWAY THEATRE

Many of these plays were first produced in the off-Broadway theatre, the growth of which has been a phenomenon of the past decade. The hit-and-miss situation on Broadway, where most productions fail and a few are great successes, where costs of production have rocketed, partly through union practices, salaries, and high rents, has turned many writers toward production of their plays in the "little theatre" movement. For the audiences, the steep rise in admission prices on Broadway has made the Broadway production an occasion only for a special outing or the entertainment of out-of-town visitors.

The solid, intelligent audiences who desire a regular experience of drama, have been attracted to the small experimental theatres, few of which can seat more than three hundred patrons, which are mainly converted from old warehouses, night clubs, stables, lecture halls, and defunct cinemas. Most of them are situated around Greenwich Village, and at first they attracted mainly a local patronage. But since their productions began to be noticed and reviewed by the New York critics, many of them have attracted much wider audiences.

Of the many deserving notice, only a few may be selected for mention. The Phoenix Theatre, at 344 East Seventy-fourth Street, has built up a subscription audience for its seasons of great drama of the past by productions of Ibsen, Pirandello, Aristophanes, Gorky, and notable works by American playwrights Robert E. Sherwood, George S. Kaufman, Moss Hart, George M. Cohan, Frank D. Gilroy, Aldyth Morris, Robert Ardrey, and Arthur Kopit. It is associated with the A.P.A. seasons at the University of Michigan in Ann Arbor, and it has been so successful that it plans to take over the Lyceum Theatre on Broadway, where it can run a true repertory season to much larger audiences.

The Circle in the Square, of 159 Bleecker Street, has given many interesting productions, which Jose Quintero has directed and in which Jason Robards, Jr., and Geraldine Page were first seen. The Cherry Lane Theatre has, among other offerings, given a season of nine plays under the collective heading of Absurd Drama, including a premiere of Beckett's *Happy Days*. The Provincetown Playhouse, of 133 MacDougal Street (of early O'Neill fame) still operates. The Actors Playhouse, the Sheridan Square Theatre, Theatre de Lys, the York, and the Sullivan Street Playhouse are others which have made a contribution to the demand by actors and audiences alike for a regular intake of serious drama which Broadway has not been providing.

The off-Broadway theatre has given opportunities to players and dramatists at the beginning of their careers, many of whom have subsequently become famous. Apart from those already mentioned, it has provided acting debuts in New York for Kim Stanley, Jacqueline Brooks, Ben Gazzara, and George C. Scott, among many others. It has provided audiences with a chance to see the work of new writers, including Leslie Stevens, Arthur Kopit, Ionesco, Jean Genet, James Forsythe, Bernard Kops.

Off-Broadway theatres have also revived some important American plays which were only partly successful on Broadway, such as Arthur Miller's *The Crucible,* Tennessee Williams' *Summer and Smoke,* and O'Neill's *The Iceman Cometh.* It is also presenting revivals of popular successes of thirty years ago, which are unlikely to be seen again on Broadway, such as the Kaufman and Hart *You Can't Take It with You.*

REPERTORY COMPANIES

There is also a growing demand for the permanent repertory, where actors are employed for the season or longer, to give a program of plays which audiences may see on alternate evenings, as in London's National Theatre and the Royal Shakespeare Theatre Company. This has been furthered by Ford Foundation grants totaling over half a million dollars to several theatres to enable them to establish resident repertory companies.

Among these is the Arena Stage of Washington, D. C., whose director, Zelda Fichandler, began in 1950 in a decrepit old movie house and now operates a brand-new theatre on the edge of the Potomac. It presents eight plays in a season, from October to June, on a rectangular stage surrounded on four sides by rising rows of nearly eight hundred seats, with entrance tunnels at each of the four corners. It has given an extremely varied program of plays, including works by Shaw, Chekhov, Brecht, Giraudoux, Anouilh, Andreyev, Edward Albee, Denis Johnston, John Arden, O'Neill, Thornton Wilder, and new works by American writers such as Wallace Hamilton and Millard Lampell.

Another repertory theatre which has benefited from a Ford Foundation grant is the Actors Workshop of San Francisco, established

THE WASHINGTON ARENA THEATRE　A regional professional theatre, The Washington Arena Theatre was one of the first theatres in America in which professional actors performed "in-the-round." Most early efforts at arena staging had been confined to colleges. Established in 1950, the theatre performed on a makeshift stage until 1961 when it moved into its permanent home: the first theatre designed exclusively for arena staging. The rectangularly shaped stage is bounded on all four sides by the audience.

STAGE OF THE TYRONE GUTHRIE THEATRE   Established in 1963, the Tyrone Guthrie Theatre was frankly inspired by the Shakespeare Festival Theatre in Ontario, Canada. An open stage projects into the auditorium, assuring intimate contact between actor and audience, no seat being more than 52 feet from the stage. Note the balcony stage playing area in the rear, and the amphitheatre-shape of the auditorium. A system of tracks and trap doors within the playing area affords increase flexibility in staging.

in 1952 by Herbert Blau and Jules Irving (then both faculty members of San Francisco State College) in the loft above a judo academy with a production of Philip Barry's *Hotel Universe*. Other presentations followed, and with a highly successful production of Arthur Miller's *The Crucible* two years later, the company took on professional status at the Marines' Memorial Theatre, where it remains at present. Now a full-scale permanent company with a solid subscription support from the Bay Area, it has produced some distinguished work, including the staging of Brecht's *Mother Courage*, Beckett's *Waiting for Godot*, O'Neill's *The Iceman Cometh*, and Genet's *The Balcony*. In 1965, Blau and Irving departed to direct the Lincoln Center Repertory Company, taking some of the company with them, but the Actors Workshop continues with new directors, Kenneth Kitch and John Hancock, and a similar policy of presenting dramas of distinction, whether past or new, to high artistic standards.

THE MINNESOTA THEATRE COMPANY

An object lesson in what can be done by awakening and harnessing the enthusiasm of the local residents for intelligent drama has been the founding of the Minnesota Theatre Company, now firmly established in the new Tyrone Guthrie Theatre in Minneapolis–St. Paul.

With funds raised mainly by the citizens of the Twin Cities, and with the aid of grants from both the Walker and Ford Foundations, a new theatre was built, designed by Professor Ralph Rapson of the University of Minnesota in consultation with the directors of the company, Tyrone Guthrie, Oliver Rea, Peter Zeisler, and the resident stage designer, Tanya Moiseiwitsch. It is of unusual design, with an asymmetrical pentagon arena stage backed by a shallow apron (used mainly for entrances and exits) and fitted with large sliding doors. These allow wagons, with preset furniture and props, to be pushed onto the stage when opened, and when closed form a corrugated wall. The auditorium is on two levels, although a third of it slopes down uninterruptedly from balcony level. It holds seats

GEORGE GRIZZARD He appeared as Henry V in the Minnesota Theatre Company's production at the Tyrone Guthrie Theatre, 1964.

for 1,437. The story of the creation of the theatre is well described in Tyrone Guthrie's lively book, *A New Theatre* (1964).

The first season began on May 7, 1963, and a program of four plays was given—*Hamlet, The Miser, The Three Sisters,* and *Death of a Salesman*—until September 22. The company was led by Hume Cronyn, Jessica Tandy, George Grizzard, Rita Gam, and Zoe Caldwell. The success of these productions lengthened the 1964 and 1965 seasons from May to October and then to November. The permanent company was enabled to present four or five plays, with sufficient time to achieve productions of a very high artistic level.

A link with the University of Minnesota was forged by the McKnight Foundation, which has awarded twelve Fellowships annually to graduates, which enables them to work for a season at the theatre as actors, designers, or in administration. The plays chosen were either classics or modern American plays now regarded as classics, with the object of building up an audience experience on which to form its taste for drama in the future. It is hoped later, when the audiences know what the company can do and what it should do, to perform and even commission new work. A nonprofit organization, the theatre is well established in the community, with a women's organization, "Stagehands," to help in liaison between the theatre and the expanding subscription membership. This is furthered by lectures, forums, workshops, and other off-season activities.

The success of this venture has led to two unexpected developments, one being the increased interest in drama throughout the urban areas, many new groups having started their own little theatres, and the other that visitors from all parts of the country are attracted to the theatre. Groups with a common interest in drama are organizing journeys by air and bus for a weekend of playgoing.

THE LINCOLN CENTER REPERTORY COMPANY AND THE VIVIAN BEAUMONT THEATRE

The new Vivian Beaumont Theatre at Lincoln Center opened in 1965, the first new theatre to be built in New York for over thirty

years. It was made possible by a two million dollar donation by
Mrs. Vivian Beaumont Allen. A Ford Foundation grant helped in
the formation of the Lincoln Center Repertory Company which, as
has already been mentioned, began in a temporary home in the
A.N.T.A. Washington Square Theatre. Although Arthur Miller
and Elia Kazan had been actively engaged in its beginnings, they
left the company with the departure of Robert Whitehead, an experienced Broadway producer who had been an administrator in its
early days, due to disagreement with the Managing Board of Gov-
ernors. Miller has also withdrawn his plays from the repertory.

In the 1965–1966 season, Herbert Blau and Jules Irving, the new
directors, produced Büchner's *Danton's Death*, Wycherley's *The
Country Wife, The Condemned of Altona* by Jean-Paul Sartre, and
Brecht's *The Caucasian Chalk Circle*.

The theatre is only part of the great cultural center, which is to
house the Metropolitan Opera, the New York Philharmonic, and
the Juilliard School of Music. It was designed by Eero Saarinen, in
association with Jo Mielziner. The theatre has many exciting new
features. It has a thrust stage, which can be moved forward at the
press of a button, and a flexible arrangement of panels to make a
proscenium for a traditional stage if desired. The thrust stage can
be dropped, elevated, or rotated. There is a cyclorama at the back of
the stage and two turntables. Labor difficulties and expenses of
scene-shifting have largely been dispensed with by automation.

The complicated lighting system is operated automatically by a
punched-card system. Once the lighting plot for the complete play
has been programmed, it is always available for immediate use. The
theatre can easily store the settings and props for five productions.
It provides seats for 1,083 playgoers (and when the thrust stage is
retracted, for 1,140), none of which is more than sixty-five feet
from the stage. There is also a smaller auditorium, seating 299, for
experimental plays and rehearsals.

For so many years, Broadway directors, actors, and designers have
been toiling with equipment from the horse-and-buggy age, and at

last they have been shown what can be made available. The tickets are sold by subscription, and range from two to six dollars. Already more than 40,000 members have subscribed. With the continuation of this good will, and the talent and resources already available, there is every reason for supposing that the Lincoln Center Repertory Company will become a major influence in the American theatre.

SHAKESPEARE-IN-THE-PARK

New York City has an outdoor Shakespearean company, the New York Shakespeare Festival, which gives free performances in its own recently acquired Delacorte Theatre in Central Park and tours many neighborhoods, presenting performances in playgrounds, school auditoriums, and outdoor theatres. The touring company is called the Festival Mobile Theatre.

Joseph Papp, the producer, began the theatre on a shoestring several years ago. The generally high caliber of the productions and the value of Shakespearean productions given without charge to a wide cross section of audiences have since attracted both municipal and private financial support.

Macbeth was presented in both English and Spanish in the summer of 1966, as was a children's show entitled *Pot Luck,* which New York's young playground and theatregoers found enchanting. Mr. Papp and his companies have been responsible for reaching one of the widest and most diversified audiences of any Shakespearean productions in America.

THE PASADENA PLAYHOUSE AND THE CLEVELAND PLAYHOUSE

Outside New York, there are two first-rate companies with their own permanent theatres which have been established for over fifty years. The Pasadena Playhouse, founded in 1916 by Gilmor Brown, has grown over the years and now has five auditoriums, extensive workshops, a new experimental theatre, a complete television studio, and operates a school of the theatre which has produced many distinguished actors and directors.

The Cleveland Playhouse, founded in the same year by Raymond O'Neill, is now run by Frederic McConnell along similar lines.

Other repertory companies of note are The Alley Theatre in Houston, the Miller Theatre in Milwaukee, the Loeb Theatre at Harvard, the U. C. L. A. Extension Theatre in Los Angeles, and the Izenour-Schweikher Theatre at the Carnegie Institute of Technology in Pittsburgh.

AMERICAN SHAKESPEARE FESTIVAL THEATRE AND ACADEMY

The Shakespearean repertory group at Stratford, Connecticut, The American Shakespeare Festival Theatre and Academy, presents three or four of the Bard's works in repertory during a summer sea-

BERT LAHR   The actor is shown in the costume of Autolycus, in the 1960-61 American Shakespeare Festival Theatre production of William Shakespeare's "The Winter's Tale."

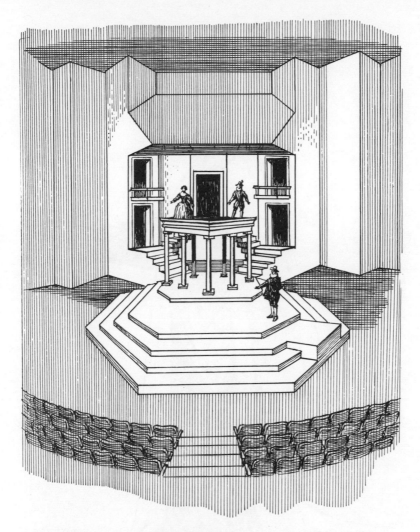

THE SHAKESPEARE FESTIVAL THEATRE OF ONTARIO, CANADA Here is a modern version of an Elizabethan stage. The platform stage is a permanent structure embellished with balconies, trap doors, and multiple playing levels. The auditorium rises in a sharp incline, surrounding the stage on three sides. Inspired by the combined talents of Sir Tyrone Guthrie and Tanya Moiseiwitsch, the Shakespeare Festival Theatre has been a model for two other important new theatres: The Tyrone Guthrie Theatre in Minnesota, and the The Chichester Festival Theatre in England.

MORRIS CARNOVSKY AS KING LEAR The actor performed in this role in the American Shakespeare Theatre Festival production, Stratford, Connecticut, in 1963.

son and tours various educational institutions during the fall and winter months. It has a beautiful theatre patterned after the Globe, in a rustic setting, where playgoers often picnic between a matinee and evening performance. The quality of its productions and acting has varied, but it has provided actors, designers, directors with a place in which to try their ideas, a training ground for American actors in Shakespearean interpretation (which has been sadly lacking in the American theatre), and the public an opportunity to see intelligent presentations of Shakespeare's work.

COLLEGE DRAMA DEPARTMENTS

Finally, there is the vast activity of college drama departments. As well as providing degree courses in speech and drama, some of the departments maintain a professional theatre. The University of Washington in Seattle, for example, with three theatres, operates a professional schedule of twenty-five productions throughout the year for six nights a week. It also operates a touring company with a repertory of three plays—a classic, a modern play, and a children's play.

Other universities that operate touring companies are Stanford, Indiana, North Dakota State, and North Carolina. Apart from producing the classics and well-known modern plays in their theatres, one-act and even full-length plays written by students are produced. Productions are directed by the faculty, with students working in all the various phases of lighting, costume and scenic design, properties, acting, and stage management.

There have been some interesting new theatre buildings in the colleges in recent years, including Frank Lloyd Wright's Dallas Theatre Center for the graduate school of Baylor University, and the University of Arkansas, Fayetteville, which has two theatres, one indoor and one outdoor, part of a cultural center containing as well a concert hall, sculpture court, exhibition gallery, library, and studios.

The architect, Marcel Breuer, is also responsible for the fine theatre at Sarah Lawrence College, Bronxville, N. Y. A 500-seat theatre, it has been designed for great flexibility of use. The auditorium is arranged around three sides of a thrust stage, while there is also a proscenium and traditional stage. At the rear of the stage are large sliding doors which, when opened, enable the stage to be used as an open-air theatre, with the audience seated in the adjacent area.

The University of Washington in Seattle, which for many years operated an arena stage in its Penthouse Theatre, now has a new theatre with a ring stage, with various revolves and hydraulic lifts, backed by a plaster cyclorama, and with two shallow side stages.

Much of the progress in solving the technical problems of staging today in the new theatres with thrust or arena stages has been inspired by experimental college work, just as in the past the colleges have produced eminent playwrights, directors, designers, and actors.

DESIGNERS

America has produced some of the best designers of settings and costumes in this century. It has been accepted that the designer has a positive contribution to make, not only by providing the background for the actors but by his work to illuminate and clarify the main theme. The designer thus cooperates rather more closely with the director than he does in Britain, and is generally given rather more freedom.

The pioneer work of Adolphe Appia and Gordon Craig, who used simple and rather abstract settings which by a flexible use of stage lighting could quickly be changed to suggest a different mood or atmosphere, has been absorbed into general practice. This has also been understood by contemporary playwrights, and many of their more recent works have made use of the dramatic possibilities of rapid changes of scene and mood, the dissolve and flashback. While this applies chiefly to conventional proscenium stages, the new form of arena stage, on which the problems of setting have multiplied enormously, has also offered much scope in the development of a new style of design in which lighting and costumes become more important.

ROBERT EDMOND JONES

The first designer to reach eminence in America was Robert Edmond Jones. His single setting at Wallack's Theatre (during the Granville-Barker season in 1915) for the production of *The Man Who Married a Dumb Wife,* a medieval comedy written by Anatole France, was in somber tones of gray and black, which served as foil to the brilliantly colored costumes and yet contained an element of symbolism. This element in Jones's designs has sometimes been overplayed, as in his designs for *Macbeth* at the Apollo Theatre, in which Lionel Barrymore and Julia Arthur appeared in 1921. In this production he introduced three enormous masks, which appeared high up in the sky and symbolized the forces of evil associated with the appearance of the witches. Most of the scenes in the castle were made up of arches set at rather odd angles, which gave a disturbing look to the whole setting. This unusual treatment of a traditional tragedy was considered at the time to have too powerful a quality of symbolism for the excellent, though conventional, acting. It did excite much interest, however, and made it easier for the work of later designers to be accepted.

Jones has made many dignified and simple settings in which detail is kept to an absolute minimum, and in which the boldness achieves a dramatic value complementary to the play. Notable among these were the settings for Marc Connelly's *The Green Pastures,* and for *Othello,* originally staged by Jones in Colorado's Central City, but revived in New York in 1937.

A most unusual production was *Oedipus Rex* (1931), which was arranged by Leopold Stokowski for music by Stravinsky, in which the action was played out by puppets, a conception already expressed in the theory of Gordon Craig's *über-marionette.*

Jones has also designed in a more conventional style, such as in the small-town settings for *Ah, Wilderness!* in the Theatre Guild's production of 1933. But plays of a musical character have inspired some of his best work, as in the Chinese temple set for *Lute Song* at the Plymouth Theatre in New York in 1946. The design, a composite set altered in different scenes chiefly by the lighting alone, and the costumes, were freely adapted from the authentic style of fourteenth-century China in a manner which retained the essence without laborious introduction of detail.

Jones, perhaps feeling that his designs were never used in a way that he had intended, also took on the task of directing plays, and thus achieved a greater artistic unity, particularly with *Love for Love, Patience,* and *Camille.*

NORMAN BEL GEDDES

Norman Bel Geddes, a contemporary of Jones, was a designer who also felt the influence of Gordon Craig and, like Jones, directed as well as designed. He has made much use of multiple settings entirely composed of steps and rostrums. His design for *Hamlet* (which he also directed) at the Broadhurst Theatre in New York in 1931 was based on a series of small playing areas set at different levels, linked by steps with a few plain flats set at different angles, masking the back and sides of the stage. The various levels could be occupied together, as in the play scene, or singly, as in the closet scene. Lighting was the means of giving accent to the various parts of the setting.

Bel Geddes had earlier conceived of a vast production of Dante's *Divine Comedy* in a special theatre to be built at Madison Square Garden, the designs for which were produced but remained unfulfilled. He also designed the settings for Reinhardt's production of *The Miracle,* in which he converted the whole proscenium and stage into a soaring cathedral apse, achieving the effect of medieval architecture, stained glass, and carving with great realism.

Apart from *Hamlet,* his realized designs of note include O'Neill's *Lazarus Laughed,* and *Lysistrata* for the Theatre Guild, and Sidney Kingsley's *Dead End* at the Belasco Theatre in 1936, in which Bel Geddes turned to extreme realism in his remarkable setting with its riverside tenements and warehouses, catching the general air of lost hopes and despair.

LEE SIMONSON

Lee Simonson began with the Washington Square Players, and achieved his reputation chiefly through his work with the Theatre Guild. Like Bel Geddes, he used simple rostrums, ramps, and steps of different levels (as in Ernst Toller's *Man and the Masses*) in which the grouping and movement of the players is considered an integral part of the setting. In *Liliom,* he devised simple stylized settings which had the authenticity of being based on realism, yet with a dramatic effectiveness. The robbery scene was designed to be enacted under the arch of a railway viaduct, which added considerably to the tension built up by the players. In the Heavenly Court scene, in which Liliom has to answer for his earthly misdeeds, the accent was on the very ordinary treatment of the walls, doors, and windows; yet there was no ceiling—the sky alone was seen above and when doors were opened in the background.

In his designs for *Heartbreak House* he worked directly under the guidance of Bernard Shaw, who himself made several sketches indicating the kind of setting (something like the poop deck of an old sailing ship) which he had visualized for his play.

O'Neill's *Marco Millions* gave Simonson splendid opportunities, not only in devising an ingenious solution to the problem of the many short scenes which must be changed swiftly, but in capturing something of the flavor of Venetian, Chinese, Indian, and African art in the detail of his settings and costumes. He created a permanent setting with a large portal in the center and two smaller ones on the sides. The portals could be changed rapidly by small additions, which completely altered the silhouette and contained appropriate design motifs which symbolized the different localities.

Another remarkable setting which Simonson created for the Theatre Guild was for *Roar China,* a Soviet play by Tretyakov which had been produced in Moscow by Meyerhold. In this play on the revolt of Chinese coolies against imperialism, the dominating element of the setting was a great representation of a warship, complete with turret and guns pointing out from the back of the stage.

Between this and the forestage, where a good deal of the action took place, was a shallow tank on which several sampans floated. When moved into the center, their fully rigged sails masked the warship and served as an effective curtain to punctuate the various scenes.

For O'Neill's *Dynamo,* Simonson devised a constructivist setting showing four rooms without walls, combined with elements of extreme realism in his representation of the generator and equipment of a modern power station for another scene. In his designs for *The Adding Machine* by Elmer Rice he used a few symbolic motifs which were strangely distorted to convey the mood of the play.

Simonson has always attempted to catch the mood and atmosphere of the play, and never more aptly than in S. N. Behrman's adaptation of Giraudoux's *Amphitryon* 38, which was so successfully produced in 1937 with the Lunts, in both London and New York. This witty and sophisticated retelling of the old Greek story of one of Zeus' many amatory excursions, caddishly undertaken in the guise of the lady's husband, was an opportunity for Simonson for a remarkably stylish *jeu d'esprit.* Other notable productions he has designed have been Claudel's *The Tidings Brought to Mary,* Ibsen's *Peer Gynt,* Shaw's *The Apple Cart,* and Sherwood's *Idiot's Delight,* as well as excursions into opera and ballet: *Faust* and *Lac des Cygnes.*

DONALD OENSLAGER

Donald Oenslager is a graduate of Professor Baker's 47 Workshop, and later became a teacher at Harvard. He has designed settings for many Broadway productions of importance, such as *You Can't Take It with You* and *Born Yesterday,* which were sympathetic renderings of varied backgrounds. But he made more imaginative essays with his designs for the Shaw plays, *Major Barbara, The Doctor's Dilemma,* and *Pygmalion.* He has also done much designing for college theatres, which designs have been more broadly experimental—as in the settings for *Prometheus Bound* by Aeschylus, an imaginative symphony of projected lighting, and for O'Neill's *The*

Emperor Jones for the Yale University Theatre.

MORDECAI GORELIK

Mordecai Gorelik was the designer for many of the Group Theatre's earlier productions—including *1931, Men in White, The Case of Clyde Griffiths,* and *Casey Jones*—in which he created convincing if unusual settings which added much to the interpretation of the main theme. Although these settings were broadly realistic and suited to the type of play, his later designs for more imaginative dramas gave him greater scope for attempting the creation of mood and atmosphere. This was beautifully done in the lighthouse setting for Ardrey's *Thunder Rock,* and in Odets' retelling of the story of Noah in terms of a contemporary Jewish household in *The Flowering Peach.* In the setting for Gazzo's *A Hatful of Rain,* Gorelik made a positive contribution to the theme of drug addiction—its victim and the criminal suppliers—by his skilled distortion of architectural elements.

OTHER DESIGNERS

Aline Bernstein created some sensitively realized settings for period plays, as in *Camille* for Eva Le Gallienne and *The Game of Love and Death* for the Theatre Guild.

Raymond Sovey, Cleon Throckmorton, Stewart Chaney, and Lemuel Ayres have produced colorful and exciting settings for many Broadway productions.

Boris Aronson has designed impressive settings for many of the important plays of the last decade or so, including Odets' *The Country Girl,* Tennessee Williams' *The Rose Tattoo,* Inge's *Bus Stop,* MacLeish's *J. B.,* Irwin Shaw's *The Gentle People,* and particularly Arthur Miller's *A View from the Bridge.* In the latter, he attempted to give the Brooklyn tenement scene overtones of a monumental and classic quality, recalling a setting for a classical tragedy.

Off-Broadway, William and Jean Eckart have produced some imaginative work for the Phoenix Theatre in, for example, *The*

Golden Apple by John Latouche.

Oliver Smith has been responsible for the stylish settings of the great success *My Fair Lady,* among many other productions including *Night of the Iguana* and *A Clearing in the Woods.*

Ralph Alswang has contributed settings to many unusual productions, such as the all-Negro *Lysistrata,* the *King Lear* of Louis Calhern at the National Theatre, *Peter Pan, Blood Wedding, Courtin' Time,* and *The Last Dance* by Strindberg.

JO MIELZINER

The most consistent designer, whose long list of productions spans forty years of the vital development of the American theatre, is without doubt Jo Mielziner. During this time, he has shown a great range of style, from the realistic tenement front of Elmer Rice's *Street Scene* to the fragile, semitransparent settings for *The Glass Menagerie* by Tennessee Williams; from the heavy Victorianism of *The Barretts of Wimpole Street* to the brash vulgarity of *Guys and Dolls.* His settings for Katharine Cornell's production of *Romeo and Juliet* made possible a rapid flow of the drama by having preset scenes, while the action was performed on others in front of them. He used the simple architectural treatment of the Italian primitives rather than the traditional Renaissance manner, using pure color in a light key. His *Hamlet* settings for John Gielgud were ingenious in their simplicity, governed by the need for a swift flow of action from scene to scene.

For *Winterset,* by Maxwell Anderson, he created the vast brooding shadow of Brooklyn Bridge, which characterized the inexorable and tragic fate of the young lovers. In Maxwell Anderson's *Journey to Jerusalem* Mielziner devised an exciting method of projecting scenery. This was further developed for Anouilh's *The Lark,* which had a single permanent set, including a circular wall across the back of the stage on which the various scenes of village, countryside, court, and public square were suggested by means of light projections. For Tennessee Williams' *Cat on a Hot Tin Roof* he made use of symbolism, a simple set capturing the character of the old mansion of the South, in which a few items of furniture were emphasized to strengthen the impact of the story.

For Arthur Miller's *Death of a Salesman,* he created the remarkable composite set of Willy Loman's house, surrounded by towering angular shapes of apartment buildings crowding onto it on all sides. In the center of the house was the kitchen, which had a table, three chairs, and a refrigerator, but no other fixtures. To the right, stairs led to the upper bedroom of Loman's two sons. The roof was indicated by the outline of the gable, but there were no walls and no actual roofing, although there was a fully built-up dormer window at the rear of the room. Another bedroom was seen to the left of the kitchen, on a slightly higher level, again with a window. There were also curtained recesses which suggested that they led to other parts of the house. Before the house was a large apron stage, which fulfilled the dual purpose of representing Loman's backyard and the locale of his imaginings and his scenes in the city. The whole set aptly expressed the strange mixture of dreams and reality which made the play so memorable.

Jo Mielziner, more than any other designer, has developed the importance of lighting on the stage in a very positive way. To him, lighting may suggest the passage of time by its changing values, or a change of locale by differing intensity, by projected shadows or color or transparencies. He can paint a scene with light, in a moment, more powerfully than with any pigment. He has always had the underlying theme and message of the play foremost in the creation of his designs. For this reason, his settings have been as varied in style as the plays themselves.

Mielziner has his own studio theatre where he works out his lighting effects, which can rarely be appreciated as drawings or photographs. He was associated with the beginnings of the Lincoln Center Repertory Theatre in its earlier seasons at the A.N.T.A. Theatre, Washington Square, and was largely responsible for the design of the thrust stage and the modern equipment for the Vivian Beaumont Theatre, their ultimate home at Lincoln Center.

MUSICAL COMEDY

The growth of musical comedy in America is one of its most exciting contributions to the world of theatre. It is one of the liveliest
and most compelling of entertainment forms, and has grown and
thrived consistently since *The Black Crook,* the first successful
American musical, was produced in 1866. It was based on the *Faust*
legend, and while quite crude by our current standards, was enormously successful in its time. Later, in 1954, a Sigmund Romberg
musical, *The Girl in Pink Tights,* told the story of the production
of *The Black Crook.*

The American theatre is laced with the names and work of bril-
liant musicmakers. The early trend was toward the Viennese operet-
tas of Franz Lehár (*The Merry Widow,* first produced in New
York in 1907), Oscar Straus (*The Chocolate Soldier*), and Johann
Strauss (whose *Die Fledermaus* was produced in New York as *The
Merry Countess*). Victor Herbert was very much in this tradition,
with *Naughty Marietta, Princess Pat, The Red Mill, Babes in
Toyland.*

Rudolf Friml and Sigmund Romberg continued the trend. Friml
had his first big success when he substituted for Victor Herbert
writing the score for *The Firefly* in 1912. He wrote constantly for
the musical stage after that. *Rose-Marie* (1924) was something of a
milestone, for it was among the first attempts to achieve some unity
between score and plot. *The Vagabond King* had François Villon
as its hero, and *The Three Musketeers* was based on the famous
Dumas story.

Romberg was very much influenced by Johann Strauss, Lehár,
and other Viennese composers. *Maytime* (1917) was his first great
success. He did several songs for Al Jolson productions. His other
most famous operettas were *Blossom Time, Bombo, The Student
Prince in Heidelberg, The Desert Song, New Moon, Rosalie, May
Wine, Up in Central Park,* and *The Girl in Pink Tights,* the last
being produced over two years after his death.

There are many other great names and memorable productions

in the American musical theatre: Jerome Kern (*Sally, Sunny* [both starring the celebrated Marilyn Miller], *Show Boat* [his greatest achievement], *Music in the Air, Roberta, Very Warm for May*); Irving Berlin, who has also written innumerable popular tunes that will probably continue to be sung by many generations (various *Music Box Revues* and *Ziegfeld Follies, Face the Music, As Thousands Cheer, Louisiana Purchase, This Is the Army* [a World War II show with an all-soldier cast], *Annie Get Your Gun* [revived in New York in 1966 with its original star, the inimitable Ethel Merman], *Miss Liberty, Call Me Madam*).

George Gershwin, the immensely talented composer of much serious music, made many memorable contributions to musical comedy: *Lady Be Good!, Oh, Kay!, Funny Face, Girl Crazy, Strike Up the Band, Of Thee I Sing, Let 'Em Eat Cake,* and his immortal "opera," *Porgy and Bess.* His brother, Ira, was his lyricist.

Among the wealth of the American musical stage are the contributions of Vincent Youmans (*No, No, Nanette, Wildflower, Hit the Deck, Two Little Girls in Blue, Rainbow, Great Day!*); Richard Rodgers, perhaps the giant of the American musical stage, with his collaborators Lorenz Hart and Oscar Hammerstein II (*The Girl Friend, A Connecticut Yankee, On Your Toes, Babes in Arms, I Married an Angel, I'd Rather Be Right, The Boys from Syracuse, Too Many Girls, Pal Joey* [with Hart]; *Oklahoma* [a milestone in musical theatre, with its complete integration of story and music, its farm setting, its balletic dances], *Carousel, Allegro, South Pacific, The King and I, Me and Juliet, Pipe Dream, The Flower Drum Song, The Sound of Music* [with Hammerstein]; and *No Strings,* in which Rodgers served as his own lyricist after the death of Hammerstein).

We can go on to Cole Porter (*The Gay Divorcee, Jubilee, Red, Hot, and Blue!, Leave It to Me!, DuBarry Was a Lady, Panama Hattie, Let's Face It!, Something for the Boys, Mexican Hayride, Seven Lively Arts, Around the World in Eighty Days, Kiss Me, Kate* [based on Shakespeare's *The Taming of the Shrew*], *Can-Can,*

ZERO MOSTEL The actor is shown in the star role of
Prologus, in the 1962 production of "A Funny Thing Happened on the Way to the Forum."

Silk Stockings); Jule Styne *(High Button Shoes, Gentlemen Prefer Blondes, Bells Are Ringing, Peter Pan, Say, Darling, Gypsy* [based on the autobiography of Gypsy Rose Lee]); Frank Loesser *(Where's Charley?, Guys and Dolls, The Most Happy Fella* [which was very operatic in its structure, with arias, recitative, duets, quartets], *Greenwillow)*; Meredith Willson *(The Music Man)*; Frederick Loewe and Alan Jay Lerner *(Brigadoon, Paint Your Wagon, My Fair Lady* [the champion of all musicals]); Leonard Bernstein, the brilliant pianist, conductor of the New York Philharmonic Orchestra, and composer of classical and concert music *(On the Town, Wonderful Town, Candide, West Side Story)*; Richard Adler and Jerry Ross *(Damn Yankees, The Pajama Game)*; Marc Blitzstein *(The Cradle Will Rock)*; Arthur Schwartz and Howard Dietz *(The Little Show, Band Wagon, A Tree Grows in Brooklyn)*; Harold Arlen *(Bloomer Girl, St. Louis Woman, House of Flowers, Jamaica)*; Burton Lane *(Finian's Rainbow)*; Harold Rome *(Pins and Needles, Call Me Mister, Wish You Were Here, Fanny, Destry Rides Again)*; Kurt Weill, whose works were more socially significant than much of musical comedy *(Johnny Johnson, Knickerbocker Holiday* [with Maxwell Anderson], *Lady in the Dark* [with Moss Hart], *One Touch of Venus, Street Scene, Love Life* [with Alan Jay Lerner], *Lost in the Stars* [again with Anderson], and the immortal *Threepenny Opera*, which Marc Blitzstein adapted into English, and which had first been presented in Berlin in 1928).

In addition, the American musical stage has been studded with revues (the *Music Box Revues*, the *Charlot's Revues*, imported from England) and spectacles (the various *Ziegfeld Follies, George White's Scandals, Earl Carroll Vanities, Jumbo)*, largely featuring beautiful girls and good music. But the musical comedy has come of age, and today is probably the most vital musical theatre in the world, encompassing everything from the brassy, colorful vehicles that used to be indicative of musical comedy to the beautifully integrated musical dramas and operas of more recent vintage.

THE AMERICAN SHAKESPEARE FESTIVAL THEATRE IN STRATFORD, CONNECTICUT This famous structure, erected in 1955, was designed by architect Edwin Howard. The exterior polygonal shape of the auditorium resembles the Old Globe Theatre of London. The theatre premiered with "Julius Caesar" on July 12, 1966.

Index